Shipping Out

Shipping Out

Race, Performance, and Labor at Sea

Anita Gonzalez

University of Michigan Press
Ann Arbor

Copyright © 2025 by Anita Gonzalez
Some rights reserved

This work is licensed under a Creative Commons Attribution-NonCommercial 4.0 International License. *Note to users:* A Creative Commons license is only valid when it is applied by the person or entity that holds rights to the licensed work. Works may contain components (e.g., photographs, illustrations, or quotations) to which the rightsholder in the work cannot apply the license. It is ultimately your responsibility to independently evaluate the copyright status of any work or component part of a work you use, in light of your intended use. To view a copy of this license, visit http://creativecommons.org/licenses/by-nc/4.0/

For questions or permissions, please contact um.press.perms@umich.edu

Published in the United States of America by the
University of Michigan Press
Manufactured in the United States of America
Printed on acid-free paper
First published February 2025

A CIP catalog record for this book is available from the British Library.

Library of Congress Cataloging-in-Publication data has been applied for.

ISBN 978-0-472-07724-3 (hardcover : alk. paper)
ISBN 978-0-472-05724-5 (paper : alk. paper)
ISBN 978-0-472-90486-0 (open access ebook)

DOI: https://doi.org/10.3998/mpub.12123587

The University of Michigan Press's open access publishing program is made possible thanks to additional funding from the University of Michigan Office of the Provost and the generous support of contributing libraries.

Contents

Acknowledgments	vii
Introduction	1
1 Onboarding	10
2 Play at Sea, Space, and Meaning	55
3 Ports: Transactions and Cultural Encounters	123
Coda: Improvisations and Cultural Reflections	179
Appendix	187
Notes	189
Index	209

Digital materials related to this title can be found on the Fulcrum platform via the following citable URL: https://doi.org/10.3998/mpub.12123587

Acknowledgments

I am grateful to all who have supported and encouraged my scholarship in this area. Thank you especially to LeAnn Fields for advocating and carefully vetting the work. Glenn Gordinier and the National Endowment for the Humanities' America and the Sea Institute first introduced me to the potency of maritime scholarship. Archivists at the American Antiquarian Museum, the Mystic Seaport Collections and Research Center, the Merseyside Maritime Museum, and the University of Bristol Theater Collection gently guided my inquiries into nineteenth-century port lifestyles.

I am grateful for the inspired leadership of the cruise entertainment directors who modeled versatility and adaptability as they orchestrated entertainment across dozens of venues.

I am grateful for my traveling companions who helped me to navigate the thin line between tourism and onboard work—John R. Diehl Jr., Amelia Gonzalez-Govan, and Xochina El-Hilali-Pollard. Mia Massimino deserves special mention for her detailed editorial comments and copyediting. I appreciate the developmental editors who engaged with the project: Meghan Drury and Mike Levine.

Finally, I want to acknowledge the support of the Paul Cuffee Fellowship from Mystic Seaport and the University of Michigan Humanities Center fellowship, which allowed me to deeply engage in writing the manuscript with an interdisciplinary cohort of scholars during my fellowship year. Last, but not least, thank you to the Black Studies writing group at Georgetown University who helped me to see how to place myself in the core themes of the manuscript.

Introduction

> The American "race question" is inherently theatrical. From the arrival of the first African slaves on American soil, the discourse on race, the definitions and meaning of blackness have been intricately linked to issues of theater and performance.[1]
> —Harry J. Elam Jr.

Harry Elam writes about race in the context of the United States and how performances of race are theatricalized. A student of mine once responded to this quote saying: "We arrived enslaved and naked in the United States and they gave us some clothing and ever since we have been performing a role imagined by others."[2] But what if you could sail away from localized imaginations about your identity or potentiality? What if you could live in a place in the middle of the ocean where notions of race, home, and work continuously shifted and reconfigured—a place where at every stop or with every encounter you could reconsider your social expression?

This book, at the intersection of African American studies and performance studies, looks at how race, performance, and labor interconnect on cruise ships in the Caribbean. The cruise ship uniquely encapsulates both workers and guests in the same physical space. While paying passengers are free to disembark and reboard the ship at will, the crew members, many of them from the Global South, remain on board in their respective service roles. Cruise ships are simultaneously work spaces (for the crew) and leisure spaces (for the passengers). When passengers pay and step on board to vacation, they expect to be entertained and receive a plethora of services. The cruise experience, like any other theatrical entertainment, is deliberately crafted by the cruise ship management to deliver the best possible immersive performance by its workers. However, the workers never leave the theater, they merely move below deck—and like ships' stewards and cooks from previous centuries, they work within an imaginary where Blacks are envisioned as servants.

This book uses ethnography and archival materials to illustrate what it is like to work for extended stays on a contemporary cruise ship, contrasting those circumstances with the experiences of workers on historical merchant ships. I'm concerned primarily with Caribbean cruise ships and transatlantic merchant ships from the long nineteenth century into the twenty-first. Performance, and particularly the performance of racialized labor, links these two worlds. Explicitly, Black and brown individuals perform servitude when they labor on cruise ships, and historical disenfranchisement has normalized service workers from the Global South in this role. Performance intervenes in this space; identities become less fixed, more fluid as crew members interact through vernacular performance forms that have the potential to establish new relationships.

The book's title, *Shipping Out*, responds in part to a *Harper's* magazine article with the same title by David Foster Wallace that describes a voyage the author took on a seven-day passenger cruise. His satirical essay uses a tongue-in-cheek tone to deride most aspects of a cruise experience. Wallace, traveling as a passenger, tracks his immersion into a pampered world of onboard amenities and his "re-entry into the quotidian, land-locked real-world life."[3]

As this book will demonstrate, Wallace was responding to a series of carefully crafted staged experiences designed to give twenty-first-century travelers the illusion that they are part of an elite passenger class from the nineteenth century. I seek to turn Wallace's notion of "shipping out" upside down. Instead of focusing solely on the experiences of the passenger seeking leisure at sea, I write about how workers and passengers, during their brief time on board, interact with one another through performance. The ship's container creates its own stage for cultural performance.

Passengers are drawn into experiential exchanges with cruise members that reinstate class hierarchies even while offering opportunities for experimentation and reimagination of self. The historical precedents for these embodied cultural exchanges were established within merchant shipping cultures of the eighteenth and nineteenth centuries. *Shipping Out* moves fluidly between descriptive analysis, archival referents, and ethnographic accounts to deepen its engagement with contemporary cruise ship culture.

For over twenty years I have worked as a destination lecturer for a variety of companies cruising the Caribbean by participating in the entertainment offerings on board.[4] Destination lecturers function as part of the entertainment staff, informing guests about destinations they are sailing to. Generally, lecture programs are part of the "edutainment" offerings guests may choose to attend during days at sea. The position of "lecturer" is a liminal role, neither passenger nor crew member. My subjectivity as an African American woman complicates how I "pass" as a passenger among a primarily white group of vacationers while working with, and being serviced by, primarily Black and brown-skinned crew members. This subjectivity allows me to interact with crew and passengers from a unique perspective, while as a destination lecturer I share knowledge about the histories and socioeconomic contexts of African diaspora people. I primarily lecture on larger ships holding about 3,000 passengers and 1,200 crew members. Ships in this class contain dozens of sites of performance where guests may interact with crew members trained to offer diversions during the voyage. In writing this book I have complemented my onboard experiences with research in Caribbean cruise ports. Analyzing the various performative exchanges negotiated by island people has added considerably to my analysis. There I've observed how islanders who make their living laboring for cruise ship clientele—merchants, tour guides, cab drivers, and others—organize their lives around the comings and goings of the megaships. On both land and sea and in both historical archives and in contemporary practice, maritime spaces are sites of cosmopolitan encounter where people from various social and cultural backgrounds interact.

Race

Christina Sharpe tells a maritime story in her book *In the Wake*. She illustrates how Black lives are swept up and animated by the afterlives of slavery, focusing on the Middle Passage and its impact on Africans who were taken by ship by European immigrants to be enslaved in the Americas.[5] Her analysis is strong yet metaphorical as she describes the residues of trauma on African diaspora people. However, even as the enslaved were transported across the Atlantic, they were not the only African diaspora people on the ocean. Free Black men and women labored on Atlantic and Caribbean waters, serving and smiling, navigating vessels, washing clothing, cooking food, and changing bedpans. Their labor and their performances of servitude endure in the funhouse environment of the twenty-first-century cruise ship, where Black and brown-skinned workers execute these same tasks; they serve and smile, clean and cook, and manage bedding for shiploads of passengers who change every week or so. Unlike texts that employ theory and metaphor to envision an experience of being at sea and between cultural worlds, *Shipping Out* describes the world of flesh-and-blood African American sea workers and other people of color who live below deck. Their presence on these ships complicates notions of freedom and enslavement, home and journey, place and space.

Within the African American context, scholars tend to define freedom as counterpoint to slavery. We *picture freedom*,[6] consider the *horrible gift of freedom*,[7] or articulate freedom through performances on the *captive stage*.[8] From the perspective of the global nineteenth-century mariner, the horrible circumstance of slavery with its capitalist oppression was merely an extension of a global network of encapsulation and extraction based upon maritime trade. Situating Black bodies in relationship to the ocean opens a space for discussing how bodies of all ethnicities have used migration and liminality to access inclusion. I think of fugitivity not solely as an escape from chattel slavery of the Deep South, but rather, in global perspective, as a fugitive desire to travel away from whatever economic and political constraints prevent a person, an "actor," from having agency over their own survival. The liminal spaces of ships and ports allow paradigms of race and gender to be reimagined. Sea workers are neither "here" nor "there," therefore social codes shift.

In *Picture Freedom: Remaking Freedom in the Early Nineteenth Century*, Jasmine Cobb highlights how an ideal of freedom was linked to the ambiguity of race and ethnicity during the nineteenth century. She joins other scholars in describing the circumstances of the *Amistad*, a slave ship overtaken by a group of Mende people[9] who redirected their vessel away from the Caribbean islands toward an uncertain freedom in New London and New Haven, Connecticut.[10] After wandering transnational waters, the ocean travelers were brought to trial in New England seaport towns where no one was quite sure if they should be free or enslaved. Since they had passed through Cuba and followed the Atlantic Gyre north, it was difficult to determine where they belonged within the social and racial structures of land-based laws. Their liberty and freedom were inextricably linked to an unstable location on the maritime circuit.[11] In *The View from the Masthead*, Hester Blum claims that "part of the attraction of standing at the masthead . . . is the lure of losing his 'identity.'"[12] Black and brown workers had the same aspirations even though, for the racially marked, no shore or ship was a guaranteed safe haven.

Encapsulated in the ship, laborers learn to interact because there is no escape. When they land, each port offers a unique, temporary landscape for social negotiations. In ports, on sailing ships, and on cruise ships workers use performance as a way of managing work and social relationships. However, cruise ships are more than transport vessels or work environments. In essence, they are a carefully designed entertainment venues that amplify the performativity of cruise ship workers. Customers pay to experience the maritime world, often through lenses tainted by stereotype, when they embark on an entertainment-laden Caribbean cruise. The application of methodologies from the field of performance studies can bring greater legibility to analysis of cruise ship entertainment dynamics.

Performance

Shipping Out brings together the broadly interdisciplinary field of maritime studies with the field of performance studies.[13] My introduction to maritime studies was through a National Endowment for the Humanities seminar, "America and the Seas," held at Mystic Seaport in Connecticut. Under the tutelage of historian Glenn Gordinier, my scholarly cohort studied primary texts within the field, including *The Way of the Ship*, *America and the Sea*, and *The History of Seafaring*.[14]

At the time, I was always interested in the life of the common sailor and curious about where African diaspora workers might be accommodated within a maritime paradigm. Some of our reading, including W. Jeffrey Bolster's *Black Jacks: African American Seamen in the Age of Sail*[15] and Ray Costello's *Black Salt: Seafarers of African Descent on British Ships*,[16] addressed Black presence in the maritime world. Sowande Muskateem and Marcus Rediker[17] also eloquently and astutely examined the traumatizing and dehumanizing experience of slave ships and the slave trade. But there was only partial discussion of the day-to-day life of Black seamen and limited information about historical vernacular performance. Only the pictorial volume *Jack Tar: A Sailor's Life*[18] illustrated how gesture and play were incorporated into nineteenth-century maritime lifestyles. As the NEH seminar's sole performance scholar, and the only African American, I quickly realized how my field could contribute to a better understanding of the maritime world as a transformative space for cultural exchange, and a transitory space for reimagining identity and affiliations.

Increasingly, maritime studies, reframed as oceanic studies, has gained prominence in academic circles. Two volumes in particular investigate oceans from increasingly interdisciplinary perspectives. Eric Paul Roorda organizes the edited volume *The Ocean Reader: History, Politics, Culture* around metaphoric perceptions of the ocean, gathering essays about "piracy," "battlefields," "laboratories," and "shipwrecks" into a reflective volume that situates oceanic imaginings across historical time frames. Kimberley Peters, Jon Andersen, Andrew Davies, and Philip Steinberg contrast this work by compiling an anthology of essays, *The Routledge Handbook of Ocean Space*, that utilizes social science methodologies to discuss how oceanic studies intersects with pressing contemporary political issues like migration, labor, race and gender inequities, scientific measurement, fishing industries, and climate change.[19] They foreground economies of labor, noting how organizational structures within maritime industries impact international policies. The lengthy volume examines "the diversity of relationships and connections between people, ocean and place, building on a growing discourse around the role of social sciences in understanding these relationships."[20] The previously mentioned *In the Wake: On Blackness and Being* by Christina Sharpe delves deeply into intersections of memory and history in a book about transatlantic slavery, work that resonates with that of other scholars invested in performance studies.[21]

Investigations like *Moving Islands: Contemporary Performance and the Global Pacific* bring oceanic interpretations of cultural studies to Pacific seascapes. Author Diana Looser proposes *transpasifka*, a conceptualization of a heterogeneous set of islands in motion where interconnected spaces of resistance innovate across cross-lingual and cultural communities.[22] Looser's writings are in dialogue with the scholarship of Jordan Waiti and Belinda Wheaton who, in the aforementioned Routledge handbook, turn to indigenous Māori oceanic epistemology to contest colonial systems while asserting self-determination over their own watery highways.[23] Writings that consider indigenous engagement with oceanic space increase the diversity of approaches to oceanic studies. These scholarly investigations advance interdisciplinary analyses of oceanic space, while consuming cruise ship passengers who pay for vacations generally view the ocean not as a site for investigative inquiry but rather as mere backdrop to entertaining onboard activities. Consequently, this book foregrounds labor and the performance of servitude as an organizing trope to examine how workers craft identities and associations on cruise ships.

Performance studies is uniquely situated to examine this liminal arena of working-class maritime performance because the field of performance studies extends beyond literary analysis and engages with architecture, embodied acts, sonic "phonographies," symbols, and cultural migrations.[24] When I discuss historical performances on ships, I apply theoretical concepts from performance studies to situate working-class sea culture in historical and contemporary contexts.[25] The spirited sounds of the sea shanty singer or the physicalized labor of rolling a barrel onto a ship communicate a classed, gendered, and raced perspective on work, migration, and identity. This *dramaturgy in motion*[26] reveals the communicative power of hands, eyes, and posture, because expressive acts of sea laborers articulate their social status within a capitalist class system based on exchanges of human cargo and material merchandise.[27]

The long nineteenth century was a particularly fertile time for unscripted, nonverbal performances that ranged from variety shows to dog races, and from street festivals to parades. Shipboard performances were part and parcel of a larger panorama of street performances popular among working-class individuals. The embodied performance of sailors expressed their thoughts and aspirations,[28] in dialogic performances closely connected to behavioral aspects of socioeconomic class.[29] Dance and performance studies scholars describe specific social settings where working-class performances occurred, many of them in port environments like New York or Philadelphia. For example, Gillian M. Rodger, in her book *Champagne Charlie and Pretty Jemima: Variety Theater in the Nineteenth Century*, poses the question: "What kinds of entertainment were available to those who did not qualify as the 'upper ten' or aspire to join them?"[30] She identifies variety theater, saloons, and acrobatic shows as core sites for working-class entertainment to prosper, noting how singing and storytelling communicated cultural histories. I posit that working-class performance perpetuated itself beyond national borders and expanded its reach through transferences across and within maritime spaces.[31] At the same time, I am attentive to how performance modes manifest in contemporary, embodied practices in oceanic spaces.

Labor

This book is primarily about the people who labor on ships and how they interact. Cruising is a lucrative industry that employs tens of thousands of workers who actively toil to produce the type of vacation that passengers have been sold through commercial marketing. The industry employed approximately 178,000 people in 2019.[32] Some laborers work with limited public visibility, physically cleaning and maintaining the vessel, while others more actively interact with passengers, maintaining an emotional façade of gratuitous service. Even while working, they are part of an immersive entertainment experience. This book grapples with the incongruities of laboring while entertaining. Once cruise workers sign a contract, they remain on the ship until their contract ends. During their work contract they serve at the pleasure of the captain, the management team, and each area head; however, the effectiveness of their performance is ultimately evaluated by the passengers.

Equally important, ship work situates workers within a community of displaced laborers, while releasing them from land-based circles of attachment, that is, family members and community bonds that previously shaped their identity. Notably, workers rebuild their persona and social codes through iterative performances based upon the minutiae of everyday encounters in their work world. As Dorinne Kondo maintains, "identity is not a fixed thing." During the process of shipping out, over the course of the journey, working-class passengers and employees participate in an "anthropological hermeneutic circle where participation gives way to observation and reconstruction."[33] Crew members come from many countries, but at their worksite they morph into friendly faces whose nationalities and cultural experiences are expressed only through their name tags. Their work thus shapes how they present themselves, in a performance of both labor and identity.

Shipping Out draws broadly and deeply from performance studies to track how individuals craft selves through iterative song, dance, and play while working within the maritime space. I focus on passenger engagement with performative environments on the cruise, and on performance spaces where crew members labor to create immersive experiences for passengers.

The book's narrative shifts back and forth between scenarios on contemporary cruise ships and historical scenarios from the long nineteenth century, and uses both historical and contemporary illustrations to familiarize readers with paradigms of the maritime world and its unique cultural codes.

The Structure of This Book

Chapter 1, "Onboarding" begins with a description of the experience of settling into a ship as a destination lecturer, explaining the entertainment structures of staff and personnel that support the experience. It highlights how performance and labor intersect in that immersive setting. Next it describes how the diversity and the internationalism of the maritime world creates a "motley crew" of service workers. Finally, I recount the historical circumstances of Black seamen who worked on merchant and packet ships as cooks and stewards during the nineteenth century.

The second chapter, "Play at Sea, Space, and Meaning," concerns itself with performance spaces in the cruise ship and their semiotic meanings within the architecture of the cruise ship. I center my discussion around David Wile's concepts of processional, public, cosmic, sympotic, and cave spaces. Architectural spaces unique to cruise ships allow passengers to participate in playful activities that pass the time. Next, I describe how the raucous and ridiculous Crossing the Line ceremonies of previous centuries were a precursor to the playful events on contemporary cruise ships. Finally, I analyze historical song and dance traditions, focusing on how African foot sounding coupled with sea shanties effectively transferred cultural knowledge. Sea shanties in particular express the rich cultural histories of transitory sailors and can serve as a literature of the sea.

Chapter 3, "Ports: Transactions and Cultural Encounters," analyzes how ports, historical and contemporary, function as spectacles, trading zones, social settings for dialogic exchange, and touristic sites for transactions that are facilitated by performance. In addition to discussions of Caribbean ports, the chapter considers historical movements between the cities of Liverpool and New York, two bustling commercial centers where Black and Irish populations negotiated presence through performance.

Each chapter ends with a "Snapshot" or a description of a social moment in my cruise ship experience when disturbing realignments of place, culture, or identity occurred. These ethnographic moments illustrate how the experience of traveling with a racialized, multicultural crew creates moments of disjuncture, moments that unsettle land-based presumptions about space, time, place, and, most importantly, identity. It is within these moments that the liminality of the oceanic space surfaces most clearly. I end the book with a short chapter, "Coda: Improvisations and Cultural Reflections," that contains short descriptions of cruise ship experiences where unpredictable circumstances created moments for passengers and crew members to experiment with identity and fantasize new worlds for themselves within the temporary and precarious circumstances of cruise ship travel. Together the chapters serve to investigate how ships create a unique liminal space for cultural performance and exchange.

One

Onboarding

The Destination Lecturer

I enter the ship through the doorway of the fifth-floor lounge for my first introduction to the cruise ship staff. I wear my sporty casual outfit because I know it will match the clean military look most of the workers will have on to greet the onboarding cruise ship guests. Before heading to Miami, I packed several "looks" to wear during this cruise, each designed to enhance the various "roles" I will play this week—lecturer, dinner guest, poolside dancer, or international traveler. Boarding a cruise ship involves a lengthy intake process where scores of locally hired employees examine passports, tag and cart luggage, review credit information, and eventually allow passengers to board the ship. I have just completed that process, skirting through by presenting papers that document my role as a "Destination Lecturer" working with the "Entertainment" staff. At the registration desk, the port staff gave me my ship card, a plastic identification card that keeps track of my spending during the all-inclusive journey. A three-story ramp brings me to the entrance of the ship where I am greeted by smiling servers holding trays with glasses of champagne. They invite me to settle in and explore the ship. I head to my cabin where the housekeeping staff, now serving as porters, will have deposited my heavy bags, turned back the bedsheets, and placed an envelope with work instructions on my desk. I am ready to settle into my temporary job as an onboard specialist offering presentations to passengers. The business of cruising has begun.

The business of cruising is a performance engagement where my own labor as an academic intersects with the labor of staff hired to deliver a vacation experience to a cross-section of middle- to upper-class consumers. All of us are imbedded within a maritime culture where Black and brown bodies have been historically associated with servitude or enslavement. Because of

Figure 1. Gonzalez on stage as a Destination Lecturer. Photo courtesy of the author.

the persistence of traditional maritime hierarchies, we are expected to participate in what I call "performances of servitude." Many people cruise for leisure or exploration, but few cruise as a Black destination lecturer. I was introduced to the role of destination lecturer when a recruiter from a Florida talent agency contacted me at my university in 2001, asking if I might be interested in working on a cruise ship. They were specifically reaching out to theater professors because they thought they would be able to provide the kind of "edutainment" labor that cruises require. At first, I was cautious. I had never cruised before, and I wondered why anyone would. I agreed to try it out, and two decades later, that journey has led me to this book. Destination lecturers, as the title implies, provide information about regional histories and cultures, in my case by giving short forty-minute talks, usually during "sea days."[1] In my role, I occupy a liminal position—neither fully paid laborer nor vacationing guest. I receive a free sleeping cabin and free food for sharing my expertise, but my interactions with the guests are moderated and monitored to ensure I am presenting an appropriate persona for the paying travelers. My identity as a Black female academic complicates this role.

Cruise ship hierarchies are clear. Black and brown bodies primarily labor in subservient roles—as waiters or housekeeping staff—while higher-level staff members are generally white-presenting managers from Europe or Australia, Canada or the United States. Contemporary cruise hierarchies arise from earlier maritime social structures where Black and brown people prepared food in the kitchen, offloaded barrels at maritime docks, or were cargo transported in the holds of ships. Many continue to work on cruise ships in variations of these roles. Historically, shipowners managed maritime merchant trade from distant locations while a hired captain directly managed the onboard laborers. Within the context of contemporary cruise hierarchies of race, my appearance as a higher-ranking Black woman, an entertainer with brains, is an anomaly. There are usually other Black women on the ship, but most of them will be in the business of serving passengers, not educating them. I also self-identify as a woman, while maritime work has traditionally been performed by men. With few exceptions, navies recruited male conscripts, and oceanic adventures and explorations were conducted by male captains presiding over male crew members. Women traveled primarily as captains' wives or, by the end of the nineteenth century, as privileged passengers seeking respites in exotic settings. Black women were never a part of this maritime landscape. So, when I enter a ship as a destination lecturer, my presence brushes up against historical framings that are both exclusionary and intimidating. Lecturing offers me an opportunity to observe and study the role of others on the ship and consider how past shipping cultures intersect with twenty-first-century paradigms of race and labor. For me and others on the ship, performance serves as a mechanism for functioning within a contained, hierarchical, and very structured entertainment venue. I use performances of intellect and humor to intervene and succeed.

Performance Paradigms

Performance operates within this space on several levels. First, I take on an imaginary role when I cruise, deliberately marketing a character called "Dr. Anita" that simultaneously identifies me as a highly educated Black woman while also somewhat diminishing my academic title by only referencing my first name, similar to the way that plantation owners referred to their enslaved workers by first name only—calling the cooks Betty or Sally instead of Mr. or Miss. "Dr. Anita" also implies that I am somewhat informal, willing to converse with passengers as equals even though I have a PhD. My character is friendly but knowledgeable; always approachable. As an African American who has been educated in public, primarily white universities, I am well schooled in the multiple behavioral codes needed to function within primarily white environments. Doubly conscious sensibilities allow me to easily adapt to the unfamiliarity of the cruise ship ambience. Double consciousness, a term coined by W. E. B. Du Bois in the 1903 edition of *The Souls of Black Folk*, describes the sensation of feeling as if your identity is divided into several different parts.[2] Adjusting to multiple external expectations about Black performance is one aspect of living in a doubly conscious way within a work setting.

A secondary way in which performance operates within the cruise ship environment is through performances of servitude. By this I mean that cruise ship workers, following historical precedents, labor on ships in service to a leisure class of passengers who pay to ride the ship for entertainment. Performances of servitude are not unique to cruising—those involved in hotel or restaurant industries also serve and respond to visitors' whims, but the cruise ship is a twenty-four-hour immersive environment where the housekeeping staff is expected to serve continuously and where waiters are always on call. Unlike hotel or restaurant workers, they do not have time away from the ship to recover with their families and then resume their role of servitude. If they are not physically below the waterline and in their cabins, then their performances are ongoing. The historical precedents for divisions between workers and guests, captains and laborers, investors and crewmen are explored throughout this volume.

Finally, certain types of performances on cruise ships are designed and coordinated by cruise operators and managers to provide passengers with ongoing entertainment throughout a cruise journey. Vacationing passengers pay a single, all-inclusive fee to be entertained by staff members like myself who create educational and fun activities to pass time between destinations. Ship activities are "free" in that no money transfers at points of sale or entry, yet the entire cruise experience is monetized through the use of the onboard ship card. Crafted performances range from theatrical entertainments in main-stage venues to impersonations of pirates and mermaids on destination docks, and from shore excursions controlled and managed by cruise operators, to technologically inspired events where passengers listen and dance to playlists provided by crew personnel. Coordinated and crafted performances are imbedded throughout the cruise experience.

The elements of race, performance, and labor intersect in distinctive ways throughout cruise journeys. When traveling as a destination lecturer, I am an unpaid worker performing the role of an educated academic within a space where most of the paid laborers are involved in physical, manual, service work. We are all working for passengers who may themselves be workers escaping their own jobs by taking a cruise vacation. My clientele, depending upon the cruise line, can range from primarily white and middle- or upper-middle-class retirees to working-class teachers and service workers. What performance of leisure and work are each of us enacting as we encounter one another in our common liminal space at sea? Most of the ship's laborers live on the ship, so their work environment is also their home environment. Still, they maintain connections with families on land, or friends whom they may see only when their contract ends or when they are able to take shore leave. Our encounters with one another throughout our journey are crafted to ensure that each move in our dance of entertainer, laborer, passenger, voyager, educator, guest, and servant is managed within unspoken codes of behavior. Some of the codes evolve from norms of service and hospitality, some from maritime histories, and some from theatrical innovations unique to cruise ship protocols.

Throughout the journey I will be concerned about the efficacy of my performance. By this I mean that as a laborer within this environment I will need to perform in a manner that the cruise personnel deem to be "excellent." Excellent behavior conforms to norms of the maritime trade, including a sense of masculine efficiency based upon militaristic expectations drawn from naval traditions. On higher-priced vessels, men will wear standardized haircuts and women will wear jackets with ties. Service is expected to be crisp, functional rather than friendly. Excellent behavior is evaluated through customer surveys coupled with the observations of the permanent cruise ship staff. All cruise personnel are scored by passengers on a survey distributed at the end of the journey, and passengers rate their vacation experience in all service areas including entertainment. For me, the impact of the ratings is minimal; if my ratings are poor, I won't be able to book another cruise. But for full-time contracted staff, good performance ratings might mean additional shore leave or time off, while bad ratings could mean the loss of a job. Consequently, all laborers are invested in performing roles of service and entertainment excellently. My family trained me to strive for excellence, therefore I tailor my lectures to match the interests of each unique set of passengers, working to find a comfortable balance between education and vacation entertainment.

My specialty is the Caribbean, but there are destination lecturers for ports of call throughout the world. In addition to destination lecturers, many ships also support "special interest" lecturers who speak about topics unrelated to the ship's itinerary. Popular subjects delivered by this category of lecturer include astronomy, nature, celebrities, or world affairs. The ability to entertain is as crucial as the presentation topic, and as a result, talent agencies select only dynamic speakers to place on their ships. This makes cruise ship gigs particularly attractive to those trained in theater or public speaking. Cruise-critic.com author Dan Benedict explains it succinctly: "On a cruise ship, audience members attend lectures out of curiosity and for fun; they don't need to pay attention or take notes in order to pass an exam. They are free to walk out when their interest wanes, and they will—the casino may be only a few steps away, the lido grill is open most of the day, and there are always other activities and options."[3] It makes sense that on cruise ships, lecturers are a part of the entertainment team.

The lecturers complement other "enrichment" positions that differ from cruise line to cruise line. Cruise directors and their entertainment staff have creatively designed positions that run the gamut from expert card player, to "Bridge" experts who talk about landscapes visible from the ship, to "distinguished gents" who dance with single women in club venues. Enrichment offerings change as each cruise line develops it brand. For example, Carnival Cruise Line will have more dance instructors and fewer historical lecturers because their clientele tend to prefer party and sports activities. Cruise lines with more elderly guests will have more academic lectures. Enrichment staff are not contracted workers on the ship but rather function as temporary workers who cruise for only a week or two. Their only compensation is airfare, complimentary cabin accommodations, and meals. Complementing the enrichment staff volunteers are a paid cohort of "Activity" staff who are under six-month contracts. They work with the cruise director to deliver more high-energy, active events like pool splash parties, dance classes, carnival parades, or Bingo playoffs.

So why do I cruise? There are several reasons. First, cruising allows me to perfect my lecturing skills, because I must communicate my content to an audience who is probably not that interested. They came to vacation. My content must be crafted to effectively engage listeners, a skill I find useful in all presentation venues. Second, I want to learn about perspectives outside of academic bubbles in order to test the relevance of my research and scholarship. Cruise ships, as popular cultural sites, bring me into contact with people I might never meet in my normal social circles. Lecturing on ships allows me to expand my horizons by participating in cultural exchanges with those outside of my comfort zone. There is something about working in a liminal zone where daily routines are forgotten and the traveler is able to reflect upon what it means to be in a nowhere zone between and betwixt the familiar and the unfamiliar. This liminality of place and space, race and labor, home and destination links the experience of sea travel across time. And it is my engagement with this liminal space that has catalyzed my interest in this research and writing this book. When I travel through the Caribbean, where Arawak, Caribe, English, French, Spanish, Dutch, Indian, and Portuguese cultures have shaped encounters, experiences of cultural exchange seem simultaneously pertinent, historical, and performative.

In addition I cruise because as a theater director and producer, I am in awe of the coordination and improvisational skills of the creative artists and management staff who craft entertainment spectacles on board ocean liners. The ship's architecture facilitates entertainment events throughout all areas of the megaship. In some ways, the experience of the cruise ship replicates elements of immersive theater because the entire vessel provides a full-scale, nonstop, alternative environment. James Frieze, in his edited volume *Reframing Immersive Theatre*, establishes that "immersive experiences depend on the creation of an event bubble that excludes the reality of the wider world." Maintaining the experience requires removing referents to reality-based life events.[4] This principle of immersion is particularly apt for cruise ships. Entertainment and hospitality staff design the guests' entire entrance ritual to quickly establish that they are entering an alternative seascape where their needs, and indeed their desires, will be attended to. Frieze writes, "The crux of participatory performance lies not in the object of our attention, what might normally be called the 'content,' but in the ways that our attention is managed, the ways in which our engagement is co-opted *with and as* content."[5] Ostensibly, the intention of a Caribbean cruise is to experience the Caribbean with the ship functioning as the means of transport. Instead, passengers' attention is redirected from destinations to onboard activities; the cruise industry manages the journey by focusing activities on the ship itself as an immersive entertainment environment. A well-coordinated team collaborates on this trick of redirection. From an economic perspective, one goal of immersing passengers in onboard activities is to keep the money on the ship. Drinks, food, spa treatments, Bingo boards, upgrades, shore excursions, photographs, clothing, artwork—in short, anything and everything is available within a cashless environment managed through internal financial systems, with the cruise ship card documenting all transactions.

The creation of an all-inclusive, commercial fantasy spectacle of this kind is certainly not unique to the cruise ship industry. Theme parks like Disneyland or Universal Studios have deep experience monetizing immersive entertainment experiences. However, on a cruise ship, the experience is even more immersive because the guest cannot simply exit the environment—even the shore excursions are crafted to continue the fantasy of vacation immersion. The experience also has elements of immersive commercial theater: even though the audience's interactions are planned and scripted in immersive commercial theater, guests still make choices about what they want to do and how they want to do it. The ability to re-sort elements of an immersive theatrical experience gives participants a sense of agency as they invent their own expressive response to the environment. Cruise guests can fashion a unique and pleasurable experience for themselves because there are so many options. Ship managers, like Disney executives, do not attempt to re-create actual structures or to simulate authentic experiences. Instead, they use themes and visual references to maritime iconography to create something altogether new. Cruise lines strive to design contemporary experiences while giving a nod to the past. As new lines emerge (like Virgin Voyages[6]) experiences become even more tailored to specific audiences.

Taking codes and cues from these designed environments, guests make daily decisions about how they want to craft the offerings. If guests prefer to immerse themselves in a drinking, fun-in-the-sun fantasy, they can, or they might instead imagine themselves as art connoisseurs, shopping at art auctions or taking classes in glass blowing on the upper deck. Vacationing guests have agency and the ability to construct, resist, recast, and dream within the codes and cues of the fantasy world. Like Disney guests, they "participate far more actively in the onstage experience than many assert."[7] Cruise passengers are able to construct a vacation experience that matches their imagined cruise experience, be it the *Love Boat* or the *Titanic* crossing, but they do it within the theatrical imaginary constructed by the cruise companies' entertainment formula. It is no accident that management offices for Carnival, Norwegian, Royal Caribbean, and Disney cruise lines are all headquartered in Florida, and near Disneyland, where infrastructure for populist fantasy entertainment abounds.[8]

One might think that passengers cruise because they want to see new countries or experience new cultures, but that is seldom the case. Even though cruise companies advertise various destinations in the Caribbean cruises, the ship itself is the mainstay of the experience. Shore stops are brief—usually six to ten hours—and the air-conditioned vessel is the passengers' home base.

Many passengers never leave the ship at all, preferring to eat and take advantage of amenities they find on board instead of venturing out into the hot and chaotic experiences they might find in the ports. For those who do disembark, the primary draws are frequently the same—sun, beach, and shopping. Any distinctive cultural aspects of each port are brought to life only through the storytelling of the destination lecturer and the expertise of local islanders if passengers choose to pay for a cultural shore excursion. Within this context, the role of the destination lecturer becomes essential in fulfilling passengers' perception that they have actually traveled somewhere other than the container ship and its ancillary shore excursions. The passenger experience of the twenty-first-century cruise vacationer is meticulously managed, differing considerably from earlier centuries when boarding a ship was a fraught, risky necessity. Crew workers who support these leisure travelers encounter a different set of challenges.

Shipboard work has changed substantially across the centuries. Maritime historians differentiate between sailors connected to the military (naval seamen) and those involved in shipping goods (merchant seamen). Modern cruise ships evolved from merchant ships that moved goods from place to place. Seen as another form of freight, passengers are merchandise and the vessel of the cruise ship operates as a contained mobile environment for transporting them through oceanic landscapes. The cruise ship needs workers, thousands of them, in order to fulfill its function as a mobile transport unit filled with hotel, dining, and entertainment options. All workers live below deck; only some of them come to the upper decks to interact with passengers and service their needs. Others stay below deck to work in the kitchen or the laundry or with the engineering staff and remain effectively invisible to passengers. Workers who do interact with passengers are trained to interact in a performative and functional manner. By this I mean that cruise ship workers specialize in performing an attitude of service and responsiveness that differs considerably from what one might expect on a different type of vessel. On a naval vessel, crew members respond to military hierarchies with an imperative of defending the nation. On a cargo ship, workers manage the weight and load of their goods especially when moving across waters known to be treacherous, such as the Great Lakes or the Cape of Good Hope. However, on cruise ships, work demeanors are similar to those employed in the hospitality and service industries. Consequently, micro performances—small acts of service and servility—impact how passengers experience the all-inclusive cruise experience.

For example, when I enter the ship and arrive at my cabin, a member of the housekeeping staff will introduce themselves, ask how and when I would like for my bed to be made, and offer to get me ice or water. At first, it's disconcerting; I have never had a butler before. This deliberate first moment establishes that the staff member is at my service and ready to accommodate my every need. I mark this moment as a performative moment of servitude where the housekeeper and I establish how we will relate to one another. If I were a normal passenger, I would simply say "thank you" and begin to unpack. But I am actually a fellow crew member, albeit temporarily. So, I usually say thank you, and mention that I am a destination lecturer delivering programming for the ship. The housekeeper may already know this, because on many cruises my cabin is located just behind the door that separates the crew from the passengers. It's a borderline space where I receive upgraded services including wine and chocolates, while simultaneously functioning as a worker. Nevertheless, the two of us move through a choreography of service and introduction as we explore the boundaries of our now-nebulous roles of worker and passenger. Once the housekeeper leaves, I unpack and arrange my traveling dressing room.

Even though my accommodations are comparatively luxurious for a crew member, it's still a pretty small space, somewhere between 170 and 240 square feet. Once I close the cabin door, I settle in to prepare for my meeting with the cruise director who manages the entertainment staff. We will discuss timing and venues for my lectures after the ship sets sail; my plan is to discuss each of the Caribbean destinations through the lens of music, dance, and cultural studies, explaining the unique cultural mixing—indigenous, African, European, and Asian—that characterizes the Americas. This approach to lecture content allows me to link history with folklore and tourism, and to raise awareness about how historical subjugation impacts the very landscape the travelers will move through, even if they have no interaction with Caribbean people during their journey. As cruise passengers, they may encounter more Caribbean islanders in their dining room than they do on their shore excursions.

Diversity and Internationalism

During my time on board, I will interact with an international set of crew members who come from the Caribbean, the Philippines, Greece, the United Kingdom, India, and Australia, as well as other nations. Collectively, their experiences represent a broad swath of cultures and class locations. They are working in a fairly secure job where room and board is provided, and consequently are able to save their wages and, for many who have families, send support back home. Most travel with six-month contracts, yet many have worked on cruises for years, even decades. Most paying passengers will never learn much about the men and women who serve them and guide the ship through the Caribbean waters. The workers are a "motley crew" who create an immersive onboard atmosphere of leisure. The experience of working on board a ship connects me to histories of others who have traveled this way, other workers who traveled seas and oceans within a multicultural environment. Some were lured by the promise of experiencing new destinations; most were trying to earn money through employment in the primary transportation industry of their era. Workers on cruise ships generally come from economically challenged countries and hope to advance their social and political circumstances by leaving homelands, often located in the Global South, for lucrative employment within the cruise industry. Through their work on international waters, they learn how to strategize success alongside international crew members from other cultures. I'm interested in how performative interactions within the contained work environment of ships (past and present) transfers knowledge across these cultural communities.

On the ship, I watch, and participate in, micro performances of cultural engagement throughout the journey. The West Indian housekeeper encounters the Filipino food service worker. They meet and greet in the hallways of the ship, and while the common language is English, their native languages are different so they use gestures to augment their conversations. Their nonverbal communications and the knowledges they transmit are instructive, and different jobs hold differing statuses within the social ecosystem of the ship. Coworkers, through onboard interactions, participate in what Dorinne Kondo calls "the complex dance of domination and counter-domination, of approaching and drawing back."[9] Through a process of interactions with different national or ethnic communities, crew members shape themselves and their identities for what will be future cultural adaptations. This back-and-forth of cultural adaptation is something I've also witnessed in my university work, whenever I orchestrate exchange programs with students or artists seeking to communicate across cultures in foreign countries. For a maritime worker who has service skills and but limited access to social mobility, the stakes of cultural exchange are even greater. While cultural exchange certainly happens in land-based communities, the unique circumstances of traveling in a modified container ship for extended periods of time with workers from various cultures amplifies the tone and intensity of the exchanges. Learning cultural fluency allows workers employed by international enterprises to advance economically as they educate themselves about diverse cultural paradigms.

Shipping companies have been practicing segregation based on ethnicity since the globalization of the seafarer market starting in the 1970s. According to an International Labor Organization report, "the composition of the multinational crew is the result of clear policy and not chance."[10] On the one hand, cruise lines pride themselves on the international and multicultural identities of the crew and staff members. Passengers can experience the diversity of the world through their interactions with entertainment and service staff. On the other hand, there is a troubling tendency to replicate hierarchical identities, where male seafarers from the Global North dominate senior officer positions, while those from the Global South are lower-level staff members.[11] The majority of seafarers are recruited by crew agencies in their countries of origin. "White-collar" crew positions, like hotel lead staff, cruise directors, and destination lecturers, tend to be direct hires.

Front-facing staff on higher-end Caribbean and European cruises tend to be American, Canadian, or European—white faces to make the primarily white guests feel comfortable. Services like the spa require intimate contact and spa staff tend to have strong English skills and come from the Global North. Workers who staff specialized small-scale entertainment areas (e.g., glass blowing, art auctions, wine tasting), are also usually white. Below deck, Asian workers and Black workers are employed in food preparation, laundry, and housekeeping. Engineering staff tends to be Greek or Italian because of their historical dominance in the shipping industry.[12] In general, people from developing countries occupy the lower positions, and employees from similar ethnic groups tend to work together. About 80 percent of the staff is male with women occupying more service-oriented positions.[13]

Because cruise ship companies recruit internationally, they can hire cheap workers while avoiding legal restrictions. They cut financial corners much like the captains of earlier centuries who scrimped on sailor's uniforms and rations.[14] The industry justifies its use of international labor by promoting the internationality of crew members. Management insists that each staff member's name tag must bear their country of origin and invite guests to chat with the workers about their home countries. Ester Ellen Bolt and Conrad Lashley, two researchers specializing in hospitality on cruise ships, have written extensively about crew members' perceptions of their work environment. They explain how making and maintaining friendships on board is somewhat fraught and crew members from the same country tend to stick together: "Different ways of greeting, behaviours, language and impressions were seen to be interesting to employees working on board a cruise ship. However, crew members seemed to be acting more sensitively to others, to find out what approach is expected from others in order to gain mutual respect."[15]

The authors interviewed workers who were attempting to communicate across language boundaries, and who were confused about tasks and frequently had to demonstrate with embodied gestures. The performative use of gestures to explain tasks is typical of cross-cultural communication. Inherent in such communication is disjuncture—moments when meanings are muddled or communication is incomplete. Some crew members admitted they were racist and disliked working with crew members of other ethnicities.

> "Most of the utility Galley are Caribbeans. So, but, if they see one Philippines in the area they take care more about him. But if it is Caribbeans they just don't care about that." (Interview 3, Galley employee, Nicaragua, male).[16]

I received similar observations in speaking with entertainment performers about how they interact with other staff members. One Black dancer described how, when eating in the officers' dining room, the Russians and Croatians would exit the dining room because they did not want to be around other Black entertainers. Nonverbal clues and informal microaggressions help crew members to understand where and how they are to interact with other nationalities while working on the ship.

The past informs the present and it is useful to look back to the era when global sea traffic on merchant sailing and steamships peaked. Across the long nineteenth century, sea workers, migrants, the enslaved, and leisure passengers traveled across ocean waters to establish themselves in new destinations. Their interactions in vessels and ports created contested social hierarchies where, ultimately, new class structures were negotiated. Within this process, acquiring information about new locations was essential for success and, indeed, survival. Musicologist and maritime historian James Revell Carr writes: "The sea for the nineteenth-century world was what the Internet is for the world today, a seemingly boundless communication network that transmitted information, commerce, news, maps, art, music, literature and the like from person to person, across great distances."[17] For sailors, the maritime network allowed crew members to learn from one another about how to navigate culture and employment. Crews that were diverse could better educate one another about how to navigate challenges of social mobility.

Archives document the labor activities of these multicultural crews in images and ledgers. As merchant trading expanded during the eighteenth and nineteenth centuries to include new goods—cotton, sugar, wood from the Americas, and enslaved Africans—more workers were needed first to support sailing ships, and, later, steamers. Some voyagers sought new opportunities in the "New World," but many were merely mobile workers performing tasks like cleaning or carpentry that they could have done on shore. However, working at sea—traveling across maritime highways with a diverse set of laborers—enabled exchanges of innovative practices and survival strategies in ways that doing the same job on shore could not. Much of this communication network flowed across nonliterate bodies, bodies that utilized gestures, songs, and chants to unite with unfamiliar foreigners around common tasks. Performances, quotidian and embodied, were, in this context, a way of establishing dialogue with strangers. In a nineteenth-century merchant ship, a white New England barrel maker might sleep within inches of a Black steward charged with gutting chickens to feed the workers. Thus, cultural and social worlds collided for extended periods as workers, laboring under the control of the captain, moved across ocean waters.

It is difficult to access the perspectives of disempowered laborers by relying on written narrative. Literary writings that document histories of the underclass, and particularly the Black or ethnic underclass, describe their activities through a racialized lens usually tainted with Euro-American cultural and class bias; however, viewing these histories through the lenses of dance studies, folklore, and musicology somewhat illuminates underclass epistemologies. I draw upon methodologies from these fields to access information about how merchant seamen interacted with one another, methodologies that include the analysis of cultural expressions depicted in historical images, examinations of merchant trade logs, and tracing musical traditions documented in song lyrics and popular performance practice. Unfortunately, the historical, theatrical, and maritime archives in England and the United States yield only a few images of ethnic communities working on merchant vessels.

Figure 2 depicts the crew of the *Moel Ellian*, a packet or merchant cargo ship that traveled between England and Australia during the late nineteenth century. I'm struck by the way in which the working men gather on the deck of the sailing vessel posing for the crew portrait. Each of them wears a distinctive hat, defined by their personal taste or, perhaps, their ethnic community. With their arms crossed, the subjects pose facing the camera. The captain sits down in front, perched on a seat, his status marked by his casual hands and rough-hewn suit. The others who wear suits are probably mates who assist the captain with navigation. The ropes and rigging surrounding the men are symbols of their watery occupation. For me, this photograph

Figure 2. Workers on a merchant ship bound for Australia. Seafarers career papers of Hugh Thomas of Port Dinorwic, c. 1888–1897. Courtesy of the Merseyside Maritime Museum.

represents the enigma and challenge of the maritime world. How did men from such varied ethnic and national backgrounds come to live and amuse themselves together for extended periods? How did they translate and share experiences? How did they accommodate one another? What was the theatricality of their daily encounters?

The "motley crew" of the nineteenth century operated within an expansive network of transatlantic and transpacific commerce routes. The merchant trade industry drew (and continues to draw) from international communities. Shipping networks included many ethnicities who moved through even more culturally complex shore cultures. The notion of a "motley crew" infuses imaginations about the world of maritime travel. What actually happens when men crowd together on a wooden ship for months at a time seeking a better life? I sit in my stateroom on the cruise ship wondering what it would have been like to sail while Black during the nineteenth century. Because I am a theater professor, I am most familiar with the Black stewards of the African Grove Theatre who worked for packet ship lines running between New York, Liverpool, and the Caribbean. Their story captures one aspect of migration and social mobility.

Black Stewards

The African Grove Theatre, touted as the first African American theater company in the United States, was founded by free Black stewards who shipped out of New York City during the early nineteenth century. Their history drew me into this investigation of how free Black seamen found employment by serving others on transatlantic journeys.

> Nearly half a century ago—in 1816–17, to wit—there sailed from the port of New York, in one of the Liverpool packets, as steward thereof, a tall black man named Brown. He belonged to the class which, at that time, and for years afterward, even to the present day, occupied a respectable and responsible position. The steward was then, next to the captain, the most important personage on the ship. Dressed in his brilliant-colored morning-gown and red slippers, he was wont to receive passengers with "stately courtesy," which was duly reciprocated by those who went down to the sea in ships. The stewards of the different lines of packets vied with each other in their style on board ship, and in their private houses. They were all colored, and sailed to every port at home, or abroad—Liverpool, Canon, Bremen. Charleston, New Orleans, Savannah, &c.[18]

This passage, written by Thomas Hamilton in the January 1860 issue of the *Anglo-African*, describes the colored freeman and seaman named William Brown who founded the African Grove Theatre in 1821. William Brown was a retired ship steward and his main actor, James Hewlett, worked as a tailor and a steward on the Liverpool packet ships, vessels that transported mail and passengers between New York and Liverpool. Brown likely relocated to New York City from the Caribbean, sailing up the Gulf Stream to settle within a community of free African American and Caribbean domestic workers. There, he established a summer entertainment garden that offered weekend entertainment to the free Black working class. The history of the African Grove players highlights how maritime migrations contributed to the movement of ideas across transnational ethnic communities. Actors in this company, which operated during the height of slavery, performed works by Shakespeare, Richard Brinsley Sheridan, and other European playwrights as well as new work about Caribbean politics. The African Grove's original play *The Drama of King Shotaway* described a revolution on St. Vincent island led by indigenous leader Joseph Chatoyer.

The creation of this play is significant because it captures a history of rebellion embedded in the story of the Garífuna or Black Caribe communities. When a slave ship wrecked off the coast of Honduras, the survivors intermarried with local Caribe indigenous communities, forming a unique Garífuna nation. The Garífuna fought against the British for their freedom and were eventually exiled to the coasts of Honduras and Belize. Their multilingual communities contributed greatly to Afro-Caribbean expressive cultural forms that may have informed the original production of *King Shotaway*.[19] When I cruise through the British Caribbean, I can see the lasting impact of the Black Caribe uprising because contemporary Garífuna cultures extend from the coast of Nicaragua, across the island of Roatán, and on to Honduras and Belize. Cruise ship guests are exposed to Garífuna cultures through island tours and folkloric exhibitions where they observe traditional *punta* dancing, food products using the native cassava plant, and hand-carved dugout canoes. Garífuna cultures are one of the few Black ethnic communities in the Americas to maintain their traditional language. Their expatriate communities extend to New York, California, and other sections of the United States.

In 1821, the African Grove players incorporated histories of the Garífuna into their performance repertory to document the history of the rebellion and perhaps to celebrate the nobility and diversity of African American experiences. Because the African Grove players worked both on land and on ships, they were able to share and compare experiences in England, the Caribbean, and the United States. Indeed, the coastal sea currents would have directly propelled the merchant sea trade along this route making exchanges of information facile. Consequently, the social encounters of Black seamen working the maritime routes extended beyond what they would have experienced living solely in the United States as members of racially marked cultural communities. James Hewlett, for example, the lead actor from the company, built a career as both an active steward and an up-and-coming actor. He used his skills as an entrepreneur to market his Shakespearean performances in New York City, Liverpool, and Trinidad. Historian Marvin McAllister maintains: "Hewlett refused to concede his career to the historical accident of being born black . . . and decided to create opportunities and representational freedom in a less culturally restrictive locale."[20] Working on ships enabled him to subsidize his passion for acting while exposing him to cultures and fashions of the Caribbean and the United Kingdom.[21]

Other members of the African Grove players also participated in transatlantic economies by working as stewards, cooks, or able-bodied seamen on ships. Most learned on the job or through word of mouth, but there was a seaman training program at the African Free School in New York City that included navigation and cartography.[22] Stewards were basically servants; they served the captain and his mates by cleaning cabins, helping with dressing and laundry, repairing clothing, and serving meals. The cook served meals to all the seamen, working round the clock to provide viable rations to an often-surly crew. Even though African American men occupied these subservient roles, it is likely that they used their proximity to the main cabin to advance their knowledge of cultural practices and global events. The materiality of the ship, and the architecture of the vessel itself, demonstrate how the stewards and cooks could closely observe the captain at work. In order to serve the captain, the steward, especially on passenger voyages, would need to sleep in a crude berth on the upper deck. It was within this space that stewards would spend their time serving. Rendered largely invisible by their race and social status, they were nevertheless privy to intimate conversations of officers and first-class travelers. Like the African American Pullman porters of the early twentieth century who used their proximity to passengers on railway lines to develop intellectual networks,[23] stewards on packet ships used their access to upper-class cabins to their advantage.

Thomas Hamilton's description of the steward above, referencing a steward wearing a brilliant-colored morning gown and red slippers, romanticizes the role. In reality, stewards dressed as other seamen and were considered a part of the crew. Michael Sokolow describes the life of a New England–based African American steward in detail in his book *Charles Benson, Mariner of Color in the Age of Sail*.[24] Compiling information from a collection of archival materials housed in the Beinecke Library at Yale University, Sokolow explains how Benson was a career mariner who sailed for over two decades to Zanzibar and Madagascar off the eastern coast of Africa. His travel writings reflect the life of a man comfortable with his role as a steward—a man respected by his captain and entrusted with managing trade goods on the ship and in the ports. Benson began his life as part of a small African American community in Framingham, Massachusetts. Eventually, as he spent more and more of his life at sea, he distanced himself from his town, his family, his community, and particularly the racial politics of the century. Like house-

Figure 3. Black crew members sewing on the forecastle, starboard side, circa 1864–1865. Courtesy of Naval History and Heritage Command.

keepers or service workers on the modern cruise ship, his day-to-day labor of traveling and working away from home distanced him from familiar connections. After a while, the quotidian circumstances of onshore life become a distant memory. Benson lived and worked within a maritime community united by their dislocation from land-based social constrictions placed on African Americans, as he found a kind of freedom in his career-based identity as an independent seaman.

The occupational status of stewards changed significantly between 1818 and 1850. Between 1818 and 1825, stewards were respectably employed and newspapers advertised for colored seamen with specialized skills. An 1820 advertisement in the *New York Daily Advertiser* reads: "Two likely colored men wanted as waiters on board the steamship *Fulton*—those who speak good French and Spanish will be preferred. Apply to the steward on board at the end of Cherry Street."[25] The advertisement indicates free, Black, multilingual stewards were both available and desirable. Although work was hard and journeys unpredictable, employment as a steward at sea enabled free Black people to acquire income and intellectually engage with a polyglot crew while exploring various ports. Maritime historian W. Jeffrey Bolster reports that before 1839 many Black seamen were able to sail with crews where other Black men also labored, a situation that would have provided a sense of camaraderie or fellowship.[26] But by midcentury the Black sailor, if he was able to find a job, would sail with a primarily white crew. The majority of Black seamen worked in the whaling industry or on packet ships where the shorter runs between, for example, New York and Liverpool, would have ensured a return trip home every sixteen to thirty days, allowing for some stable, onshore social interactions.

Packet ships, named for the packets or packages carried by the vessels, were originally organized within the British Isles to connect mail service across the islands. They were a specific type of merchant ship, built smaller and faster so they moved more quickly from port to port, ensuring a parcel would arrive at its destination in a timely manner. Packet ships aimed for speed, navigating quickly through storms and rough waters. In North America, domestic packet ships ran short journeys up and down the Atlantic coast and were called "coasters." They proliferated as new ports developed[27] and by 1702 there were packet service lines in Barbados, Jamaica, Florida, California, Charleston, and Pensacola. In addition to packages, the ships sometimes carried passengers who would pay for steerage tickets to settle in below deck amid the cargo. At first, during the late eighteenth century and early nineteenth century, accommodations were rough and passengers were required to bring their own bedding.[28] Later, as better accommodations were provided, stewards were needed to service the passengers as well as navigate the ship.

One of the first packet lines to sail between New York and Liverpool was the Black Ball line. The shipping line, founded in 1817, outrageously proposed regular sailings, on schedule between North America and the British Isles. To prove their point, they launched in January, subjecting their workers, later known as "packet rats," to the harsh realities of sailing North Atlantic waters during the winter season. These were the packet lines that the stewards of the African Grove worked on. The Black Ball line initially consisted of four vessels, the *Amity, Courier, Pacific,* and *James Monroe,* but the success of the industry expanded the fleet quickly. By 1820 multiple shipping lines were offering regular service between the eastern coast of the United States and the United Kingdom. While these shipping lines became occupational opportunities for free Black and other crewmen, working on packet ships was an undesirable position within the maritime work world; only the most disenfranchised white seamen would view it as a viable work opportunity.

Whaling ships, by contrast, provided lucrative opportunities for profit sharing, and Black men were keen to participate. The downside was the length of the journeys. Whalers would travel for as much as three to five years following migrating sea animals. Because seamen spent hours stalking whales on the open ocean, the daily work varied from intense periods of hard work to long periods of enforced idleness.[29] However, capturing the whales required working as a coordinated team to subdue the large mammals. The laborers developed a sense of community where each man's effort would ultimately be rewarded. After the hunt, part of the job was to boil blubber fat in an iron try pot set atop an onboard oven. The product, whale oil, used for lanterns and soap, was a much-needed and expensive product during the nineteenth century. When the journey ended, the entire crew would receive a percentage from the sale. Men who worked on whalers in many ways exemplified the motley crew—they came from a variety of cultures and backgrounds. Native Americans were active in the industry[30] and African Americans appear in photos and lithographs[31] depicting whale captures. Herman Melville's *Moby Dick*[32] offers a remarkably accurate account of life on this type of vessel. Because of their relatively small crew and the extended amount of time crew members spent together, the culture of the whale ship was less hierarchical. This sense of equality would have appealed to African American seamen seeking respite from the violent and racially polarized social life of the early nineteenth century United States.

Even though sailing while Black in the nineteenth century was lucrative, it was also undoubtedly fraught. Free African Americans needed multiple skills to survive during a time period where slavery knocked on the doorstep of every Black individual. For those who chose to work at sea, situations in ports varied considerably. Mid-Atlantic and New England ports in the United States—Salem, Boston, Baltimore, Philadelphia, and New York—had communities of free Blacks that could provide services to itinerant sailors. In these communities, boarding houses accommodated domestic workers of all industries. Churches and entertainment centers like the African Grove were social meccas where news and gossip fueled social activism.[33] Some ports, like those in the Caribbean, were suited for information exchange across nationalities, and social life within these ports required multilingual skills. For example, a New Orleans port in the 1700s would have been an international French province. After the Louisiana Purchase, however, landing there would have been dangerous for a free Black sailor working as either a cook or a steward.

Even enslaved Blacks would sometimes take advantage of variable port environments to escape. One of the most renowned maritime escapes is

Frederick Douglass's departure from the shipyards of Baltimore using borrowed papers from a free African American seaman. Douglass worked as a caulker[34] and acquired a knowledge of sailor vocabulary, which made his assumed identity credible. He writes in his autobiography about how he managed to realize his escape. "I had one friend—a sailor—who owned a sailor's protection, which answered somewhat the purpose of free papers—describing his person and certifying to the fact that he was a free American sailor. The instrument had at its head the American eagle, which at once gave it the appearance of an authorized document."[35] The narrative of his departure demonstrates how working at sea offered a somewhat liminal space for contested Black identities. W. Jeffrey Bolster succinctly sums this up: "He succeeded that September day in 1838 largely because free Black seamen were then so common as to cause few second looks."[36] Sailing while Black in the nineteenth century meant negotiating a racial construct that was fluid and relative. Crew lists record people of color as *black, mulatto, colored, brown, dark, very dark*, and so forth. Since maritime waters cover multiple nations and postcolonial ports, cultural definitions of race varied widely. Black in one port was brown in another, colored in another, and so on. While these records are confusing to the researcher, they were undoubtedly advantageous to the Black traveling mariner.

On the one hand, as political and social systems shifted, Black sailors were able to literally navigate themselves away from one port and into a more favorable territory, albeit at the loss of familial or friendship circles. On the other hand, the dangers of the waters complicated life for Black sailors as much as any other Jack Tar.[37] Notices of drownings include mentions of colored stewards along with everyone else. The *Norfolk Beacon* of 1827 describes how the schooner *Xenophon,* coming from Havana and carrying sugar, coffee, oranges, and sweetmeats, was lost off the coast of an inlet. The crew was stranded on the ship for twelve hours. During that time five men, all colored, including the cook and steward John C. Williams, took account of the incident.[38] On another voyage a colored steward, John Taylor II, was not so lucky. *The Evening Post* of 1824 reports how he accidentally fell off the wharf in Savannah and drowned.[39] Considering the role of the steward during the early part of the nineteenth century provides context for the African Grove players. William Alexander Brown, who managed the enterprise, was financially successful and settled down after international travels. His theater, which lasted for three years, marked a high time for free Black seamen. The entrepreneurial skills of the free Black working-class domestics allowed them to achieve some degree of notoriety and freedom both on land and at sea.

Imagine how shifting identities and perceptions of self-worth might impact a man's choice of work environments. Black seamen made strategic choices, carefully weighing the dangers of being at sea against the dangers of being Black onshore.

The contemporary cruise ship's version of the steward is the housekeeping staff. On Caribbean cruises, most of the housekeeping staff members are Black. Housekeeping staff are responsible for the upkeep of each passenger's cabin during their time of occupancy and each worker manages about twenty cabins—changing bedding, filling ice buckets, picking up discarded clothing, and rearranging bedding for "turndown" service. Their presence is part of the performance of service hospitality essential to the leisure cruise experience. On the cruise lines where I lecture, many of the housekeeping staff are from the Caribbean. Consequently, their knowledge of both the passengers and the islands we travel to is acute. When possible, I tend to check in with the housekeeping staff about the ship's journey to keep myself up-to-date on new developments at the various ports.

On one engagement, as I settled into my cabin, a male member of the housekeeping staff entered with a name tag that read "Edward—St Vincent." St. Vincent, as mentioned earlier, is where the Black Carib nation helped to fight against the British. Noting his name tag, I mentioned to Edward that today my lecture would mention St. Vincent and I asked if he had ever heard of the African Grove. With a hint of exasperation, he said "no" and turned away. Perhaps he was annoyed that I would mention his country of origin when all he was trying to do was bring in the water. The efficacy of his service depended upon him servicing a large set of cabins in a very short amount of time during a long port day. But I wanted to chat. I asked Edward if he knew about a play called *The Drama of King Shotaway*, a play some historical African Americans wrote about a rebellion in his home country. With a bit of an eye roll and a hint of surprise Edward responded, "Shotaway?" he asked, "Do you mean Chatoyer?" "I guess . . ." I responded. Now I would get my comeuppance from Edward. "His name is Chatoyer, and everyone knows him. He is a very famous king who fought the British. His statues are all over the place on my island." I sat subdued. While the story of King Shotaway sits as a footnote in European-focused theater history books, this maritime worker, this modern-day steward, was deeply connected to histories of intercultural knowledge. This transference of knowledge has long been a part of the way in which laboring communities explain presence across waterways that have transported them as enslaved, as immigrants, and as performers. Histories of resistance especially resonate within a contained labor setting.

As Edward travels across ocean waters, his knowledge about his island and its history intersects with multiple stories shared by multiple service workers about their homes and their communities. This is a core component of the maritime world: the ability to exchange histories and broaden cultural competencies through work.

The Black Cook and the Black Imaginary

The contemporary counterpart of the Black steward is the cook. Historically, and on present-day cruises, this is a position usually occupied by Black and brown-skinned people. Food service is one of the most expansive spectacles on any cruise ship. Impeccably trained waiters, servers, and cleanup crews surround passengers with exquisitely staged presentations of food. In the pool bar, in the passageways, in the dining rooms, and in the coffee shops, passengers are offered food delicacies prepared by an extensive set of workers, most of whom labor below the waterline. Those who do work on the upper decks and interact with paying guests are asked to actively perform their job in servitude. They wipe and (especially post-COVID-19) ladle food onto guests' plates. In the dining room they carry large trays of food directly to tables, bringing even the most obscure ingredients in response to guests' requests. I have seen guests ask for ketchup and hot sauce to season up French cuisine, or for up to six plates of lobster. On some cruise lines dining room staff are asked to sing and parade for passengers after serving them meals. They pass through the dining room banging plates, singing songs, and twirling napkins. As an entertainment insider, I can see the weariness of the staff as they prepare for this sometimes-demoralizing spectacle. On a good day, this is an opportunity to shake out the kinks, cavort, and play. On a bad day, it's an extra expenditure of energy for an already exhausted worker. The public presence of the food service staff on a cruise ship underscores the importance of food within an environment where the only available food is what has already been stored on board. The archetype of the cook as a service-oriented worker who interacts with others has historical precedents. Modern cruise ship food service is a professionally regulated industry while in the past the ship's cook survived through his own ingenuity.

Historically, cooks on merchant ships were responsible for preparing food for the captain, his mates, and the crew. Men of all races worked in this position, but it was the primary work opportunity for African, Indian, and Asian men. On ships' crew lists that would often notate the race and the role of the seaman, the cook was frequently listed as Black. In the photograph of the

Figure 4a and 4b. Two images of Galley cooks on a modern cruise ship. (All photos are by John R. Diehl Jr., unless otherwise noted.)

motley crew above, a Black cook sits squarely in the center of the group of white men. He is distinguished by his white apron, which he wears on top of clothes similar to the other workers. It's an accessory that doubly marks his difference. He is both Black and gendered by his apron. Within the hierarchy of the ship, duties that required a man to service another man were considered subservient, and cooking for the crew was one of the more subservient roles. Early American historian Charles Foy, in his essay "How Blacks Became Ship Cooks,"[40] maintains that older men and disabled men were employed as cooks because they were too weak to "man" the sails or climb the ropes. Within a hypermasculine world, tropes of inadequacy and femininity mapped onto this position. Both men of color and those with limited physical prowess were gendered into feminine servitude in relation to other ship workers. The cook and the steward both occupied these domesticated roles.

The disempowered cook was especially subject to abuse. "Given the importance seamen placed upon food, cooks were often the focus of their colleagues' attention, for better and worse. With limited authority to alter what was generally a dull and repetitive diet, cooks stood responsible for a crucial element in crews' lives and therefore the anger of the crew when food did not meet expectations."[41] On the other hand, the cooks controlled the sustenance of all of the men on board and had the power to poison or nourish. Their job was difficult and required ingenuity. Cooks worked in a tight cramped space, usually on the top deck where they prepared meals for a disgruntled crew with limited supplies that were highly perishable. Animal and insect infestation only intensified the challenge of making palatable dishes. Written journals frequently describe the person in this job as a thief or deserving of a beating for "poisoning the food" or stealing rations. Similarly, archival depictions of cooks are dehumanizing.

Figure 5. 1831 Thomas McLean caricature of two cooks on the deck of a ship. Image courtesy of the National Maritime Museum, Greenwich, London.

For example, in a caricature drawn by Thomas McLean, two Black cooks commiserate with one another on the upper deck of a steamship. They look disheveled and stereotypically ape-ish as they sit preparing food. The cook's depiction replicates other stereotypes of African diaspora men, the Sambo, the Uncle Tom, the cuckold, or the comic buffoon. He is docile, subservient, stupid, perhaps bestial. This image of the cook was disseminated in London during the early nineteenth century, around 1831, when 20 percent of transatlantic seamen were Black. Within the maritime world where the captain runs the ship, the hypermasculine seamen "man" the sails, and the captain's mates navigate, the servile cook and his coworker, the steward, represent the bottom rung of the ladder. Even though the racial representation of the two men is biased, their activities were typical. One de-feathers a chicken, while the other carries what looks like a plate of potatoes. The chicken would have been a rare delicacy on board the ship while potatoes, even moldy ones, were staples. Maintaining fresh stock was a major challenge in the damp environment of the ship's hold as the temperature fluctuated drastically depending on where the ship traveled.

A revealing document about a cook's lifestyle is the *Nautical Cookery Book* published in 1896 by Thomas Francis Adkins.[42] The author describes the volume as an "Alphabetical Guide to Sailor's Cookery for the use of Stewards and Cooks on Cargo-Carrying Vessels." Adkins insists the volume is meant for "sailing ships, ocean tramps, and small craft, where the stores are entirely up to the captain's supervision, and where there is little facility for keeping provisions." The cookbook's recipes are sequenced from "A to Z," and items like stews with potatoes predominate. Included in the volume are instructions about how to use salt water to make bread, how to prepare deviled bones, how to use potatoes as yeast, instructions for oatmeal cakes, and a special section on how to cook for people with food poisoning. The manual includes a large section on how to care for livestock on board a ship with instructions about when to best kill and preserve pigs, fowl, or cattle. The two men depicted in the drawing by McLean look stupid and incompetent, but the realities of their job would have required ingenuity and perseverance.

A contrasting illustration by R. F. Zogbaum in 1892 more naturalistically depicts a Black cook on a U.S. Navy ship.[43] The seaman stands on the upper deck conversing with women from a foreign port who have come on board to sell local goods to the ship's crew members. The cook is easily recognizable in the lithograph because he wears a white shirt and an apron over his pants. The other men in the image are dressed like navy men. The cook smiles while holding an opened woman's fan. The other men look on, slightly amused. The groupings within the painting somehow accentuate the femininity of the Black cook within a cluster of seamen performing more typically masculine behaviors. The image highlights the fluidity of gender within the liminal world of the ship and contrasting racial norms. The Black cook, centered prominently in the image, reads as different from the other men in both skin color and gender. The white shirt accentuates the darkness of his skin. His smile, amid the stern faces of the other sailors, accentuates his female-gendered acquiescence. Yet the cook is also an example of gender fluidity on the ship and how male/female polarities can be disrupted within the liminal contained culture of maritime settings. Away from the shore, the land-based strictures of gendered social norms loosen. The encapsulated men have an opportunity to play with behaviors associated with men and women. In another print by the same illustrator titled *All Hands to the Skylark*, two men dressed in naval garb dance a hornpipe, a popular folk dance, with one another. On the side, a Black cook and a white fiddler accompany the men.

Figure 6. Black cook and navy men inspecting goods on the deck of a navy ship. Magazine illustration by R. F. Zogbaum in *Harper's Weekly: Souvenirs*, 1892.

In both Zogbaum illustrations, the cook is humanized in the way he is depicted but isolated from the other sailors who perform heteronormativity as they go about their daily routines. He is a seaman marked with difference not only because of his skin color but also because he acquiesces to the physical desires or needs of the other men. I riff on gendered interpretations of the cook's status because other stereotypes of African diaspora men, the Sambo, the Uncle Tom, the cuckold, or the comic buffoon, also draw from imaginations of Black men as docile, subservient, stupid, and emasculated. Working against the grain, the cook, like the steward, resists the limitations of white expectations about Black intellect. Kowtowing, cooking, wearing an apron, all of these performances of servitude belie double consciousness, a cultural awareness that the performance is not the thing. I view this as a kind of performative minstrelsy.

Blackface minstrel performance enacted by African Americans evolved during the latter half of the nineteenth century and persisted into the early twentieth century. The theatrical form was a way for African Americans to adopt the white racial imaginary and work within its paradigms to advance themselves economically. African American minstrels traveled to Europe and beyond wearing the minstrel mask and learning about foreign social codes and modes of behavior. And they traveled by ships across transatlantic waters. Theater historian Douglas A. Jones Jr. characterizes this phenomenon as a characteristic of the "Black Below." "Despite its racist degradations and grotesqueries, the minstrel stage appealed to Black performers and entrepreneurs because it offered them work other than the drudgery African Americans were accustomed to as well as outlets for their creativity."[44] Both African American minstrels of the late nineteenth century and African American seamen of the early nineteenth century were aware that the performance does not contain the identity of the lowest worker of the underclass. By this I mean that both racialized performers and racialized service workers perform gestures and behaviors to accommodate to the imaginations of the employer, the audience member, the overseer. They enact a Black identity that is not necessarily how they perceive of themselves or their potentiality. Workers thoughtfully and skillfully manipulate their performance to access greater mobility, a slice of freedom, and in the case of the Black seaman, perhaps the breeze near the stove where he can find a moment of peaceful solitude. The cook, the steward, and other Black seamen acquired, while working, active membership in a transnational network of workers gaining international fluency in world affairs.

By the end of the nineteenth century, being a steward or a cook on a merchant ship was fraught. As systems of slavery expanded and became more institutionalized, the risks for a Black sailor, identified by his melanin, increased. The same circumstances that earlier allowed for free navigation were more likely to result in a misinterpreted identity that would result in enslavement. Black codes, terrorism, and other legal and illegal mechanisms were used to disenfranchise and wreak violence upon Black bodies. Even though the War of 1812 validated the nobility and capabilities of Black sailors, the continued use of enslaved labor after the slave trade ended put free Black men at greater risk. The violence of post–Civil War Reconstruction additionally dehumanized Africans seeking participatory democracy in the United States. An influx of Irish workers to the United States who sought to escape the potato famine increased tensions between Black and Irish seamen as they vied for employment as dockworkers and seamen.

For example, the New York draft riots of 1863, initially a working-class response to the nationally mandated draft, turned into a race riot that destroyed free Black neighborhoods, forcing them to migrate out to the boroughs. Tensions were already high between Blacks and the Irish; the Irish had driven Black longshoremen away from employment at the docks because of labor competition. The Irish had immigrated to the United States and moved into the dock areas as a result of the potato famine. Once settled, they monopolized waterfront trades in part by forming the Irish Longshoremen's Benevolent Society (1852). By 1855, Black men were seen working the dock only if they were strikebreakers.[45] The draft riots began when bands of Irish longshoremen who lived within blocks of the pier began the first attacks.[46] They attacked waterfront dance houses, brothels, and boarding houses that catered to Black laborers; by midweek they had emptied the harbor area of Black men. Historian Iver Bernstein describes in vivid detail the violence inflicted on Black bodies by longshoremen defending their turf.[47] Individuals were battered, dismembered, and burned at will. After the riots, Black stewards would avoid at all costs the shipyards and their potential racial violence.

For the first half of the nineteenth century, the merchant sea trade provided a place of homemaking for Black men who strategically managed their fugitivity. By the end of the century, however, there was no safe haven. Because racialized capitalism limited the productivity of Black mariners, many stepped away from maritime occupations to find employment in urban port centers where other free Black men and women were living in community. Within these havens, some free Black individuals aided distressed seamen in their relocation and settlement. Records from the Colored Sailor's Home managed by two African American entrepreneurs in New York City document an escalating impoverishment of Black seamen between 1839 and 1860. Albro Lyons, pursuing a passion for religious temperance, partnered with William Powell to found the home on Pearl Street near the East River, where wayward seamen were welcomed if they were willing to participate in pious practices. The home owners enforced temperance and encouraged readings and conversations about elevating the Black community.[48] Powell and Lyons's Colored Sailor's Home offered inexpensive meals and a bed to those who could not afford to pay for the few costly boarding houses that allowed Black men to freely drink and carouse. The Sailor's Home owners were interested in documenting and empowering homeless Black seamen while keeping detailed records of their comings and goings.

Powell left New York City during the 1850s but later returned and relocated his home to 20 Vandewater Street. Upon his return, he noted an increasing destitution of the sailors as more men were barred from sailing on the more lucrative merchant and whaling journeys. While the Sailor's Home hoped to provide a sense of stability, many of the men ran away either because they could not afford even the nominal lodging fee or because they preferred to indulge in behaviors prohibited in the home. Through Powell's ledger I can see the names of the men and their ships and track their occupations. Most of them were cooks: Frances Washington on the ship *Stephen Bracers*, William Riley on the frigate *Elquigdamo*, Thomas Clark on the ship *Caroline*, or Burnett Buckley who deserted the ship *Typhoon*. Powell and Lyons estimated that 3,271 men passed through their doors. The situation of the seamen was so discouraging that Powell wrote a letter to the American Friends Society in 1861. The letter gives a sense of the desperate circumstances faced by African American cooks and stewards in an increasingly antagonistic maritime environment.

> Gentlemen—Since my last report Seventy Stewards Cooks and Seamen, have boarded at the Colored Sailors Home No. 2 Dover Street. Of this number eight from various causes were totally destitute of money and clothing, four were formerly slaves of rebel masters, but were liberated by government, and taken to the United States Naval services. Subsequently they were discharged and arrived at their port. Unfortunately, they fell into the hands of white and black landsharks, and stripped of all their clothes and money. In this predicament they found their way to the home, and were received and cared for. Also three others, who had been discharged from governmental service, fell in among a gang of runners and landlords, and were made to pay each four dollars for breakfast, and with an intimation (when they expressed dissatisfaction) that they must pay each seven dollars more, before they could leave the premises; they however escaped, and with some difficulty managed to save their baggage, and were brought to the home; efforts were made by the police to ferret out the gang of imposters, but failed; the men, being strangers, were unable to identify the house.[49]

I would characterize the status of Black seamen at midcentury as human outcasts in a state of fugitivity. Men were stripped of clothing and money, accosted by landlords, and forced to pay exorbitant prices for basic needs. As new ethnicities entered the labor market, the caste system realigned and other ethnic laborers excluded Black men from maritime jobs, prioritizing brethren from their home countries. Irish immigrants, for example, created a hostile environment for Black seamen who wanted to work on ships or as longshoremen. At the same time, a shift in the slave trade industry encouraged owners and merchants to capture and sell free Black men into enslavement. Even though the slave trade was abolished by the British in 1834, Black bodies were still traded for an expanding plantation market that needed even more field laborers after the invention of the cotton gin. Powell, himself an undesirable member of the African American caste, found his efforts to appeal for support on behalf of the colored seamen to be largely unsuccessful. He became a victim of the Draft Riots of 1863 and was forced to abandon his home along with his appeals for colored sailors. The rioters stripped him of his possessions and scattered them to the four winds.[50] He became, like the homeless men he sought to shelter, a fugitive.

The downward economic spiral of the cooks and stewards, the Black underclass of the maritime world, underscores how identities become negotiable within a world where intercultural crews are ranked based upon race and ethnicity. I experience and respond to this variable sense of race and class when I witness how cruise ship crew members interact with other men and women on various vessels. On some vessels, primarily the larger ones, I see men and women who are part of a large cohort of Black waiters, servers, entertainment staff, and hotel personnel. Conversations and exchanges elicit laughter, the pool staff throw towels and joke with one another, sharing commentary in their native patois or creole tongues. On other ships a single Black maintenance or cleaning person walks among a group of Filipino workers speaking Tagalog. The Filipino workers exchange a word or two with their Caribbean coworker, but they seem to prefer the camaraderie they find in others whose cultural experiences are mostly aligned with their own. I wonder how this plays out below deck.

The engine revs up and I can see the water outside of my cabin begin to churn. As the voyage gets underway, I can feel the back-and-forth rock of the ship that means we have left the sheltered harbor and are making our way into open waters. The physical precarity of the ship in motion reminds me of the precarious nature of identity politics and how racial and ethnic boundaries that seem fixed within distinctive national contexts are actually imagined ways of aligning power, class, and labor. My academic grounding in African American studies and performance impacts how I reimagine myself in the play space of this destination lecturer role. I will shape-shift into the role of the ethnic entertainer and perform the act of Dr. Anita on the open seas, lecturing within what was once an all-male merchant shipping environment for the benefit of cruise patrons whom I will never meet again. Such is the world of shipping out.

Cruise Ship Histories

Cruise ships offer travelers an opportunity to experience the imagined lifestyles of an elite passenger class who long ago crossed the Atlantic on steamers. Movies like *Titanic* create theatrical portraits of privileged travelers immersing themselves in a world of glitz and fine dining where servants tend to each passenger's every whim and passing need. Twenty-first-century passengers attempt to immerse themselves in similar splendor in the dining room of a mega cruise ship, where passengers dine while listening to classical string quartets, or perhaps the hand-clapping of Southeast Asian waiters performing a scripted enactment of joy as they bring in plates of steak or lobster. However, most cruise ship passengers are not the elite, with average salaries between $75,000 and $115,000 per annum.[51] The clientele varies according to the corporate sponsor, with some cruise lines, like Carnival, offering excursions for as low as $50/day while others charge upwards of $500/night for a journey on what is essentially a container ship with amenities. The historical precedents for viewing the ships as leisure locales were set in the late nineteenth century when upper-class passengers traveled to vacation destinations, and continued into the early twentieth century when cruise opportunities expanded to include the middle class.

As in previous centuries the captain on a modern cruise ship heads the organizational structure and sits at the top of the labor hierarchy. He manages the vessel's navigation and is responsible for the safety of all passengers and crew members.[52] Other departmental managers oversee day-to-day operations in hospitality, engineering, dining, and entertainment units. Collectively the staff in these departments take care of most components of onboard operations and often contribute to entertainment offerings. Even as they craft their daily operational activities, they report to the captain who oversees the navigation of the ship and sets its itineraries and destinations based on safety protocols and passenger needs. The professional environment on modern cruise ships differs significantly from the circumstances of the nineteenth century: jobs are automated, regulations are in place to assure worker safety, and codes of behavior are managed to ensure a collaborative and collegial environment. Still, hierarchies between those who work with passengers and those who maintain the ship are stringent. Then and now, captains navigate ships owned by foreign investors who profit from selling onboard cargo and merchandise.

Commercial Caribbean cruise tourism began with bananas. Sailor Dow Baker first imagined transporting bananas in 1878 when he brought a load of bananas to Boston and resold them for a profit. Recognizing a business opportunity, he formed the Boston Banana Company with partners. Later, United Fruit Company acquired the business, introducing the Great White Fleet in 1907. To improve business efficiency and to prevent fruit from rotting, the corporation installed air-conditioned holds on their vessels and marketed it as a "Tropical Fruit Steamship" company that could transport both bananas and passengers aboard air-conditioned vessels. While transatlantic passenger trade was well established by the second half of the nineteenth century, the notion of cruising through warm waters for the experience of the ocean was a unique innovation of the banana industry.[53]

Industrialization fueled a burgeoning middle class that was interested in navigating ocean waters for the experience of the natural world. "Between 1840 and 1880, the ocean ceased being a wasteland and a highway and was transformed into a destination, a frontier, an uncivilized place ripe for conquest and exploration."[54] Open water and nautical thoroughfares accommodated late nineteenth- and early twentieth-century leisure travelers who could afford free time and transport fees. The deep blue ocean unfolded as a backdrop for imagined manifestations of human desires and potentialities. Dozens of combination passenger and cargo ships appeared during the 1930s and continued to sail through the 1960s. While carrying cargo, they also offered luxurious quarters for between fifty and 300 passengers as they transported goods. William Miller honors the materiality of these ships in the volume *First Class Cargo*, displaying images of passenger berths and promotional posters.[55] Although most of the industrial-looking ships seem ill-fitted for passenger accommodations, these ships, like the merchant ships of the nineteenth century, increased the economic efficiency of maritime trade.

Passengers preferred the leisurely pace of these journeys and the opportunities they offered for restful recuperation. The early combination cargo-passenger ships developed standards for luxury suites within a container ship. Israeli businessman Ted Arison, capitalizing on consumer urges for uncomplicated travel experiences, founded Norwegian Cruise Line in 1966. By 1972 he acquired Carnival Cruise Line whose empire of corporate subsidiaries expanded and merged into clusters of cruise ship ownership that consists of Costa Cruises, Royal Caribbean, and Celebrity enterprises.[56] In the twenty-first century, the passenger cruise ship industry is a $38 billion business.[57] Megacorporations work with the Cruise Lines International Association to coordinate the business practices of over fifty cruise lines and 400 partner members.[58]

During the long nineteenth century, the movement of ships across the Atlantic was a lucrative business financed by investors who either built the vessels or carefully oversaw each ship's construction at trusted shipyards. The architectural design of the ship determined human interactions and created its own culture, one that absorbed and realigned the divergent experiences of the men who helped the vessel to move across the water. Each worker was assigned a particular task within a hierarchy where captains, mates, and navigators spent most of their times on the upper decks while common seamen labored on either the sails or below the deck—both precarious locations.

The primary responsibilities of the captain were to navigate the ship, maintain order, and protect the cargo. While each investor purchased insurance for the cargo, it was the captain who, under his contract, would be responsible for staffing the ship, delivering the cargo to its destination, and returning a share of the profits to the investor. Because they wanted to ensure an adequate profit, captains would often scrimp on crew amenities. A new sailor was given a single outfit and sometimes supplies, but these items were charged against the sailor's pay. On board ship, the captain provided food and a rudimentary berth for the sailor, which made work on deck preferable to the damp, cramped quarters underneath. Finally, the captain was responsible for maintaining the ship, keeping it repaired and in good condition. Sailors helped with caulking, replacing planks and masts, or sewing sails and were much more likely to be hired if they already possessed these skills.

Because shipping was an investment, owners kept detailed records of material goods, noting where vessels were registered, how they were built, their construction costs, prices of transported goods, manifests or listings of passengers and crew, and of course records of lost ships. A captain could be hired by any businessman and, like today, he could either own his ship, borrow a ship, or be provided with a ship by the investor. Well-trained captains were familiar with the hazards of certain routes and the capabilities of certain types of ships. They worked within a network of acquaintances and colleagues who supported one another by exchanging information about sea dangers, the weather, wars, or trade news. Nineteenth-century captains were almost always male and worked with a series of mates (first, second, or third) to pilot the voyage and maintain discipline on the ship. Other sea workers on sailing ships included carpenters, cooks, stewards, and able seamen. The steamship—which appeared toward the middle of the century—needed an additional team of men, sometimes called the "black gang" because of the soot produced in the process of feeding the coal furnace. This specialized crew included stokers, firemen, water tenders, oilers, and wipers.

The Victorian Imaginary

It is truly a beautiful experience to enter the interior of a well-designed cruise ship. Many of the classier, higher priced companies design vessels that attempt to replicate the interior décor of Victorian era passenger ships that carried wealthy vacationers to getaway locations where they could relax from the industrial smog and the crowded streets full of laborers. Yet this relationship to the sea—going to sea for pleasure—was an innovative sales strategy developed by late nineteenth-century industrial capitalists who built hotels and vacation enclaves to meet the needs of a developing upper middle class. Throughout the Age of Sail (1650 to 1850) and during the early phase of ocean steamers, boarding a ship or working on a ship was an unpleasant and dangerous thing to do. Oceanic travels were hazardous and generally undertaken by those who had to go—fishermen, naval fighters, or those desperate to escape poverty or enslavement. Traveling by sea was a necessity, but not necessarily a site for pleasure. The Victorian era shifted this perception. "Between 1840 and 1880, the ocean ceased being a wasteland and a highway and was transformed into a destination, a frontier, an uncivilized place ripe for conquest and exploration."[59] Transatlantic voyages aboard steamships with upscale cabins were also popular. The infamous ship *Titanic*, which sank in 1912, was one of these luxury passenger-ships.

Victorian hotel magnates developed destination travel networks that included railroad or steamship travel followed by transfers to large "grand" hotels. The network enabled upper-middle-class travelers to seamlessly book accommodations from their home cities to leisurely summer settings. The weekend or summer getaways aimed to have the passengers experience uninterrupted leisure from door to door, then arrive at their hotel where they might play a round of croquet, walk through artfully landscaped gardens, or enjoy the fresh country air from their balconies. One such hotel is the Grand Hotel located on Mackinac Island in the state of Michigan. The destination, located in the straits of Mackinac in Lake Huron between Michigan's upper and lower peninsulas, would be reached by taking a train across Michigan, boarding a ferry to the island, and then taking a horse-and-buggy transport to the door of the hotel. Every aspect of the journey was managed by the hotel owner and designed to accommodate the Victorian leisure traveler.

This particular hotel has a unique maritime labor history because of its location on a midwestern island, but its management model was replicated in projects like the Mohonk Mountain House in New Paltz, New York; the Grand Hotel in Margate, United Kingdom; the Grand Union Hotel in Saratoga Springs, New York; and many others. In order to build the Mackinac Island hotel, representatives from the Michigan Central Railroad, the Grand Rapids and Indiana Railroad, and the Detroit and Cleveland Steamship Navigation Company first formed a legal entity, the Mackinac Island Hotel Company. Construction work (designed by the architectural firm Mason and Rice) was overseen by Charles Caskey who worked with his brother-in-law Alphonse Howe to quickly construct the buildings during the harsh winter of 1886.[60] Caskey faced a tight deadline for completing construction as rooms had already been sold.

I first learned about the construction of the hotel from its resident historian, Bob Tagatz, who is also a destination lecturer for vacation ships cruising across the Great Lakes.[61] Tagatz begins his destination lectures by boarding ships at the port in Sault Ste. Marie before the cruise vessel heads to Mackinac Island. On board, he shares histories of the hotel's construction. He tells how local workers were neither interested nor available to work on the island when they first constructed the hotel, and builder Caskey offered to pay double wages to those who would travel to the island for the construction work. He housed the workers in tents with no electricity and worked them day and night in three shifts. They transported the lumber from the mainland across the ice using sleds. When they tried to quit, Caskey refused to feed, house, or transport them away from the island. They stayed on, working by candlelight, until the hotel was complete. "The first rich and privileged Grand Hotel guests stepped off the luxury steam liner that tied up on Mackinac Island, they walked into the lobby of the Grand and checked in on July 10, 1887."[62] The building of the Grand Hotel was typical of hotel business investments during the Victorian era when railroad industrialists sought to connect water transport to railroads and hotel infrastructures.

All of these mechanical necessities and other innovations in leisure travel that made people with money feel that they could rest required teams of underpaid laborers. The class disparities inherent in this work were underscored by the ability of the upper class to take time off for aimless activities that required no output or product. Aspects of contemporary cruise ship design reference spatial considerations from these late nineteenth-century enterprises. For example, William Miller explains how Victorian travelers sought time to read and write on turn-of-the-century ships. Within the ship library guests could read a book or spend the afternoon playing cards while socializing with other passengers. A fine dining experience on board the transport ships was complemented with elegant butler cabin services. Planned immersions in elegance prepared the passengers for even-better dining and room services than they would encounter once they arrived at their hotel destinations.[63] Contemporary cruises offer amenities that somewhat replicate those of the Victorian era albeit with added modern technologies like internet access. Cruise lines designed for older and richer patrons include indoor spaces for reading and game playing, outdoor spaces for croquet or sitting by pools to socialize. The addition of personalized technology allows passengers to request even more personalized services that respond to their particular tastes in entertainment pastimes.

At this point, it's important that I distinguish between passenger travel to reach a specific destination and leisure travel where passengers simply sail to be on a ship. Throughout the nineteenth and early twentieth centuries, anyone crossing a large body of water would travel by ship. Hotel industrialists developed a new business enterprise of creating vacation destinations that would require travel by ship or rail, with class determining the reason people traveled. Working-class men and women either worked in maritime industries or used ships to arrive at new worksites. Upper-class passengers who traveled to vacation or to meet family or friends demanded comfortable accommodations. Consequently, passenger ship lines developed a tiered system of ticketing to better quarter multiple classes of travelers. Passenger travel by ship was at first very expensive, yet evolving steamship technology allowed passenger ship companies to build larger vessels capable of accommodating passengers for journeys that took less time. By the early twentieth century steamships were the primary mode of transfer for immigrating nationals seeking new lives. Millions of European immigrants arrived in the United States during this era by traveling in steerage. At first, passage on the newly developed steamers was miserable, with lower-class journeyers crowded into compartments where they were required to travel with their own rations. However, by the end of World War I ships were able to provide ventilation and offered passage at a variety of fare levels—first class, second class, and third class. Sea travel became an "affordable luxury" for passengers with some, albeit limited, disposable income.[64]

Passenger liners established during the 1930s set the standard for the type of luxury onboard service that many vacation travelers seek to replicate in their cruise experience. When I walk through passageways on board and see replicas of ocean liners or images of men and women leaning over railings with their hair blowing in the wind, I know that they are referencing an early twentieth-century time of passenger service when transatlantic voyages were the only way to cross from Europe to the United States. While the British liners *Queen of Bermuda* and *Monarch of Bermuda* ran weekly service between New York and Bermuda designed for beautiful people to live the beautiful life, New Zealand architect Brian O'Rorke established a new precedent by decorating his 1935 vessel *Orion* with modernist light, airy interiors, and a streamlined exterior. His ships were tourist-oriented liners funded with corporate money and designed to serve the public. Cunard's *Queen Mary*, which launched the following year, contrasted this discrete and functional approach to design by launching a vessel flaunting imperial majesty and a British national imprimatur. Collectively, these post–World War I vessels established design precedents for future corporate cruising during the second half of the twentieth century.[65] Passenger ships, originally designed to safely transport leisure travelers, established precedents for entertainment vessels, designed for spectacular immersion in a sense of privileged entitlement. Cruise ship architecture is deliberately ostentatious and, as I will explain in the following chapter, designed to enhance performances of leisurely "fun" that will occur in all sections of the vessel.

Entertainment Staffing

On cruises where I lecture, I am in a very privileged position compared to other staff, not only because I can leave the ship after a very short work stint, but also because I work under the direct supervision of the cruise director. Cruise directors, as the primary point of contact for passengers, play a central role within the cruise tourism business. They function like a skilled master of ceremonies, orchestrating activities across the ship's multiple venues and managing passenger entertainment experiences on board. Many of them were once Broadway or London West End entertainers who bring with them a sense of polish and pizzazz. The job requires a persona that will captivate and hold the attention of the guests. Yet the cruise director also manages a large staff in a role that parallels that of the ship's captain in terms of responsibility. It's essential for the cruise director's entertainment activities to complement the safety and destination requirements of the vessel. Utilizing theater performers, specialty guests, lecturers, entertainment staff, technical workers, and below-board staff, these entertainment managers transform ship venues into theatrical spaces. At the same time, they entertain guests by roaming the passageways of the ship, engaging in small talk and generally making themselves available for passenger complaints or compliments. They always appear on the main stage for evening entertainments where they introduce performers and provide updates about the ship's itinerary.

Cruise directors supervise contracted entertainment staff tasked with delivering activities from first light until well after dark. The staff utilizes multiple venues and performance modes to keep guests engaged. The highest tier entertainment staff members are performers hired for main-stage evening shows. Other entertainers—comedians, magicians, acrobats, or star singers—are recruited through agencies for short-term stints on the ship. While the cruise director works with company management to hire dancers and singers on standard six-month contracts, recommendations for short-term players can come directly from the cruise director. On a recent tour, I worked with Sue Denning,[66] one of the few female cruise directors I have encountered, and she focused on recruiting primarily female performance ensembles. Sue treated her entertainment staff like mentees, guiding them through the ropes of cruise ship performance. Because she was once a West End entertainer, and came from a multigenerational family of entertainers, she was especially adept at teaching her staff how to sustain quality performance within the immersive, perpetually performative environment of the cruise ship. In general, cruise directors prioritize hiring entertainers skilled at playing for vacationing crowds who like populist performances.

Entertainment venues are scattered throughout the cruise vessel. A deck plan from the *Celebrity Apex* shows fourteen levels of passenger accessible spaces. Seven tiers are reserved for cabins, but the remaining six levels of space can be used for passenger entertainment. The primary venue is a main proscenium stage equipped with motorized lights and moveable platforms for presenting review-style acts. Other venues will be animated by performance groups throughout the journey. (The next chapter provides a detailed analysis of spatial semiotics on cruise ships.) A weeklong cruise will have an ensemble of six to ten singer/dancers performing three unique musical-review-style shows that have been developed with choreographers and directors during an onshore rehearsal period. Many of the ensemble performers are recent uni-

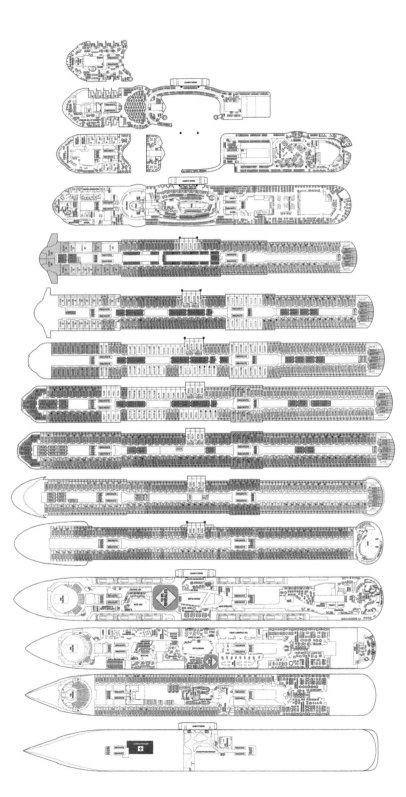

Figure 7. Celebrity Cruise ship deck plans. Courtesy of Celebrity Cruises.

versity graduates. Cruise ship performance allows young entertainers to hone their craft for musical theater performance. Ensemble members also serve in other roles. The dancer who appears behind the proscenium in a review act one night can be seen posing in a pirate costume on the dock the next morning. In his or her new position as a costumed pier-usher, the entertainer is more approachable and presents as a co-adventurer with the passengers.

Entertainment staff workers are my closest coworkers during my circuit as a destination lecturer, but I don't spend a lot of time interacting with them. They may introduce a lecture series, or invite me to join them in one of the parades or dance sets, but generally we simply smile and wave as we move from event to event. It's an odd relationship because they know I am only a temporary, drop-in visitor within a landscape that is their everyday work world. The mostly white entertainers are at the top of the cruise ship hierarchy; they are able to freely roam around the ship and they are instantly recognizable to the guests because of their stage performances. When I board the Caribbean cruise ship and step into the role of entertainer, I try to integrate into the existing hierarchies of the permanent onboard staff, but it isn't easy.

Most of my interactions will be with the cruise ship guests—some of whom are knowledgeable about Caribbean destinations, but many of whom are not. They attend the lectures, but they also interact with me in hallways and dining rooms, in onshore excursions, and by the pool. Travel as a destination lecturer is not really a vacation, because I am always on call. An added layer is my identity as a Black woman. My knowledge and credibility are often deemed questionable by my audiences. The number of Black educators on cruise ships (like the number of tenured Black professors in the academy) is very small.[67] I have never seen another Black destination lecturer throughout my twenty years of cruising although I cannot ascertain their absence because there are usually only one or two lecturers on a ship. Most that I meet are white men specializing in a scientific or economic field. I have met female naturalists and astronomers. At times I suffer from the type of racialized bias described in the book *Presumed Incompetent*[68] where passengers assume that even with my advanced degrees, because I am a Black female, I will not have anything valuable or accurate to share with them. The fact that my academic home is in the arts works like a double-edged sword. On the one hand, most audience members assume my expertise is in a "safe" entertainment area that will not disrupt the vacation atmosphere of the cruise. On the other hand, I am constantly demonstrating how pertinent the performing arts, dance, and theater histories are in revealing political, social, and cultural tensions across centuries of historical encounters.

Even though I have not met other Black destination lecturers, I have had private conversations with other Black entertainers who work on the ship as comedians, musicians, technical crew members, dancers, and singers. They recognize the liminal nature of my position, and at times envy my ability to leave the ship at will (or at least at the end of a journey's circuit). The Black guest entertainers who work under specialty contracts, like comedians or singers, and spend limited time on the ship, tend to stay in their cabins after their performances with little guest interaction. The contracted Black entertainers who work with performing ensembles under six-month contracts circulate with the guests when assigned to socializing activities, but generally stay below deck with their cast members during their time off. Only one Black performer, the comedian, openly expressed to me how challenging it is to work on board ship entertaining a primarily white audience with, in his case, humor.

But let me return to my description of the first day of onboarding for my seven-to-ten day gig as a destination lecturer. Once the ship's horn sounds, all of us—the guests, the workers, and the temporary enrichment staff—will begin our performative journey as we leave the pier and head out to sea. Now it is time for me to finally meet with the cruise director and introduce myself. The meeting is brief and, on some ships, ends with an impromptu video interview where I advertise my lectures to audiences who will view the clip on the television set in their cabins. Once I finish the introduction and the ship publishes the broadcast, I return to my cabin to prepare for the next day's lecture. Those alerted to the availability of destination lectures will now approach me throughout the week with questions and comments about my presentations. This is the beginning of my performance as a Black, female academic within a cultural environment where females have been marginalized and Black presence has been traditionally marked as cargo or servile. The next day is inevitably a "sea day" when there is no destination because the ship is sailing in open waters, encouraging passengers to explore the ship and purchase items on board. The first sea day is my best opportunity to have audiences learn about where they are going. My first day on a Caribbean cruise usually begins with a lecture about multinational encounters in the region.

SNAPSHOT #1: The Lecture

I like to introduce my Caribbean lecture series by providing a general context for colonialism in the Caribbean with a lecture titled "Tea, Rum, and Sugar in the Caribbean." The sugar trade affected almost every Caribbean island

and involved every colonizing nation. The Spanish, who were originally seeking gold, established forts in the islands to store their plunder before returning to Spain. If you examine a map of sea currents you will see that geography assisted them in their conquests, because a strong current runs off the coast of Spain, past the Canary Islands, and propels ships directly toward the northern coast of South America and the Caribbean islands. Another current, the Gulf Stream, merges with the North Atlantic Gyre to propel vessels back toward Spain.[69]

Following the Spanish were the Dutch who used the islands as outposts for restocking supplies and taking what they could from the indigenous people. The French were interested in colonizing and competing with England for new territories in the New World. They settled and cultivated when they could, extracting wealth from sugar plantations. Continuous clashes between European naval forces for access to trade routes and territories created the patchwork of colonial nations that today characterize the Caribbean.[70] Embedded in all of the jockeying for land and sea access were pirates and privateers, and the difference between the two is negligible. Pirates stole from ships to benefit their captain and his working crew members. Privateers were pirates for hire who agreed to intercept goods and take them on behalf of a paid employer.

Throughout the Caribbean, organized indigenous people fought for their lands and continuing access to their own Caribbean Sea trading routes. Caribe, Arawak, Taino, and other nations were subjugated or murdered by the various European colonizers who needed land and labor in order to cultivate and process products for export. My "Tea, Rum, and Sugar" lecture first touches on these historical contexts, and then describes how sugar cane is harvested, milled, distilled, and transformed into the rum drinks that many will consume during their vacation. Within this context, I talk about the triangular slave trade and the movement of ships to Africa to find human laborers, then to the Caribbean where the enslaved were traded for processed sugar and rum, then to North America where sugar and rum were traded for wood and cotton, and finally to England where wood and cotton were offloaded and traded for finished goods (arms and clothing), which were traded, once again, in Africa.

Cruise directors and their staff prefer for the lectures to be lighthearted and entertaining but really—the institution of slavery has to be discussed. I do this by showing images of plantation layouts and Black men and women laboring over bins of steaming or evaporating hot sugar cane syrup; mentioning, of course, that they will be able to see remnants of this industry when they take a shore excursion to the sugar cane plantations. Finally, I mention how the need for sugar was driven by the British need to serve something with tea when bread and milk were scarce. This very broad historical tour is usually followed by an in-depth explanation with photographs of the history of the specific islands they will see on their itinerary and the tourist sites they may wish to visit.

On one cruise, perhaps it was a western Caribbean circuit through St Maarten, as the talk was ending, a woman approached the stage to speak with me. She looked concerned and emotional. Quietly, she waited until all of the other guests had left the venue. "May I help you?" I inquired. "I just have one question for you," she spoke with a decidedly British accent. I await the question, tired, but curious. She asks: "Are there Black people in the Caribbean?" I wonder how culture and history can morph to create a perspective about the Caribbean where the world majority of laborers, Black and brown, enslaved and free, are imagined as inactive contributors to world economies. I wonder how I have presented a history of colonialism and conquest that has somehow landed on my audience as a story about the absence of Black people. I wonder how the more privileged think global economies exist without the exploitation of primarily Black labor. I wonder how anyone can travel to the Caribbean and not realize there are Black people there. "Yes" I say, "there are Black people in the Caribbean. Most of the Caribbean is Black."

I hope this cruise ship guest will indeed explore the island when we land. I hope she will take the historical bus tour instead of the half-day beach excursion. My first twenty-four hours as a destination lecturer are complete. And we are shipping out.

Two

Play at Sea, Space, and Meaning

Performance and Space

I feel exhilarated when I move through the corridors of a cruise ship. Traveling the hallways and breathing in the artwork—be it Victorian or modernist abstraction—I am embraced by a sense of luxurious harmony as the curving designs coupled with the rocking of the ship lulls me into believing that I will always be a part of this magnificent world of transatlantic travel. I get to decide if I will sit with fellow passengers at the leather-edged couches in the coffee shop or find a quiet corner on the upper pool deck where I can bask in the sun. If my muscles ache, I can exercise with others by taking a yoga class on the golf green with its prickly fake grass or indulge privately in one of the secluded steam rooms hidden behind the spa's appointment desk. I know that when I walk these same corridors at night, I will become a part of a well-appointed, smart-casual parade of guests who can observe and nod to one another as we pass from the theater with its live spectacles to the dining room with its personal performances of choreographed servitude.

As a theater director I know that the first consideration in staging a production is the venue. It determines how the story will be shared with your audiences, who will attend, how pre- and postengagements will be scheduled, and, most importantly, the story's meaningful impact. Cruise line architects like Gem[1] or Wilson Butler[2] design architectural spaces to accommodate ongoing spectacles while leaving spatial options for a variety of small-scale interactions between passengers and crew, between passengers and other guests, and between crew members. Their goal is to keep passengers happy on the boat while offering a variety of entertainment options. Management succeeds when passengers decide to book another cruise. Much of this success can be attributed to the effective transformation of a sterile oceangoing vessel into a luxurious and fun environment. Visual décor referencing maritime themes converges with elements of contemporary modern design to create efficient public gathering areas that nod to the past. Inventive designs of architectural spaces facilitate safety while establishing immersive entertainment environments that support theatrical activities.

For example, the central atrium of a cruise ship functions like a "theater in the round," a theatrical arrangement that engages audiences in ways that a proscenium theater does not. And the ship also has proscenium spaces for large format presentations. Mechanisms for performative engagement are always linked to spatial designs that can contain, amplify, or limit interactions. Theater practitioners generally consider relationships between audience members, between performers, and between performers and the audience, but these relationships are disrupted in environmental settings where boundaries blur. The immersive, contained space of the cruise vessel not only manages performative spaces but also deliberately manages class hierarchies by determining who can access which sections of the performance space. Although most public areas of the ship are available to all passengers, there are sections of ships that are only accessible to first-class or concierge class clientele. Historical precedents have normalized divisions of upper- and lower-class travel and distinctions between crew, passenger, and cargo, and a look back at them can illuminate today's hierarchies.

For instance, Figure 8 show an architectural plan from the packet ship *Rosseau*. The vessel weighed 305 tons and was built in 1801 in Philadelphia for Stephen Girard's packet ship line. It became a whaling ship in about 1845 and was dismantled in about 1896. The image illustrates the separation between those who work on the top deck—the quarters of the captain and his mates—and those who work or live below—immigrants, second-class passengers, and crew members. A lot has changed in ship architecture since packet ships transported goods, yet some specifics remain. The architecture of any ship continues to dictate where passengers gather and how they experience their time encapsulated within a vessel. Today, on a cruise ship, the top floor is where the spa staff and the dining staff work or where passengers enhance their suntans near the pool. They have little to no relationship with the captain who also sits near the upper deck, but works from a protected bridge platform where he, along with his conavigators, run a control panel of automated devices to guide the craft.

But there is still a sense of an upper deck and a lower deck. The vertical architecture of the cruise ship replicates some aspects of the socially hierarchical structure of earlier vessels. In the past, the bottom hold of the merchant ship needed to carry enough weight for the craft to remain stable with

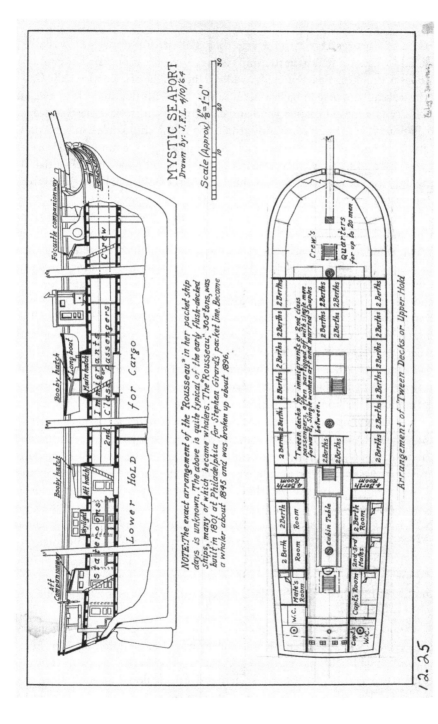

Figure 8. Deck plan of the *Rousseau*. Courtesy of the Collections and Research Center at Mystic Seaport.

the hull submerged beneath the waterline. Ballast, or extra weight, was often added to cargo to maintain the ship's balance and flotation.[3] Ballast could be stones or anything heavy enough to add to the weight of a wooden ship. Captains carefully managed ballast because the ship, as a floating vessel, needed stability as it fought against wind and currents. In a historical merchant ship, ballast and cargo were constantly readjusted as the ship landed in each port. Human cargo, whether enslaved or paying passengers, counted as a part of the weight, so managing the transfer of humans and goods was essential. In the drawing below it is clear how the cargo in the hold, and below the waterline, sustains the stability of those who ride on the upper decks.

Imagine the maritime circuit of a slave vessel traveling round trip from England. A sailing ship loaded with firearms and crew might travel to Ghana where it offloads weapons and trades them for human cargo who rebalance the ship with a different weight. The ship then crosses the Atlantic Ocean to the Caribbean where the enslaved Africans are offloaded and traded for rum and sugar, cotton or tobacco. The ship is once again rebalanced and goods transported to New York harbor where they are exchanged for lumber. The lumber and cotton bales are readjusted and then transported to England where the cotton is manufactured into clothing and the lumber is used for buildings, or perhaps for more wooden ships. The load and its weight continually shift and only the crew remains stable. In both economic and physical contexts, the human cargo balances the ship.

On a contemporary cruise ship, water stored in tanks at the stern or aft of the ship serve as ballast. This water, which is regularly pumped in and out of the tank, adjusts the draught or height of the ship in the water.[4] On modern cruise ships, most of the people who manage the functional services of the ship are housed below the waterline. Like workers of previous eras, they sleep near the cargo and the engineering sections of the vessel. In a sense, they are part of the weight-based ballast system, because everyone who sleeps below the waterline is a worker and not a passenger. Their performative interactions in the underbelly of the ship remain hidden from most passengers, including the guest lecturers. Historically and in contemporary practice, the architectural layering inherent in ship design keeps some crew and cargo out of sight while others have access to the upper deck.

Standard cruise ships generally accommodate 1,500 to 3,000 passengers who occupy what is effectively a small town or a large hotel. Smaller, more elite ships will hold between 200 and 700 passengers. In contrast, vertically oriented megaships have between ten and fifteen floors located above the waterline. The performative spaces of the cruise ship are carefully designed

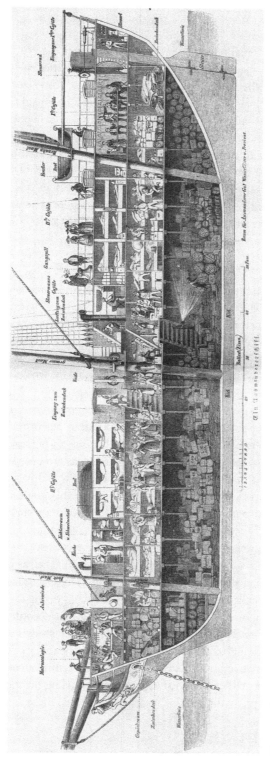

Figure 9. Cross-section of a packet ship. Courtesy of the Smithsonian Institution.

environments that enable particular types of interactions. Not only do the ships' architectural spaces determine what kind of activities the cruise director programs, but they also reference spatial designs from past eras of sea travel such as the plush wood paneling of passenger ships from the Victorian era or the billowing sails of wooden ships. Maintaining the upkeep of exquisite architectural designs requires labor. Ships have always involved some element of crew labor to support passenger needs; however, on modern cruises the labor force also participates in maintaining the illusion of luxury travel through demonstrative acts of service. I am interested in how cruise ship space, as performance space, determines how passengers, who are now audience members, interact with onboard activities and make them meaningful.

David Wiles and Cruise Ship Space

To amplify my argument, I draw from analytical frames presented by David Wiles in his book *A Short History of Western Performance Space*, which draws from Western historical paradigms to designate semiotic frames for theatrical performance. Wiles discusses eight types of theatrical space, indicating how each evokes a particular relationship between audience and performer. He is a historian "trying to make sense of a pluralistic world" while looking at "spatial practices involving 'performers' and 'spectators'" where bonding supports particular kinds of narrative structures. Drawing from Michel Foucault, he examines power structures within quotidian performance environments.[5] Spaces of encounter range from sacred spaces to processional spaces, and from cosmic circles to interior caves. Wiles's ideas are constrained by the Eurocentric context of his materials as he draws from archives of theatrical presentations in Greek amphitheater settings, medieval squares, French and Italian palaces, and public opera houses. Still, his writings suggest parallels between traditional theatrical spaces and populist entertainments on floating vessels. First, I am drawn to his assertion that "the context for a history of performance space is a history of space."[6] His focus on space as a meaningful contributor to audience engagement in theatrical events is a second strength of his analysis. Finally, he broadly considers inside and outside spaces, and natural as well as manmade structures, as organizing spatial configurations for performative experiences. My own background in dance studies and choreography also positions me to consider spatial contexts as a way of categorizing multifaceted activities programmed within the architectural areas of the ship.

Below I simplify Wiles's expansive project by focusing on those elements particularly resonant in the case of cruise ships. First, there is processional space or areas where passengers repeatedly cross between the front and the back of the ship to arrive at various onboard destinations. Second, there are public spaces or town plazas where passengers gather in large groups to hear, see, and respond to public presentations orchestrated by the cruise director. Third, in cosmic circles, audience members gather to observe one another while viewing or competing in an event as a collective. Passengers collaborate with entertainment staff on "fun" programming to pass the time in the places I designate as cosmic. Fourth, there are sympotic spaces where small interactions between individuals and small groups contribute to the overall experience of luxury and service. These are dining spaces and bar lounges where passengers experience theme-based personal service. And, fifth, in cave spaces, passengers go to retreat, reflect, or dream within their own individual imaginations. The ship library is one such space and sometimes game rooms, where passengers, unmatched with activities personnel, can pursue various activities without being watched. Within the cave, passengers read and relax, but they also learn. Finally, Wiles describes the empty space. I interpret that space as the sea, an ecological and environmental space. Ecological because it surrounds all performance activities. On a cruise ship the sea operates as an impenetrable, natural backdrop for all guests traveling by water across the Caribbean.[7] While these are broad adaptations of Wiles's core propositions, adjusted to suit my investigation of the specialized space of the cruise ship, they advance my analysis of the unmoored, liminal cruise ship as playhouse.

Processionals in the Central Corridor

Because of the horizontal layout of each floor, passengers constantly walk back and forth on a cruise ship. There is a "fore" and an "aft" meaning the front and back sides of every vessel. The "port" side is the left side and the "starboard" is the right when you face the front of the ship. The fourth, fifth, and sometime sixth floors of most megaships have a long passageway connecting the front of the ship to the back. This uninterrupted walkway serves as a public arena where passengers pass through as they move from the "fore" to the "aft" of the ship. I call this passageway Main Street because it functions as the floating vessel's main thoroughfare and connects the large theatrical venue at one end of the ship to the dining room at the other end. Throughout the cruise, passengers will make an unavoidable journey through the main passageway that brings them past stores and drink establishments, the photo vending area, the casino, and sometimes an art display. This is similar to the way that museum pathways often end with passage through a gift shop with items for sale. The difference is that passengers on cruises will walk through the main shopping areas multiple times each day for several days, and as they walk, they are lured to use their ship card for purchases. Each venue—the retail store, the coffee shop, the photo exhibit or the bar—may be staffed by a worker who entertains by taking photographs, tossing drinks like a juggler, manipulating cards in the casino, or offering appetizers in front of specialty restaurants. Modes of theatrical engagement in the processional corridor are multiple.

Royal Caribbean ships contain a particularly grandiose Main Street with multiple stores and pubs situated on both sides of the thoroughfare. Guests can pop into the coffee shop or stop by the pub as they make their way from dinner to evening entertainments. The ship *Oasis of the Seas* calls this strip the Royal Promenade, suggesting either that the passenger is royalty or that the vacationer will pass royalty when walking down the thoroughfare. Everyone who walks the promenade will see the rich display of corporate consumer products available for sale, from designer handbags, jewelry, and watches to T-shirts, ice cream, and lattes. The main processional passageway is also a staging area for indoor entertainment events. Cruise directors will sometimes program costume parades or initiate an indoor carnival along the promenade, encouraging passengers to dress for the occasion. A special event like a Mardi Gras or Caribbean-themed festival event enables the stores to sell specialized products such as half face masks or Hawaiian shirts to complement the ship-sponsored special event. Similar to a Hallmark card shop, the cruise ship offers guests an opportunity to purchase holiday-related items to match these advertised onboard events.

Other cruise lines, for example the more sedate and more expensive Oceania cruise line, downplay the commercial intent of the promenade passageway. Their vessels contain only a few stores and a small casino. Instead, customers encounter the majesty of the artwork on display between the restaurant and the theater. Comfortable living room chairs are set up along the passageway so that elderly guests can easily sit and watch as others move through. Visual splendor provides a scenic backdrop while accentuating the upscale cruise ship's elegant connection to Victorian maritime décor. On these ships, safety precautions play a more prominent role in design. All ships, including cruise ships, rock in response to wave action, a situation particularly dangerous for the elderly or mobility challenged. I have seen cruise ship passengers in orthopedic casts newly acquired after a fall on a wet deck. To avoid this, architects tend to use carpets to reduce the slip and slide. Accessible handrails placed in passageways ensure that those with unsteady footing are able to stabilize themselves. Even though wheelchairs and motorized vehicles are encouraged in order to accommodate differently abled people, narrow passageways can make locomotion difficult. When a wheelchair passes, guests walking through the hallways can sometimes barely fit through the narrow space between the sidewalls.

Several types of performances occur along the Main Street passageway. Organized spectacles initiated by entertainment staff animate during peak dinner hours, but during the daytime smaller acts of servitude populate the space. Some service activities are maintenance-oriented: grooming of the floors, banisters, and carpets, for example. Passengers' eyes are drawn to continual acts of cleaning so that they can appreciate the pristine upkeep of the vessel. In contrast, higher end vessels will situate espresso bars along the passageways. The espresso bars are extremely popular. I have seen crew members wearing jackets with epaulettes over white uniforms socializing in this area. Even though waiters and other low-end personnel are not allowed to dine in public places, members of the management team, the entertainment team, and the navigation team are encouraged to make frequent public appearances, reminding guests that they are sailing with a professional team of maritime experts. This circumstance also applies to me, the guest lecturer. I sit in public areas so that paying passengers can chat with me about their shipboard experiences. While service workers may occupy the same spaces, they are not encouraged to have extended conversations with guests unless they are serving them. Floor managers constantly observe servers and maintenance workers to ensure they look busy and are not idle in front of passengers. In other words, service laborers constantly scrub and clean the tables, decks and chairs of the central corridor, while my job is to look attentive and friendly when I sit anywhere along the very public processional corridor.

A few times, I have tried to break the entertainment code by bringing my work laptop into one of the coffee shops along the public passageways. This is frowned upon. Waiters will quietly ask me if I am enjoying my vacation or suggest I go to my cabin to rest. Sometimes they will mention other onboard activities that I could be attending instead of sitting in the coffee shop. Or, if it is a port day, they might ask when I will be going ashore. I usually take the hint, pack up my laptop and retreat to my cabin, aware that I have disturbed one of the ship's unspoken protocols of participating in only leisure activities in public areas.

Organized entertainments and small acts of servitude are two types of performance activities that take place along ships' main corridors, but the third type of performance is the parade of the passengers themselves. The corridor, like a public street in an urban city center, allows passengers to

Figure 10. Passengers pose for a photograph on the Royal Caribbean *Mariner of the Seas*, October 2005.

observe one another. Organized events—like parties or champagne toasts—encourage cruise passengers to get dressed up, but the ruse only works if passengers can see others participating in the game. All of the cafes and restaurants along the Main Street are, particularly during the evening hours, viewing stations for the stream of passengers who pass by as guests eat and go to and from programmed entertainments. This is participatory theater at its best. While some rules are obscure or unstated, others are clearly spelled out. My "welcome aboard" letter, a missive from the cruise director that is placed in my cabin during my first evening on board, reads:

> As a highly visible member of our enrichment team, we want you to look and feel your best. We ask you to observe the **guest dress code** which includes smart dress during the day and elegant resort attire in the evenings. The evenings are your time to shine, and as such, we ask you to wear a collared shirt, slacks or dress to dinner and any special events. More formal attire is always welcome, and you may feel most comfortable dressing one step above our guests.[8]

Figure 11. Celebrity *Equinox*, February 2016.

The letter clearly explains how I am to participate in the performance play of social decorum based upon upper-class, Euro-American expectations of cultured propriety. Because I understand the performative nature of theater, I am able to joyfully accommodate to the rules of the cruise ships' theatricality. I view the instructions as costuming notes in the stage directions for my immersion in the onboard play.

However, performance is ephemeral, and whether on board a cruise ship or elsewhere, it would not be as effective without the chance for documentation. Midlevel cruise ships hire professional photographers who capture images of passengers as they playfully engage with the ship's entertainments. Passengers first pose for photo sessions and later purchase their images in the ship's lucrative photo shop. Because most people already have a cell phone with an imbedded camera, cruise ship photo shops specialize in studio-style photography. In order to achieve a studio look, staff photographers unroll background paper painted with idealized vistas of the ship, the shore, or the nighttime sky. Voyagers stand in front of these cruise-scapes with their lovers and family members to create touching mementos of their journeys. The ship management also provides roving photographers who circulate across sundecks and dining rooms waiting with their cameras to capture moments of romance or active play. They function as personal paparazzi, allowing customers to enjoy moments of celebrity fame. Photographic imagery captures every aspect of the voyage, underscoring the importance of each individual passenger's experience. In order to enhance the photographic spectacle even more, some ships have a visual gallery area where passengers are able to sort through images of themselves that have been placed on display boards. Vacationers select their favorite photographs and purchase them in a digital form for upwards of one hundred dollars or buy individual prints for about twenty dollars each. The photo team staff skillfully transforms into scenic art the passengers' promenades through Main Street corridors, documenting ongoing performances of playful enactment.

Processionals in the Pool Deck

Flashback—I'm sitting on a pool deck, a second processional space within the architecture of the ship. This cruise was heading from Tampa to Havana only we are now stuck at sea because Hurricane Irma was heading to Cuba too. The captain announces over the loudspeaker that he has redirected the ship from Cuba to Cozumel, Mexico, as we outrun the storm. We're offered free internet, free telephones, and reduced-price everything. Some guests consider this a "once in a lifetime opportunity." The sun is shining. Pumping music wafts out over tattooed guests who recline in the hot tub, drinking specialty Caribbean drinks from cups shaped like a shark. They're playing Motown songs perfect for line dancing. Entertainment staff keep the guests partying and relaxing. They teach coordinated step patterns and arm gestures so everyone can join in. The stage bakes, the alcohol flows. Because it's a Carnival cruise programmed to appeal to the "urban" crowd, Black and Latine fashion flourishes. Carnival cruises differ from other cruise lines because they are priced affordably and marketed to attract a working-class clientele. Travel itineraries are short and activities emphasize "party" more than "escape." I see netted bathing suits and popping breasts that jiggle above legs finished with Nike high-top sneakers. Bright orange and yellow and pink swatches of fabric drape across Rubenesque stomachs and thighs. It's a wonderful party, and folks are relaxed. After all, it's been three days at sea, and we are outside of Cozumel waiting for calmer waters.

Outdoor pools, located on the upper decks of mega cruise ships somewhere between the spa and the casual dining area, are popular public spaces for soaking up Caribbean sun. Guests, when they are not seated in their lounge chairs, will process through the sunbathing area to outdoor eating cafes where it's OK to wear casual clothing or even a swimsuit. If passengers choose to spend time along this passageway, perhaps sunbathing with suntan lotion gleaming, they will be asked to purchase mixed drinks from serving staff associated with the poolside bar. When they leave, their empty chair will be cleared and cleaned by the pool's housekeeping staff. The brown-skinned service exceeds the attentiveness of most land-based pools but replicates the fastidious service delivered in other high-end resort settings. Working on the pool deck is labor intensive because, in addition to selling drinks, the staff must constantly move chairs and replace used wet towels when sunbathers leave. If it rains, they have to swab (mop) the deck, dry and change out furniture cushions, and shift furniture into covered areas. Pool deck workers tend to be male although women sometimes help to serve the drinks. For the active passenger trying to keep in shape, the pool deck has an upper, circular walk for running or walking laps. This space is similar to the running track of an indoor gym except, of course, it is outside with all-encompassing sea views. When a person sits on the pool deck, they can easily view other passengers circling in an oval pattern as they walk from the front to the back of the ship.

The upper deck processional corridor is also used by the entertainment staff for entertainment activities. Musicians are programmed to play upbeat Caribbean music for much of the day on ships designed for middle-income patrons.[9] On active ships staff members dressed in sporty outfits will lead events like belly flop contests in the pools or public line dances where passengers are able to collectively move around. Wiles described processional space as a place of pilgrimage, parade, map, or narrative. It's a bit of a hyperbole to describe the trek aross the upper deck to the casual dining room as a pilgrimage to a sacred destination, yet most passengers make this familiar journey several times a day. Cruise vacations disrupt the schedules of daily life and create new patterns of behavior for passengers at sea. The guests adjust their routines to match the call of the ship's dining hours or the cruise director's priority activities. Their movement across the sunlit deck maps their ability to lay "a claim of ownership"[10] to the fun-in-the-sun passageway between the front and the back of the ship. On a crowded ship, access to the deck chairs along the poolside processional is fraught during the midday hours when, if the weather is pleasant, guests are basking in the sun-drenched utopia they have paid for.

An observer can truly see the contrast between labor and leisure on the pool deck. Guests relax and read while the pool deck staff scrambles to provide luxuries of towels and water, food, and a dry environment at sea, acts that to me seem less performative and more pedestrian. Events programmed

Figure 12. Celebrity *Summit*, August 2021.

on the pool deck are designed to animate the flaccid guests by inviting them to play. This processional space replicates the sporty, outdoor swimming pool patio one might find in a land-based recreation center. The cruise director never advises that I hang out on the pool deck unless he or she has programmed a Caribbean themed dance event. Although guests process across the pool deck, they also settle in for moments of reading or simply resting.

Public Plazas: The Main Stage and the Staircase

On every cruise there is one public gathering space where it is assumed that all passengers will convene at least once during their time on board—the main-stage theater. The theater, located in the forward part of the vessel and outfitted with state-of-the-art technical equipment, hosts large entertainment spectacles performed by the in-house musical theater ensemble and special guests. Some of the theaters are circular and some are more traditional proscenium spaces. On large vessels they extend across two floors so they can accommodate everyone on the ship, even if guests have to be programmed to attend two separate showings during a single evening. I wrote earlier about the types of performances the cruise director lines up—comedy acts, music ensembles or soloists, sometimes a magician. Specialty performance acts featuring short-stay guest artists, coupled with two or three prepackaged professionally developed shows featuring the contracted dancer/singer ensemble, constitute the bulk of the entertainment. The goal is for cruise passengers to have a theatrical event to attend every night after they finish dining. Otherwise, there would be no spectacle after the sun sets, when the ocean with the sun shining above it is no longer visible.

I consider the main-stage theater to be the community's public plaza because this is where passengers see the cruise director in person every night and hear about updates and plans for the rest of the voyage. Like a master of ceremonies, the host performer, the cruise director, orchestrates the activities on the ship to match the weather and the itinerary. Throughout the day, the cruise director has been circulating and conversing with passengers to find out what they are thinking about. The evening show is the time when he or she can shine as the grand social hostess of the vacation immersion. The cruise director will be introduced with lights and sound before the primary performance act. A good cruise director/host will warm up the crowd and deliver a joke or two. The joke or gimmick establishes the director as accessible and fun. In my experience, the jokes have ranged from performers doing comical "bits" around mismatched socks that they wear every night, to directors performing Broadway tunes to catch everyone's attention, to something as dry as a cruise director who simply announced "now I am going to tell a joke."

After the opening bit, the cruise director reviews the day's activities and gives a preview of the following day's itinerary. This is when passengers share their opinions about their day on the ship. The cruise director will ask which activities guests participated in and generally how they felt about them. Passengers indicate, by clapping and shouting, whether or not they had a good time on the ship that day. On the first or second day, the cruise director will use some of this preshow time to introduce the cruise ship department heads to the passengers. This theatrical moment includes elaborate regalia—the lead chef wearing his high toque hat, the captain and chief engineer with their shoulder stripes, each epaulette indicating where the staff member falls on the hierarchical employee work scale. Introductions meant to familiarize passengers with the various functions on board also invite guests to participate in mastering some maritime language. Sometimes the cruise director will also explain maritime terminology, making sure everyone knows which side is "port" or "starboard" even though this knowledge will not be needed to move through activities on board. Instead, it reinforces the feeling of entering a special world with singular behavioral codes introduced in the "town plaza" of the ship to keep all involved in the rules and decorum of cruise ship play.

The middle of the ship has a parallel public meeting space, the Grand Staircase. It's called the grand staircase because, like the staircases in Busby Berkeley films, it has been designed as a place for guests and entertainment staff to promenade and perform.[11] Even though the staircase works as a public access point for movement between floors, its wide steps and circular design create an ideal performance arena for public events that are less formal

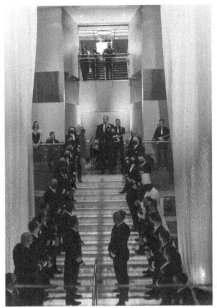 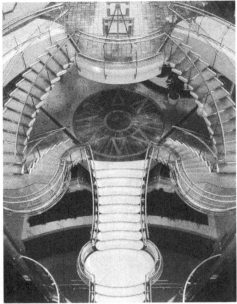

Figure 13a and 13b. Grand Staircases on the ships Celebrity *Summit*, August 2021, and Royal Caribbean *Explorer of the Seas*, May 2008.

than what would be programmed in the main-stage theater. Staff frequently use the Grand Staircase for the captain's toast, an event that occurs on formal nights when the cruise director distributes champagne so that everyone, in formal attire (or at least smart casual), will toast the journey.

Once again, this is a part of an organized spectacle crafted to encourage guests to purchase spa treatments or extra scarves or anything else to accentuate their formal dress. My role as an enrichment staff member is to participate in this display because if no one else is dressing up, then passengers will be unlikely to do so. Therefore, I make sure to carry in my wardrobe a fancy outfit so that I can join the cruise director, the entertainment staff, and the officers in a celebratory formal night toast that, if not staged on the Grand Staircase, will at least involve a processional across or down the stairs. String quartets and vocalists are similarly programmed for appearances on or near the stairway. The nature of the entertainment helps to articulate the mood or theme of the day. If it is a shore day at a Caribbean island, perhaps the steel pan player will play a forty-five-minute set in this area. Unlike the theater, where the cruise director explicitly explains the theme and activities of the day, the Grand Staircase relies upon symbolic activities to communicate its

Figure 14. Carnival *Paradise*, September 2017.

performance frames. By this I mean that costuming and scenic elements help guests to understand what the expected dress codes and behaviors are within this space. Of course, guests can ignore all of the symbolic cues and simply do what they "want to, but the intention of the staff is to lure guests into participating in games of dress and social play signaled by physical architecture and atmospheric elements.

Cosmic Circles of Communion

Flashback—The central rotunda of this Carnival cruise allows passengers to watch activities from three different levels. From the highest level, it's possible to gaze down across three decks, and tonight a few hundred people have assembled for an impromptu booty shaking contest at cruise director Matt's request. Passengers and crew members peek around columns and look down on Matt, who stands on a raised circular center platform. Music by Martha and the Vandellas blasts as he calls selected guests from the audience to the stage. This will be a karaoke night to Motown music. Most passengers have been drinking, so alcohol courses through the huddled bodies as hopeful guests wait to compete for their moment of fame. They wonder—"Whom will Matt invite to share the stage with him?" Cruise ships create a kind of celebrity culture. Cruise director Matt has adopted the role of an MC superstar, so passengers crave an opportunity to share the stage with him. One male audience member recognizes the first song so MC Matt invites him to the stage. This is a talented passenger. Even as he enters, he works the crowd, undulating to the music, dancing around the rotunda while the three floors of onlookers cheer him on. He is fantastic. He knows the words of the song and performs with panache. The crowd bursts into enthusiastic applause as he walks the steps leading up to the platform to join Matt. After he arrives, Matt presents him with a medal for his efforts.

The central staircase or circular rotunda described above can also be a site of raucous play. Because it extends across several floors, it visibly encourages passengers to gather in the site in order to get a sense of the mood and activities of the day. When it is animated as a play space it will be used for open, inclusive events. Much like an outdoor festival or party, it draws in onlookers to participate. On higher end ships the "party" will be waltzing to a classical ensemble, but on lower end ships the party will literally rock the boat with sound and dance. When the rotunda functions as a party space it shifts its semiotic impact and becomes a communal gathering space where audiences interact and create unique experiences for one another. Instead of facilitating top-down events where guests merely watch, the communal space of the staircase (or rotunda) activates interactive conversations between guests. Staff members are still involved, but they will encourage conversations across groups of guests or, like Matt above, activate interactions with passengers who "amp up" the fun. (A later section will discuss how play within the liminal space of the sea encourages passengers to act out in ways they could not imagine onshore.) The central rotunda or the open staircase enables passengers to gather in an architectural space where they can see one another cavort.

Another communal gathering space on the ship is the top floor lounge, a more understated locale that supports less-formal interactions between passengers and staff. It is usually programmed with evening or late afternoon entertainment in order to keep passengers intermingling with one another after the sun has set when sitting on the pool deck is no longer viable. While dining is a core evening entertainment activity, the upper-floor lounge functions as a gathering space that is activated after the meals and the mainstage shows are finished. Often, competitions encourage passengers and crew members to collaboratively play. They can range from sedate "guess that tune" events to raucous public humiliation games like the Newlywed Game where couples compete with one another in front of guests who laugh at their comical circumstances.

Figure 15. Royal Caribbean *Explorer of the Seas*, May 2012.

The entertainment staff generally organizes events that involve crew and guests alike. Their position as activity leaders intrinsically allows them to move easily into roles of cheerleading for guests to perform ridiculousness. Communal events orchestrated by the staff might be as simple as a beanbag toss competition or as complex as trivia guessing games, musical challenges, or games of dexterity like stacking cups or catching pick-up sticks tossed into the air. Guests truly appreciate these events, particularly on sea days when there are no port destinations to visit. When the two worlds of working ship employees and vacationing passengers collide, each learns a little more about the humanity of the other because the drive of competition releases personal inhibitions and, in moments of concentrated effort, competitors tend to drop their social pretenses. The lounge space supports informal, large-group engagements between crew members and passengers in an interior space.

The Whisper Challenge on Celebrity cruises exemplifies a passenger/crew event held in the ship's lounge where travelers commune after the dinner hour. Crew members from nonentertainment areas (like bar staff or engineering staff) may be invited to join in as a special perk. Playing games with passengers breaks the monotony of daily service work and is sometimes used as a staff reward for excellent service. The game begins when a staff member guides participants to stand in a line of four or five and wear headsets that play pop music in their ears so they can't hear anything around them. (These same headsets are also used for a different activity, a silent disco where various genres of music are played through the headsets, enabling passengers to dance to their own music in the same physical space.) For the Whisper Challenge, the music intends to distract the players from understanding words said to them during a language-based competition. A member of the activities staff gives the first player a sentence to repeat such as "I choose you." The first player speaks the words to the next player who, because of the headsets, can only read the lips of the person speaking. As the phrase makes its way down the line of players, it becomes distorted and misinterpreted. The fun of the game is to see what kinds of meanings guests draw from the words they are only able to lip-read. As the spoken text reaches the end of the route, observers can see how language and meaning have been distorted as the words moved from person to person.

Of course, this game is similar to the game of Telephone in that it reveals how language can be misinterpreted, but on the international cruise ship the game takes on new resonances. The guests who are playing the game come from different countries, different classes, and different life experiences. The night I observed the game, one of the contestants was from Liverpool, and one from South America. The way they interpreted the phrases and understood the mouthed language depended upon their lifestyles and lived experiences. "I choose you" could become "I choose shoes" or "I see you" depending upon how each guest processed mouth gestures, rhythms, and sentence structures. The after-dinner entertainment reminded all who played the game how different cultural responses can be. If the phrase was "I love Beyoncé" (one of the activity staff favorites) there was no guarantee that the seventy-five-year-old contestant from Portugal would have a frame of reference for understanding the mouthed meaning of the word. From my perspective, the Whisper Challenge game competition reminded passengers about how different cultural understandings could be in the multinational context of the cruise ship.

The Marriage Game is another guest challenge game played in lounges.[12] Couples brought to the stage are asked to predict the responses of their partners to information about their lives. The staff ask questions designed to touch upon areas of marital relationships that are seldom publicly discussed. An example might be "If I ask your wife what her favorite part of your body is what will she say?" or "What is your husband's most used tool in his shop?" The questions reveal how much couples know about their partner's habits and preferences. The answers are sometimes hilarious, but the real trick of the game is that couples traveling on vacation have time to reconsider details of

Figures 16a and 16b. Dining on the Oceania *Sirena*, November 2022, and the *Victory I* (Great Lakes), October 2017.

a relationship they may not take time to examine onshore. Because vacationing couples are released from thinking about quotidian tasks like cooking or cleaning, they have time to really see one another and recognize new truths about themselves.

On cruise ships passengers have unstructured time to reflectively engage in self-assessment. In theater training it's common for actors to do exercises where they stop "doing" and instead pay attention to what they see, hear, smell, and feel around them. The somatic process of focusing on awareness brings a new understanding of the body. Similarly, passengers on cruise ships gaze on the waters, release themselves from familiar schedules, and begin to reimagine themselves. Games like the Marriage Game, while entertaining, also encourage cruise ship guests to think about aspects of their relationships in new ways. The lounge space serves as a communal gathering area where guests, guided by activities staff, can safely interact with one another while other guests bear witness to their emotional states through the answers they give while playing the game. Passenger secrets, revealed in public spaces, contribute to the sense of communion passengers feel as they share their cruise vacation with others on board.

Sympotic Space—The Dining Room

Flashback—I enter the dining room with a chic scarf wrapped around my shoulders. It highlights the patterned blue in my silk dress while flowing with a sense of pizzazz. It will also keep me warm in the overly air-conditioned dining room. When I arrive at the podium, the hostess asks the question I dread: "Would you like to share a table?" I know the answer must be yes, because my onboarding document mentioned that conversing with guests at dinner is a part of my job. I nod and say "of course." The maître d' escorts me past dozens of tables where well-dressed guests dine. A few of them wave and nod, recognizing me as the guest lecturer from their in-room television sets. Ahead, I see our destination, a four-top table where a couple is scouring the menu. When I arrive at the table, the maître d' introduces me to my waiter, who introduces me to the already-seated guests. The waiter gestures to one of the chairs, stands behind me to pull out the seat and, as I struggle to adjust my skirt and scarf while still appearing graceful, he flips the cloth napkin and places it in my lap with a sense of practiced accomplishment. He picks up the large, twelve-by-eighteen-inch leatherbound menu from the table and places it in my hands. I look down at the eight pieces of silverware, three plates, and three glasses (two types of wine glasses and a water glass) placed in front of me and I know that the dinner performance has started. "Welcome to the dining room!," says Reginald the waiter.

In Wiles's chapter about sympotic space as theatrical space he writes about a gastro comic spectacle staged in 2001 by a local comedy troupe from Barcelona: "In a circular banqueting tent, the visible kitchen became an orchestra, with tunes played on saucepans. The waiters were assistant performers."[13] The performance took place at Olympic Village, a neighborhood in Barcelona first constructed to house athletes during the 1992 Olympic Games and now a popular entertainment destination. Wiles's description captures well the sense of an overblown spectacle that I experience in the Grand Dining Room of a cruise ship. On the largest vessels, the dining room will extend across as many as three levels and on smaller ships the single level will often have more than one entrance. White linen tablecloths and sometimes waiters in white gloves create an atmosphere of fine dining in a very special place. Micro and macro environments merge spectacle with skilled service.

On the one hand, the dining room denotes class and royalty, and on the other hand, it functions as a sympotic space where all can participate in pleasurable dining and convivial exchange. Dining room aesthetics embody the grandeur of French and English royalty. Gilded staircases wind through the room, guiding well-dressed cruise guests through their entrances. Larger tables are social gathering spots for parties of eight to ten people. While meticulous table service and extravagant food entice guests to eat grandly, it is the servile and pleasing attitudes of the staff that complete the atmospheric formula. Staff members meet and greet with questions—"How is your day?" or "What would you like to eat?" They aim to provide any delicacy requested by each and every guest. Employees express joy about each request for service. They are carefully groomed for specialty-dining-room performance. The result is an idealized world where guests are consistently immersed in dietary splendor.

Wiles writes: "The architecture of the Greek sympotic space was designed to be egalitarian, with the passing of a cup around the circle allowing each symposiast an equal share of attention."[14] The dining room of a cruise ship purports to be this kind of an egalitarian space, but the rules of maritime hierarchy prevent a leveling that would result in an equality of dialogic exchange. Dining room staff are carefully supervised, their service to the patrons is evaluated by headwaiters and the maître d', and perfected through hours of training. Over the course of the dinner, the sommelier will stop by the table several times to suggest drinks that best complement the meal. The menu will offer perhaps a dozen choices for appetizers, salads, soups, main courses, and desserts. A spectacle of service converges with an architectural spectacle, with the goal of having guests indulge and linger in the dining room. Fine dining is a core activity on the entertainment agenda.

However, Wiles also proposes that sympotic spaces are performance sites where a festive spirit arouses participants who witness performances of cooking and collective shared laughter. "Sitting at tables is crucial to the quality of this interaction, for the table allows couples and groups to acknowledge their responses to each other, and to choose whether they will give the audience their gaze, or look away in embarrassment or boredom."[15] My experience of dining rooms on the ship supports this idea. Once seated at a table and after ordering from the menu, guests generally introduce themselves to one another and inquire about which activities each of them attended throughout the day. This is an opportunity to talk about where you live, whether or not you have children, and other social niceties. Most people speak only marginally about their jobs and on upper-class cruises the clientele seem to frown upon discussing how they acquire income. My positionality as a Black woman might affect how comfortable the primarily white and wealthy guests feel about sharing their financial information. Still, this social gossip is not particularly festive or celebratory. It is instead an opportunity for cruise guests to share empathetic camaraderie around cruise-centric experiences.

On some ships—midrange and inexpensive vessels—waiters participate in a grating ritual of singing and dancing around the table while twirling napkins. The performance intends to amplify the sense of fun and to celebrate the purported joy that the staff feels about serving the clientele. It is usually done on the first or second sea day of the voyage. A headwaiter will announce to the guests that on this "special" night, the staff have decided to show how pleased they are that the guests are on board and ready for their vacation. Then the waiters seem to disappear. The headwaiter will encourage guests to clap when they hear the music. The dining room fills with a recording of upbeat music and the waiters march through the narrow aisles of the dining room led by either the chef or the headwaiter. Everyone claps and twirls their napkins to thank the waiters for putting on such a splendid show.

There was a time during the early 2000s when cruise lines offered a "grand buffet" during some part of the journey. This ostentatious presentation of carved ice statues, elaborately crafted appetizers, and sumptuous dessert trays was a particularly delightful late-night event. Chocolate fountains spewed sweets, a salmon revealed its smoky cavity, and happy chefs parted loins of lamb or beef or pork in choreographed demonstrations of articulate butchery. The grand buffet was themed with motifs like Caribbean barbecue or midnight magic. For the cruise line, the artistry of the buffet was a "signature" event. It was also an extravagant waste of food and resources. This type of grand spectacle has recently been replaced with smaller events. One consequence of the COVID-19 pandemic has been an emphasis on more intimate dining experiences carefully tailored to specialized tastes in small-group settings. Media experiences also enter the dining room. On some cruise lines, guests are able to be entertained by three-dimensional animations projected onto their plates as part of a high-tech dining experience. The table top comes to life as the projections fade away to reveal real food on the plate.[16]

More recently, in an effort to humanize and democratize the travel experience, cruise ships have offered "behind the scenes" tours to guests, providing an opportunity for them to experience the artistry of the shipboard workers. Small-scale food demonstrations give guests a chance to dialogue with galley staff and ask questions about food preparation. Behind-the-scenes demonstrations are similar to operations tours of venues like the Metropolitan Opera or theater tours for donors at Broadway shows. Some staff enjoy the opportunity to demonstrate their daily work tasks because it breaks up the boredom of the service and gives them a sense of pride about the labor they do. A "tour" might begin with a loudspeaker announcement. The cruise director will invite the guests to walk below deck and see how the kitchen serves thousands of meals every day. Passengers meet in the dining room to receive tickets for access to the galley. I might call an excursion into the lower depths of the cruise ship slumming because it exploits passengers' voyeuristic desires to see the work space of the underclass, but from the perspective of the cruise industry I can appreciate how the kitchen tour allows guests to appreciate the efficiency of the enterprise while keeping the galley staff engaged. Culinary staff, generally hidden from passenger view, demonstrate their professionalism and receive accolades that boost self-esteem as they see how much the guests appreciate their services. Undoubtedly, the presence of passengers in the galleys creates more work for the staff even as they receive special attention during the kitchen tours.

While the kitchen tour shows represent small-scale demonstrations of staff expertise, a more public performance of sympotic theatricality, one that harkens back to Wiles's depiction of the gastro spectacle of the Boccato di Cardinale at the Olympic Village, would be cooking shows staged in the main theater venue. They replicate cooking shows like *The Great British Bake Off* where contestants challenge one another as they prepare meals on the spot. Television cameras capture the ingredients from multiple angles and project all aspects of meal preparation to the shipboard audience. First, the galley staff prepares a mobile cooking set and transports it to the front of the stage. Next, a cornucopia of ingredients is placed on a table upstage of the cooking area. Finally, the activities staff, working with the cruise director, selects audience members who want to cook with the best ship chefs. Since everyone has been eating top-notch meals for days, there are plenty of volunteers.[17] The timed cooking begins and, as the meal unfolds, the audience supports their favorite team with calls and cheers. After the bell rings, new audience members are selected to taste and judge the meals. The entire sequence takes about an hour before the winner is announced. Even though tunes are not played on saucepans, as they are in the Boccato di Cardinale, recorded music keeps the cooking competition upbeat, performative, and spectacularly sympotic.

Cave Spaces: The Library

The final semiotic performance space is the cave space, a place where people retreat to create a theater of dreams, allowing them to connect to a higher, more spiritual reality.[18] On a cruise ship, one private yet publicly accessible space would be the library, where passengers can sit quietly without conversation, away from weather-related distractions. Ship libraries can vary from a single hidden alcove to a more grandiose architectural display spanning two floors. Some are extensions of internet cafes or coffee shops, signaling two different approaches to how passengers might choose to engage with the books. Internet cafes tend to have smaller book collections while expan-

Figure 17a and 17b. Celebrity *Eclipse*, January 2011, and Oceania *Sirena*, November 2022.

sive libraries will encourage guests to browse and check out both fiction and nonfiction materials. The internet, while available, is spotty on cruise ships, therefore it is unlikely that guests will spend time gaming or streaming. For many elderly passengers an ideal vacation means sitting in a comfortable chair with a good book, allowing the mind to wander undisturbed to a distant land or setting. Library architecture features high back chairs and seating spaced with distance between perches to discourage conversation.

Libraries have always been a part of the maritime experience. Even common deckhands would keep collections of books in trunks to keep them occupied during sea voyages. Captain's wives, who sometimes traveled with their husbands, were known to read at sea and keep extensive journals about their experiences on board. Passenger liners of the late nineteenth century prioritized having a small library on board. Initially these were informal collections accumulated by the ship's officers. By 1895, all first-class ships were expected to have a library. When the *Queen Mary* was launched in 1936, it had a separate library for each class of passengers. Once again, historical precedents impact cruise aesthetics and architecture.[19] The public library reading room is perhaps the area of the ship that requires the least amount of labor to sustain it. Certainly, there are shelves to be polished and books to be alphabetized, but in this section, the cave of the ship, the architecture entertains by immersing passengers in a space of quiet reflection. I have seen crew members escaping the public by slowly cleaning the inner recesses of the library corners, but the library is a space where embodied performance is unnecessary because passengers quietly immerse themselves in their own dreams and imaginations.

Each architectural space on a cruise ship deliberately mediates between historical iconography and contemporary preferences. Cruise design, a specialized architectural field, succeeds when it merges design technologies, ship safety protocols, and distinctive cruise line branding to match customer needs. The designed layouts of public cruise ship spaces directly impact how employees, trained in theatrical techniques, deploy spaces to choreograph immersive spectacles that give passengers the exotic, comfortable, elegant, entertaining, reclusive, social, drunken, full-bodied, sexualized experiences they desired when they booked their commercial cruise. From my perspective, the artistry of crafting events to match the scenic backdrops of each theatrical onboard space is what makes cruise entertainment a directorial feat.

Figure 18. Passenger play aboard the Royal Caribbean *Mariner of the Seas*, October 2005.

Play at Sea

Flashback—We are back at the Motown singing challenge. The performers are still revved up, the adrenaline from the dance competition is high. Matt, using his cruise ship iPad, brings up the next song. This is a special round, he announces—the men's group challenge. The song is "My Girl" by the Temptations. All men are eligible, but only the brave take to the stage. Ten men volunteer and rush up to the platform, gyrating, snapping, pointing, and shaking to the music. Matt knowingly invites each man to take the microphone during each musical interlude so everyone has a chance to be the lead singer. It's a fantastic performance because each man delivers the lyrics of the song in their own unique style. Matt introduces the next act. The competition will be a booty dance where contestants vie for the best moves. Black, white, and Latinx competitors line up with their backs to the largest section of the crowd and they begin to gyrate their bottoms, winding and shaking, twerking to show their capacity. One woman, possibly in her forties (I'll call her Mabel), is a clear winner. Her vibrating buttocks intoxicate and mesmerize. The crowd screams with enthusiasm and she wins the first round. A new final round begins where all previous performers are invited back to the stage. Mabel is again exceptional. She steals the spotlight of attention from everyone else on the stage. In a surprise moment, the winning male dancer, eager for his moment in the spotlight, seeks to outdo her by mounting her vibrating buttocks. This is too much. Cruise director Matt intervenes. "No, no, no," he calls into the microphone and presses the stop button on the iPad. Everyone calms down and breathes. Libidos subside.

Entertainment staff on cruise ships encourage raunchy games and jokes about sex as a tactic for amusing cruise ship passengers. Drinking and semi-nudity coupled with sun and percussive music are almost a formula for fulfilling passenger expectations about Caribbean vacations. Cruise director Matt likely stopped the twerking act not because it was inappropriate, but rather because it was infringing on the personal space of the unsuspecting female dancer. Both of the dancers who took over the stage were guests of African or Afro-Latino descent. They easily slipped into performing dance styles from Black communities where pelvic isolations and articulations of ribs and shoulders, knees and feet represent the artistic ingenuity of the African diaspora siphoned through the complex multiculturalism of the Americas. For centuries, European chroniclers and their descendants have characterized Black dances as lascivious or excessive. Now, on vacation in the Caribbean, the performers were able to "strut their stuff."

Cruise ship staff sanction excessive performances because bending rules of decorum is part of the fun of being away from home and away from normal rules. Carnival ships are known within the industry as party boats, but even more staid cruise brands like Celebrity encourage passengers to feel comfortable talking about sex and sexuality. Like the inversion of norms that happens within the carnivalesque as described by Mikhail Bakhtin, immersing in a world permeated with sexuality promotes a sense of freedom. Guests, already seduced into dressing up for evening soirées, or disrobing to don bathing suits on the pool deck, find freedom in experimenting with alternative identities in other ways. Sex talk and sex jokes add to feelings of liberation. Passengers who are couples are reminded of the sexual intimacies in their relationships. Bawdy conversations about sexual encounters remind single passengers of possibilities for intimate engagements with new partners. Some activities are fast, loud, and raucous.

Play at sea moves toward the raucous and ridiculous because passengers, unmoored from their familiar communities, cavort with one another in unexpected ways. When alcohol consumption joins the party then guests on vacation feel even freer to indulge in embodied, ludicrous play. The sea itself creates a sense of "nowhere-ness" that accentuates emotions; it underscores mortality with the presence of open water extending beyond the horizon, making it seem as if time has slowed down. For those of us tied to internet connectivity with its easy access to entertainment and surfing the web, the experience of having minimal online access and unstructured time might instill a desire for communion. On an individual level, workers and passengers occupy themselves with personal tasks—emails, letter writing, or crafts—but social activities bring people together on ships and make time pass more quickly. Across centuries, mariners have occupied themselves with ridiculous play, song, and dance as a way of coping with the repetitive consistency of traveling across open sea waters. The 2017 sea party on the Carnival cruise may not be that different from nineteenth-century escapades. Like earlier travelers, we were essentially stuck at sea and waiting for the time to pass. Instead of journals and writings, electronic music eases the boredom. When the Carnival ship diverted, the weather forced all of us to shift our expectations of a destination and cope with the realities of storms at sea. Separated from home and away from the gaze of loved ones, we reveled in a transgressive space exploring physical embodiments that would likely be frowned upon onshore.

Play at sea creates a temporary community that establishes behavioral norms distinct from normalized expectations of land-based social systems. I have already discussed how race and ethnicity operate within the hierarchical work structures of the cruise industry. However, the ship at sea is also a space where identities are reimagined and negotiated through dialogic exchange. Dialogic exchange, embodied conversations where participants exchange knowledge, occurs across ethnic communities on land, but because the cruise ship is contained, with little space for ethnic enclaves to avoid one another, cross-cultural communications intensify. This section focuses on games and rituals characteristic of ship culture. Later I will discuss song and dance and how they promote embodied, intellectual transfers of knowledge. Here, I comment on how enactments, historical and contemporary, bond communities while allowing multiple ethnic groups to perform imaginative renditions of themselves. Historical maritime rituals such as Crossing the Line and the Dead Horse ceremony are precursors of the dance rituals described above, as well as other contemporary challenge competitions like the Liar's Club, belly flop contests, and pirate photos, all activities where guests embrace the carnivalesque to participate in new experimental identities.

Crossing the Line

The most documented sea ritual from the historical archive is Crossing the Line, a maritime ceremony still practiced, albeit in a more minimalist form, on contemporary naval vessels. Sea men and women mark when a novice

Play at Sea, Space, and Meaning · 85

Figure 19. Image of a nineteenth-century Crossing the Line ritual. Wikimedia Commons https://commons.wikimedia.org/wiki/File:Crossing_the_Line_(caricature)_RMG_PU0156.tiff

sailor (or pollywog) passes over the equator or the Arctic Circle by staging a ritual that traditionally recognizes the transition of a sailor from a neophyte to a seasoned seaman. Crossing the Line ceremonies continue the tradition of initiation practices once used by medieval guilds to welcome new members into their trade, but by the eighteenth and nineteenth centuries the ritual became more codified and elaborate. It began to incorporate hazing practices with prescribed dramatic persona who represented ethnic and mythological characters.[20] Traditionally, the ceremony began when a senior sailor, bedecked as King Neptune, would appear on deck during the early morning hours. An entourage of senior officers dressed as members of the court accompanied him. Neptune the King, officiator of the upcoming ritual, would invite novice sailors to participate in pranks. Senior sailors would throw them into a saltwater bath, beat them as they traversed across darkened spaces, or shave them in saltwater with a dull blade. Men dressed as mermaids while lower status cooks or stewards would become a part of Neptune's "court."

Figure 20. Crossing the Line ceremony aboard the Royal Australian Navy ship *HMAS Melbourne*, 1926. Courtesy of Wikimedia Commons.

The ceremony incorporated myths and legends from various nations in its imagination of who would be villains or advocates. The most common personages were mermaids, turtles, cannibals, beasts, gods, witches, and unruly women. When sailors adopted the garb of the archetypal "other" through their embodied play they perpetuated racialized and gendered stereotypes within the ritual celebration. Underlings in Neptune's court often dressed like indigenous "savages" or beasts. Having already subservient cooks and stewards in these roles intensified the potential for abuse by senior sailors. One goal of the ceremony was to induct participants into an alternative maritime culture where new customs or modes of behavior would replace the patterns or cultural backgrounds of each individual sailor. Seamen who completed the ritual were inculcated into a new reality, one that would bind them to the endless sea. Crossing the Line ceremonies helped new sailors to sever ties with their homeland and establish their status as full-fledged members of the ship. After enduring the series of tests and trials, the pollywogs or novice sailors earned their way into the ranks of the "shellbacks" or veteran sailors. They "crossed the line" both metaphorically and physically.

The popularity of Crossing the Line ceremonies has continued. I find more recent images of the practice disturbing not only because of the racialization of the characters but also because of the violence involved in the actual ritual. Various participants are dumped in water, covered with mud, hit and pummeled, and forced to lick the belly button of their "masters" in order to complete the initiation—the similarity to hazing is apparent. Folklorist Simon Bronner, writing in 2006, describes elements of the ceremony that include shellbacks dressed as equatorial natives who take over the ship and force pollywogs to smear their faces; or a "bitch day" when pollywogs dress in drag and imitate women (which could be fun, but is certainly derogatory toward women in this context).[21] Crossing the Line ceremonies in the United States are currently regulated by the navy as a direct result of lawsuits. The excesses, which have included such things as being forced to participate in homoerotic sex play by dropping one's pants or licking off eggs or exposing one's buttocks for ritualistic beatings, became strictly out of bounds when women began entering the navy in greater numbers.

Masquerade and cross-dressing extend possibilities for gender play and one can assume individuals are somewhat free to morph the codes to suit their own self-perceptions. It is possible that under these specific circumstances, sea play like Crossing the Line rituals could represent a rejection of the here and now in order to find the potentiality and possibility of utopia as theorized by José Esteban Muñoz.[22] But the settings for Crossing the Line ceremonies are not, and never were, utopic. The ritual intends to inculcate sailors into the toxic masculinity of a hierarchical and misogynistic world. In his book *Sailors and Sexual Identity*, Steven Zeeland writes about how male-on-male sexual acts are not uncommon in the hypermasculine environment of the U.S. Navy and the U.S. Marine Corps, and about the dilemma this poses for gender queer men. Citing Judith Butler, he considers the contradiction between performing presumed masculinity while engaging in feminine or submissive homoerotic sexual acts. Eventually, Zeeland posits that homoerotic bonding helps to build the machismo needed to sustain the façade of the masculinized marine.[23] This negates rather than supports a heathy queer culture.

The United States Navy has somewhat shifted its sponsorship of Crossing the Line ceremonies.[24] Traditionally, navies gave a material reward to sailors for crossing the equator and participating in theatrical play to commemorate the moment. Nowadays, these crossings are acknowledged without all of the pomp and circumstance. Sailors get shellback certificates if they participate in a Crossing the Line event and maritime archives display these tokens as an honor of service. Mass communication specialist Andrew B. Church, writing about the ceremony in 2013, quotes a U.S. Navy man and explains, "The tradition has carried on, but it's carried out so that it is in line with our Navy Core Values . . . the purpose of the ceremony is to have fun, but it is strictly voluntary and Sailors can leave at any time. We keep it safe."[25] Yet the notion of safety can be relative, depending on a person's gender and cultural orientation. Although contemporary merchant and naval ships have toned down the ceremonies and adapted them to include female participants, the ritual persists as a questionable component of contemporary maritime culture.

Other maritime play rituals bear mentioning. The Dead Horse ceremony was staged on sailing ships to celebrate the end of the debt a seaman owed to the captain for his sailor outfit and onboard food. When seamen were recruited to work on a vessel, the captain would promise to pay for the worker's food and to provide him with a bunk to sleep in. He also guaranteed a work uniform for the new employee. However, like fieldworkers in the sharecropping system, the cost of the goods the captain provided were applied to each sailor's account as a debt that needed to be paid off before the sailor completed his contract. When the debt period was over, the seamen would celebrate. They began the Dead Horse ceremony by constructing a horse out of canvas and wood and parading it across the deck while singing. When the parade finished, they threw the horse overboard to represent "burying the horse" of their debts.[26] The Dead Horse ceremony no longer exists in maritime culture, but it illustrates how disempowered working-class seamen used folkways to demonstrate their collective response to wage withholding at sea. Contemporary maritime museums re-create the "Dead Horse" song and parade to entertain visitors young and old with a tidbit of maritime history. Still, the ceremony remains a part of the maritime archive of enactments. I am interested in how the existence of the Dead Horse ceremony documents, through performance, working-class sailor's response to inequities within their work environment.

Play below Deck

Historical sea play in all-male environments encouraged seamen to adapt to a lifestyle where the vessel was their space for camaraderie. On contemporary cruise ships, opportunities for workers to create rituals are more limited. In my role as a destination lecturer, I am not privy to events in crew quarters, yet there are others like David Bruns, who worked as a crew member on

Carnival lines, who have written about what happens at cruise crew parties below deck. Burns, in a book series that reads like a below-the-deck exposé about "where the crew eats, wars and parties," narrates the details of a Carnival Cruise Christmas party where staff workers imitate popular cultural icons.[27] He describes a dress-up party involving cross-dressing and ethnic/gender play similar to the outrageous character impersonations of Neptune and his entourage in the Crossing the Line ceremonies.

> Now nearly 2:30 in the morning, we impatiently waited for a Filipino housekeeper to finish his crooning of a Jon Secada ballad. Finally, the cruise director announced that his next act was from Truffles. . . .
>
> The lights remained low, and a spotlight faded in to reveal Xenia on her knees in prayer. She wore a blue hooded robe and carried a candle. The opening of the song was respectful and solemn, with all attention on the solitary figure in candlelight. . . . When the tempo picked up her melodrama began.
>
> From the shadows came the First Temptation. Leaping in . . . was a creepy man wielding a spear capped with feathers. Wearing a white toga that contrasted sharply against his dark brown skin, he rushed around the stage poking at Xenia who swooned dramatically in response to the danger.
>
> I recognized the First Temptation as Nestor from Guatemala.[28]

Bruns's short description does not provide contexts for the performances at the party. Indeed, most of his books document his personal challenges with being an American citizen working on cruise ships and his attempts to maintain a social life within that environment. I'm drawn to his description of this party because the dress-up role-playing he describes supports my assertion that ship entertainment might be a transgressive space for reimagining identities on board. Performance breaks daily routines. Maritime culture has always brought together a collective of individuals from diverse cultural spaces, and workers as actors learn new things about one another within sanctioned spaces of dramatic play.

When crew members do come above deck and integrate guest passenger spaces, they find the service economy based upon their labor to be exhausting. Crew members speak to me when I travel, usually in quiet asides or in non-public nooks and crannies. One time, the lead housekeeper for the shipboard corridor asked me to put in a good word for him because he was finally at the end of his contract. Even though, after three years on board the ship, he was finally able to travel home for the holidays, he hoped for a good referral that would allow him to return to the ship in the spring. In another encounter, a Black dining room worker found me in the casual restaurant and let me know that he had been watching my lectures on the TV in his cabin. Why, he asked, don't I talk more about Jamaica? I sometimes wonder why crew members seek me out for more personal conversations. But I know why. It's because they recognize a Black fellow traveler who is also a pseudo employee. I am someone on board in a more privileged position who may identify with what it means to be relegated to a largely invisible service role when you are in fact a three-dimensional human being with a family and a heritage. The artificial upper-class performative culture on a ship sometimes feels like a cruel funhouse reflection of a system that reiterates class divisions, reminding workers they may ever remain on the bottom rung of a service culture where one's social value depends upon how well a person pours the coffee or makes the bed. Service workers approach me because they presume I will understand the subjectivity of Black service within a primarily white environment and assist them in some way.

Ester Ellen Bolt and Conrad Lashley interview cruise ship workers about why they choose to ship out and work for months or years at a time on mega cruise ships.[29] Even though shipboard jobs, especially those in meal service and cabin cleaning, receive the lowest monthly pay and must be augmented by passenger tips,[30] salary is the main reason cruise ship workers "ship out." They sacrifice time with their families, but they are able to make more than what they would make in their countries of origin and can send funds home to their families. Some workers are embarrassed by the subservient roles they assume as they interact with passengers.

> "It's a very hard job. I always feel exhausted when I finish it and come down to my cabin. . . . The restaurant is a stage, a show. You are an actor. Believe me, you can be totally drained just by greeting people, chatting with them, smiling to them, and things like that. As an Asian, I have to work harder, I have to make more efforts to please the passengers." (Zhao 2002, 10–11)[31]

Yet there is an opportunity for workers to interact and learn from cross-cultural exchanges within this space of international commerce. One site of exchange is below deck, among the workers who dine together and learn about customs that expand their intercultural fluency. Another is with the passengers who, for better or worse, perform the sometimes-crude culture of

American exceptionalism. They drink and talk loudly, they express cultural ignorance, and they are sometimes curious about the ship's future destinations, or workers' country of origin.

However, small acts of cultural exchange also provide an opportunity for cruise ship guests to learn a little more about what it might be like to live within a different cultural paradigm. I watch guests ask ship workers about how they cope with being far away from their families. I see crew members ask guests about their homelands or their families. Corporate protocols prevent these conversations from developing into extended relationships, but the beginnings of cross-cultural communication are evident as some curious passengers seek to expand their horizons by engaging with the multicultural staff who serve their needs. Sometimes all it takes is a shared laugh or a familiar gesture in response to a mishap to initiate a cross-cultural conversation. Beneath the pretense of spectacle resides a possibility for human connection.

Some cruise activities exploit various passenger interactions with staff members. Cruise directors like to program competitions that allow favored crew members to interact with passengers by competing in structured challenge events. Having crew members compete with guests serves two purposes: (1) guests are able to meet and interact with behind-the-scenes staff in new ways, and (2) crew members receive perks of access to the upper decks and increased prominence across the ship. The activity of having cruise ship guests meet the working staff in public spaces is similar to having actors come out from backstage and mingle with audience members after a show. The public appearance allows audiences to interact with a real-life person who exists outside of their prescribed character or role. Unlike a theater, the immersive cruise experience does not have a "backstage," but many crew members are hidden from the public eye because they work below deck. When passengers see workers from the engineering staff or captain's bridge "at play," they feel as if everyone on board is at sea for the party. Bringing the crew onstage to play creates an atmosphere of fun and enhances the illusion of complete vacation immersion. Competitive events with crew members allow the guests to meet the "stars" of the vessel in an upbeat and entertaining way.

Sometimes a crew opportunity to "play" with the passengers is a reward for good service or a recognition of exceptional talent. If a crew member is selected for this opportunity, they become a celebrity across the ship. One example is an onboard event once popular with Celebrity cruise passengers called Dancing with the Stripes.[32] In this event, passengers and crew members compete in an all-out dance competition. The cruise director invites stage-worthy staff members to leave their below-the-deck stations and come to the upper-level community-engagement lounge where they can select a guest as their partner. Once dance partners are selected, each "team" will challenge other teams. Staff members are recruited from all service areas of the ship, and this is one of the few events where I have seen workers from the engineering team perform. This playful competitive event replicates structures from *So You Think You Can Dance* or *The Voice*; a panel of preselected staff and audience members chooses winners from preliminary rounds of dance performances. During competition, "mixed" couples (consisting of one staff member and one guest passenger) dance to different genres of music—tango, hip hop, waltz, or ballet. The judges eliminate teams until a winner emerges. Dancing couples are encouraged to be ridiculous—arms fly wildly, legs kick high, tiny men lift big women, and sweat flies all over the floor. Passengers view the dance event as an extension of their vacation party, while staff members utilize this performative moment to express a nonservile aspect of their personality. Dancing with the Stripes provides perks for the crew, entertains guests, and creates a carnivalesque space where everyone can break out of hierarchical roles and enjoy corporeal excess at sea. Competition is a staple for interactive play across many cruise lines, as it has been for centuries of maritime history. Once again, the past informs the present.

Competitions

One of the most evocative images from the maritime archive depicts two men, one Black and one white, boxing while tied together on a trunk. It's a caricature of life below deck, depicting presumed lower-class passengers entertaining themselves amid brawls and drunken exploits. The competitors aggressively hold up their fists while their coaches, dressed in seaman's garb, urge them on. The depiction is rife with race and gender stereotypes; Blacks, women, and seamen appear bestial and uncouth within their social landscape. Because seamen worked outside of land-based cultural norms, mannered urban socialites who published and wrote about their lives viewed their physicality with aversion.[33]

Challenging social norms is one way of establishing group identity and creating a utopia of inclusion for those relegated to the borders of society. Black on white physical competitions serve as a familiar metaphor for Black/white racial relationships. They evoke iconic events like the Max Schmeling vs. Joe Louis fight of 1936, where the much-publicized face-off between a white German and Black American foregrounded racial animosity while situating Black on white aggression as play. In the engraving, the

Figure 21. Sailors box on a sea chest. Hand-colored engraving by Thomas Tegg, ca. 1800, courtesy Bridgeman Images.

men on the trunk battle to work out conflict and perhaps achieve a truce or camaraderie after their encounter. At the same time, they sit in close proximity to one another, legs splayed as they uncompromisingly prepare for their encounter. For seamen who spent most of their time contained in tight quarters with other men, physical activities both relieved boredom and released emotional energies.

If, as Jose Muñoz argued in 1999, "queer performance . . . is about transformation, about the powerful and charged transformation of the world, about the world that is born through performance," then men who played in circumstances such as those depicted may be effectively remaking a world of "play" away from heteronormative and racialized norms, bending rules to conform to an alternative set of norms.[34] Boxing games, in this context, bring men of different races into physical competitive play that builds community. Physical competitions on nineteenth-century vessels laid a path for a continuing tradition of onboard embodied competitions. Less aggressive dance battles or belly flop contests keep modern cruise ship passengers physically active and, in the case of the Celebrity cruise dance challenge, facilitate partnerships across class rather than racial boundaries. Madcap fun has no political goal; instead, it disrupts the stasis of onboard hierarchies. It calls attention to the embodied humanity of the body resisting the containment of limited onboard space.

Physical competitions and sexy dancing lean into bawdiness or sexual innuendo that is a notable component of play at sea. Shows like *The Love Boat*, with its storylines built around romantic escapades in tropical paradises, emphasize racy, freewheeling aspects of being on a cruise ship. Advertisements for Caribbean destinations tend to display either native islanders singing and dancing or romantic couples gazing out over serene waters as they escape from home realities. Much has been written about sexualized exoticism of Caribbean women.[35] A continuing recirculation of provocative tourist imagery across commercial Caribbean tourism products encourages travelers to expect sexualized experiences to be a part of their Caribbean immersion even though, on the ship, they travel with companions from home. Once again, the liminality of the ship as a location neither here nor there encourages carnivalesque impropriety. And of course, bawdy play with sexual innuendos has been a part of theatrical repertoires since classical times. Aristotle defined the genre and writers from Aristophanes to David Chappelle have utilized techniques of sexual humor for entertainment. Cruise directors, building upon theatrical precedents of comical conventions, program and participate in bawdy play throughout the journey.

Flashback—At a late-night event on a Celebrity cruise called the Liar's Club, cruise director Sue sits on a stage with the captain and a paid guest comedian. The game they are playing is like *Truth or Consequences*. Audience members hear each contestant attempt to explain the meaning of an obscure word, then they are to guess whether or not the speaker lied in their definition. Tonight, the word is *bibcock*. The audience waits expectantly as the contestants tell exaggerated stories about what the word might mean. The comedian suggests the word means a bib to catch penis dribble. The captain looks uncomfortable but agrees to contribute a definition that makes absolutely no sense. He is not that good at the game because he's not a trained entertainer. The cruise director is deft and savvy in her response. Even though a bibcock is actually a piece of piping for plumbing, she manages to talk about bidets and uses a lot of toilet humor. It's all very inappropriate and the audience of primarily senior citizens loves it. There is nothing physical about this challenging game, but it does allow guests to revel in the inappropriate late at night. The Liar's Club is advertised as an "adults only" event, so audiences are primed to expect something naughty and outside of the norm. Since I have seen the same performance more than once I am aware of how the entire event is scripted to elicit "naughty" conversation within a safe environment.

Royal Caribbean, in a similar type of late-night event, has passengers play a game with the cruise director where he or she challenges them to work in teams to produce hidden items. When he blows a whistle, they are asked to pass pens or eyeglasses or T-shirts or bras down to the center of the arena to win points. Passengers scramble to find items in their bags or on their bodies that they can share publicly. It's part exposé, part skill, part bravado, and especially effective if passengers are well intoxicated. Participants freely indulge in sexualized comments or vulgar gestures. It doesn't matter what you do, as long as no one tells. In many of these games, a screaming crowd selects the winner. Entertainment staff assume that when everyone is making noise, they are having fun. The Royal Caribbean game is only one of a cluster of activities designed by entertainment staff and others that uniquely capture the spirit of raucous play without purpose. Of course, there are similar kinds of land-based competitive activities, such as mud wrestling and karaoke, that draw crowds. But cruise ships, especially on sea days, normalize these events, encouraging those who would never do them on land to hurl themselves into the fray.

Each incidence of "play at sea"—improvisational rituals, challenge dances, organized games, or raucous play—amplifies the sense of being away from land-based norms and in a space where different rules apply. Crew members use onboard play opportunities to escape from the drudgery of their daily work assignments, while passengers enjoy participating in activities where they are able to craft personalities different from what they express onshore. Guest vacationers caught between ports explore new sexual freedoms, or reimagined relationships, in the utopic space of the megaship; they experiment with internal and external selves through embodied acts.

Labor's Song and Dance

Flashback—I'm on the stage in the proscenium venue of the cruise ship standing in front of a twenty-foot-high screen. I've projected lyrics from the old sea shanty "Drunken Sailor." Using my wireless microphone, I approach the edge of the stage and ask the audience "What do you do with a drunken sailor?" There is no response. My audience of senior citizens looks baffled. After a few seconds, I provide the answer "Put him in the scuppers till he gets sober!" Now they are even more confused. I explain that scuppers are a hole in the side of the ship where you can force a sailor to insert his legs, exposing him to the sun. We, the crowd and I, sing about scuppers together. Next, we learn about a "hoop iron razor" so we can respond to the prompt "What do you do with a drunken sailor" with a hearty "Shave the hair off his chest with a hoop iron razor." I enjoy sharing interactive sea shanties because song lyrics efficiently teach my audience terminology relevant to maritime worlds of the eighteenth and nineteenth centuries. And I feel as if I am reenacting a history of embodiment through performance. I march around and "sound the deck" of the stage with my feet moving to the rhythmic cadence of the song. Sometimes I ask audience members to wave their hands or swing their arms as they repeat "Heave Ho, Up She Rises!" In this site of social play, we pass time on board and collectively share an embodied exchange experience. Even though there are no sweaty bodies, this event offers an opportunity for us to map cultural gestures onto our bodies as we imagine the lifestyles of historical seamen.

If I were in a college classroom, I would share even more information about how songs produced by laborers carry knowledge outside of literary traditions. Maritime settings supported sea shanties and challenge dances that captured the vernacular cultural intelligence of laborers who interacted with one another within ships and at ports where they were able to use their leisure time for dialogic exchange. White and Black, Asian, indigenous, and other Americans might find themselves in the same port or on the same whaling ship with time to share information about their homelands through song. Sonic calls accompanied by lyrics were carried from ship to shore and back again. Seamen invent ballads telling tales of their lives and histories.

In this section I discuss two aspects of performative cultural exchange between maritime workers: (1) music and dance improvisations where performers shared the virtuosity of their talents, and (2) sea shanty dialogues where mariners communicated knowledge within the storytelling lyrics of their songs. Dorinne Kondo has argued that identities are crafted in processes of work, and within matrices of power. The isolated maritime ship was a worksite where multiethnic groups of laborers negotiated power and camaraderie. They used performative behavior and oral storytelling to describe their experiences, needs, and desires. Kondo also maintains that collective and individual practices contribute to how selves are crafted.[36] I consider music-making practices on ships to be rehearsal spaces where individuals hone virtuosic skills through solo practice and then share or compete with others to improve their skills. The mutability of live performance, coupled with its corporeal capacity, makes it an ideal mechanism for negotiating and crafting allegiances within the power structure of the ship.

During a one-week stint on a sailing ship, a common seaman might trim the jib, wash the hammocks, lower the mainsail, muster at quarters, furl the sails, shift the topsail, and wash and mend clothing.[37] Each of these work activities involved physical effort where the engagement of bodies mattered. The labor of managing onboard tasks accreted; the proximity of other male bodies tested the worker's nerves. Engagement of bodies was a way of coping with difficult circumstances or reconciling differences between those who disagreed. While physical matchups resolved some differences, in other cases, performance practices such as singing and dancing contributed to complex negotiations on board. Communal singing and dancing would (1) bring seamen into conversation with one another, (2) introduce new customs or cultural contexts, (3) acknowledge the virtuosity of individual performers, and (4) simply pass time and help to relieve the boredom of ocean travel. It's important to recognize how storytelling and physicalized embodiment contributed to knowledge sharing and informational dialogues on the ship and in port towns. Embodied performative knowledge permeates popular cultural and working-class communities and work sites. It controverts performances of servitude for front-facing crew workers on cruise ships and in other settings that employ service workers.

Figure 22. Sailor dancing a jig with his ship in the distance.

Virtuosic Challenges

Historical imagery of seamen frequently depicts two or three sailors dancing together, performing a jig or hornpipe. It's a trope seen across nautical icons in popular culture, from the cartoon character Popeye to thematic costumed play at gay sailor parties on Fire Island.[38] Tapping a percussive beat while swaying hips and kicking legs from side to side, the sailor jigging to the iconic hornpipe has been a prototype for representations of British naval sea traditions since the sixteenth century. How did this image of the sailor come to represent onboard entertainment on the sailing ship? It's unlikely that sailors spent their time dancing around the deck when it was necessary for all hands to be involved in navigating the vessel. Inevitably, music and dance exchanges would have happened when seamen were off shift and waters were calm. During those moments they would be able to socialize through performance or storytelling. Competitive solo performances would be a part of these exchanges. Onboard demonstrations of singing and dancing were performative opportunities for workers of various ethnicities to exchange vernacular cultural practices through embodiment. Dancing an energetic dance like the hornpipe or sounding the deck with a jig brought workers into community for brief periods of time.

Hornpipes were a codified style of music within British and Celtic folk-dance communities with a "syncopated limping gait of a tune," accompanied by jaunty verses. Later, the musical form mixed with step dance styles and music halls appropriated the form for theatrical entertainments featuring sailors. Some land-based entertainers made hornpipe dance a specialty; for example, at Drury Lane in 1740 a performer named Yates performed "a hornpipe in the character of a sailor."[39] In practice, dancing the hornpipe was more of a commentary on the stereotype of a sailor than an actual dance that a sailor might perform. The side to side rocking steps of the hornpipe emulate the gait of the sailor on land, a gait developed to adjust to the constant rocking of the ship at sea. After the hornpipe entered the canon of musical theater and cabaret performance, it endured.

In contrast, jig dancing, sometimes called step dancing, originated in Great Britain and through cultural exchange, its high stepping knees and active foot beats were incorporated into various international folk cultures. Competitive percussive dance was performed by seamen on ships and in ports. It makes sense that jig dancing, with its emphasis on creating sounds against a wooden deck, would become a popular form of shipboard play. The wooden deck provides a natural acoustic surface for amplifying complex foot beats. The clunk of feet on percussive wood drives the cadence of the shanties and invites the possibility for dance challenges that involve foot play. Dance forms based upon complex foot beats on wooden surfaces come from multiple geographic sites, among them the Gullah Sea Islands, the ports of Dublin, the coasts of Africa, and Mexican towns like Veracruz on the Gulf of Mexico. At each of these maritime-facing port locales, feet produce rat-a-tat sounds amplified by shipping crates, inverted wooden canoes, platforms made of planking, or other invented resonators. Virtuosic dance techniques enhanced performance and raised the stakes for any dancer challenging another performer through rhythmic play. Creating the sounds requires performers to shift their weight, move their heels and their toes, in order to vary pitch and tone. Backs bend to deepen the sound or stand upright to increase the speed of the taps. Virtuosic performance would require understanding the musical complexity of polyrhythmic drumming while working within the melodic cadences of the song lyrics. A good dancer might also add a sense of style, demonstrating the "essence of cool" described by Brenda Dixon-Gottschild as a core element of African American performance excellence.[40]

Even though challenge dances could be performed a cappella, the easily transportable, melodic fiddle, often coupled with a flute, frequently accompanied performers. Sailors' melodic instruments more easily captured a variety of international folk song traditions: Irish, Italian, French, British, and American. The physicalized exchange of foot to deck or hand to instrument opened a forum for theatricalized communications that superseded language constraints. Much has been written about dialogical dance competitions between Irishman John Diamond and the African American William Henry Lane (also known as Master Juba). Both of these performers built their careers upon an ongoing battle of the feet. The two performers executed rhythmic jig and buck dance routines in challenge acts that traversed the Atlantic Ocean. The dancers competed in port pubs and on theatrical stages in London and New York, charging money for spectators to bet on their performance speed and accuracy. Their spirited performances were representative of many types of ethnic calls and responses where performers exchanged ideas through interactive, competitive dancing.

In 1841 Charles Dickens witnessed jig competitions at the Black-owned Almack's club on Orange Street in the Five Points district of New York. This immigrant, slum sector of the city housed many dance clubs and drinking establishments. In both singing and dancing exchanges, the stakes were high. Successful entertainers could receive monetary awards of as much as $500. As James Cook indicates in his lengthy article about Juba,[41] William Lane figured out how to navigate and negotiate his way not only to England but also away from his white managers. He developed his own performance act and toured throughout the United Kingdom. Eventually, he decided to abandon his manager and strike out on his own. His story is a maritime story not only because he traveled by ship to his destinations (did he compete or hone his skills as he crossed back and forth over Atlantic waters?) but also because the interethnic spaces where he competed were based in port communities frequented by seamen and newly arrived immigrants. The competitive exchanges of Diamond and Lane indicate how much audiences enjoyed seeing ethnic communities challenge one another through rhythmic foot play. The Irishness and Blackness of Diamond and Lane, respectively, affected how they were received by their publics. Both performers mixed gestural phrases and percussive rhythms of the British, Irish, and Africans to achieve acclaim for their virtuosity. Competitive arenas where wooden platforms became sounding boards for interethnic dialogues promoted intercultural exchange at multiple maritime sites in the Americas.

Hand and foot soundings trace a path back to interethnic exchanges on the African continent. African dance forms generally involve exchanges of counterpoint polyrhythms embodied in handclaps, foot beats, and the percussive use of isolated torso movements. When Africans arrived in the Americas, they used body percussion to compete in dance competitions at Congo Square in New Orleans, and within the circular configurations of the Black church. Dialogic performance exchanges across different enslaved African ethnic communities communicated unity and resistance.[42] The Afro-Caribbean music form Goombay, for example, entails dancers sounding the earth and singing in unison, making "one grand noise" to announce their presence and contest their subservience. Creole Jarocho dancers perform on overturned canoes to string accompaniments in order to maintain their cultural traditions.[43] African descendant populations on both the eastern and western coasts of Mexico show a proclivity to express themselves through dance forms dependent upon exchange across wooden platforms, as my earlier work has shown.[44] "El Marinero" (The Mariner), one of the most popular Jarocho melodies, is an excellent example of how dancers have used the sounding board of the wooden deck to entertain, challenge, and assert a right to cultural expression.

A contemporary Jarocho fandango contains all of the elements that would have made a seaman's dance jam challenging. Musicians play melodic riffs on fiddles, then a *cajon* or wooden box establishes the beat that drives the music. A singer chimes in to tell a story of someone they have lost. An individual performer, hearing the music, responds by mounting the platform where they use heel and toe beats to match the music, or create a new polyrhythmic punctuation to contest it. Finally, another dancer first joins and then challenges the competitor through a call-and-response of rhythmic play. Collectively, the crescendo of music and percussion creates a community ritual of competitive play that relieves tensions and perhaps lifts the spirits of all who have participated. Each performer contributes their virtuosity to a cacophony of cultural exchange that blends African, Spanish, indigenous, and other vernacular performance styles.

Song as Knowledge Transfer

Sea shanties circulated widely across the maritime world. They differ from the competitive dance and music exchanges above because, like African American work songs, they were sung by groups of men performing hard labor. Shanties were sung in unison, intended to ease the efforts of performing specific maritime tasks. They differ from sea ballads, which are more melodic storytelling songs sung during leisure times. In work songs, the body is intimately involved in their singing; the feet hit the deck in time to the lyrics of the songs. The voice strongly exhales on certain words to emphasize the action—as in, "WHAT do you DO with a DRUNK-en SAIL-or?" Already, possibilities for dialogic interpretations emerge. If the rhythm of work (or the syncopation of the cultural rift) becomes more complex, shanties can morph through the singers' spontaneous improvisations.

Collective singing among workers or in enslaved communities binds emotive energies, and for this reason, plantation masters in the Caribbean and the United States grew fearful when groups of enslaved men gathered to sing collectively. It is possible that sea captains also feared the camaraderie of singing seamen, because a unified and physically engaged underclass more easily foments rebellion. During the Haitian Revolution, African American collective singing spread messages for insurrection, and Black seamen were essential to the messaging. Historian Julius Scott writes: "If ships and boats sailing among the island colonies of the Caribbean brought the region together commercially, their movement also aided those seeking to escape the rigorous social control of these slave societies."[45] At the same time, European encounters with the American continent in the eighteenth and nineteenth centuries accelerated an international flow of labor that in turn accelerated the production of shipped goods. But the international flow of industrial products also supported an interchange of voices and bodies where workers transferred knowledge through vernacular embodiment.

Sea shanties and dance competitions functioned like today's sound technologies, through which records, compact discs, and music streaming bring sonic cultural histories to twenty-first-century cultural communities. Technologies of sound allow a suburban teenager in Illinois to experience the sound of Bob Marley from Jamaica. In his book *Phonographies: Grooves in Sonic Afro-Modernity*, Alexander G. Weheyliye details the intricate relationship between techno-informational flow, cultural production, and popular music. He theorizes about how African diaspora communities first used orality as a way to disseminate Black cultural production, then split sound from sources that originally produced them, using technologies to render them ephemeral, without a human source of reference.

> The invention of the phonograph at the end of the nineteenth century offered a different way to split sounds from the sources that (re)produced them. . . . Now that the space and time of audition were separated from the context of reception, both orality and musicality relied differently on the immediate presence of human subjects.[46]

In a parallel manner, sea shanty songs and their rhythmic accompaniments dispersed cultural knowledge from the songwriters to listeners. The rhythmic cadences of the chants, disembodied from their original authors, continued to circulate, transforming each singer into a repository that carried histories and culture across oceans. It is no surprise that music moves as embodied action. As Danielle Fosler-Lussier has observed, music on the move is a global phenomenon—migrating, colonizing, mediating, surveilling, assimilating.[47]

Most historians consider West African work songs to be forerunners of the sea shanty, pointing to the rhythmic cadences that are essential to both art forms. Yet sea shanties are a hybrid musical form as well. As they circulate, they collect residues of various cultural practices and refine them into complex mixtures reflective of differing homeland knowledges. Irish and British folk songs influenced some storytelling aspects of the genre. Melodic lines from England or Scotland are folded into many of the ballad compositions known to have been sung in the foc'sle or forward area of the ship's upper deck. Rhythmic percussive singing, pervasive among African work crews, was introduced to European sailors who traveled along the African Gold Coast during the seventeenth and eighteenth centuries in pursuit of trade.[48] Some histories specifically locate group call-and-response singing with the Kru people of Liberia who were early entrants in nineteenth-century transatlantic seamanship. Sailors on ships that landed in Kru territory observed local men in canoes singing in unison as they paddled along the waterways to exchange goods and services. "When rowing a boat, or paddling a canoe, it is their custom to sing; and, as the music goes on, they seem to become invigorated, applying their strength cheerfully, and with limbs as unwearied as their voices. One of their number leads in recitative, and the whole company respond in the chorus."[49] Members of the Kru ethnic group were later used as stevedores by the British in their transatlantic journeys related to the slave industry. The Kru remain an important diasporic ethnic community in the United Kingdom, migrating freely between Liverpool and Freetown, Sierra Leone.[50]

Complex sea shanties entered the canon of sea literature during the late eighteenth century when an active slave trade began to disperse African people of various ethnic origins throughout the Atlantic basin. African lexicology, rhythmic patterns, and content infused sea songs at a variety of sites, but especially in New Orleans, South Carolina, and the British West Indies. Black West Indian influences on sea shanties are particularly easy to trace because mariners in the Caribbean still actively sing them. Dialogic exchange and cultural negotiation are rich within the genre. As the songs travel with sailors through global ports, they are enhanced and adapted each time they are sung.

Stan Hugill, for example, describes how "coolie" ships that traveled through the West Indies mixed Hindustani language from the Lascari of East India with pidgin English to develop the song "Eki Dumah (Kay, Kay, Kay)."[51]

The categories of sea shanties vary according to how they are embodied, with the type of work performed defining the type of sea shanty that will be sung. If sailors are turning the capstan, then they sing a capstan shanty. If they are doing a long pull (gathering around a single rope to haul up an anchor or using a pulley to move cargo onto the ship) then they might sing a "hand over hand" song where the verses of the song help to coordinate one hand passing over the other onto the rope.[52] As with African American work songs, a caller leads the chant while men respond in verses appropriate in length to the work being performed. Sea shanty singing in its original context was improvisational, much like spoken word or rap. A skillful leader would invent and adapt lyrics for the specific circumstances of a journey or event. Melodies were revised to reflect popular tunes and a strong individual singer could influence the entire format of a song. "A good shantyman improvised, borrowing verses from different shanties or adapting entire songs to suit his purposes. British, Irish, West Indian and American seamen all brought material to the common stock, some drawn from traditional repertoires ashore and some from popular contemporary songs."[53]

Yet attempting to trace the exact cultural origins of musical phrases remains imprecise. Nina Sun Eidsheim, in *The Race of Sound*, ascertains the "voice's inability to be unique and yield precise answers." Still, she argues that there is a perceived presence of an ethnic (Black) presence in the voice, whether or not there is an ethnic (Black) body visible.[54] She refers specifically to the racialization of sound within African American communities, the way that "acoustic blackness" captures the perceived presence of Black bodies across temporal frames. Vocal differences attributed to race in the nineteenth century were commodified through recorded sound during the early twentieth century. The same can be said of other ethnic communities—British, Irish, Mexican, and Italian. The maritime trades during the nineteenth century brought seamen into the same workspace where they could hear song stories and rhythmic scores from other global sites. What to sing, and how to sing it, became part of a process of crafting new identities based upon cultural exchanges and cultural encounters. Negotiations across ethnic communities are apparent in the lyrics of sea songs as they transferred across bodies. Songs mutated and shifted as sailors from different parts of the globe sang them. Think of the game of telephone where a phrase or a saying is repeated across differing bodies, differing dialects, differing cultural contexts. Sea shanties, also known as chanteys, embodied cultural negotiations. The word appeared during the 1800s and is thought to be an adaptation of the French word *chanter* or "to sing."[55] Singing the songs of another culture might encourage an individual worker to reassess how their musical traditions relate to those of a singer from a different background. By adapting their singing or performance style, they created a new version of their experiences.

Storytelling Lyrics

Historian and folklorist Roy Palmer called sea songs a "literature of the sea." Two anthologies, Palmer's *The Oxford Book of Sea Songs* and Stan Hugill's *Shanties from the Seven Seas*, collect this literature.[56] Their volumes, published in the late twentieth century, represent a distinctive, nostalgic perspective on songs written and circulated one hundred years earlier. Two older volumes, W. B. Whall's *Ships, Sea Song and Shanties* (1913)[57] and Joanna Colcord and Richard Colcord's *Roll and Go: Songs of American Sailormen* (1924),[58] were published closer to the time when men were still actually sailing across the Atlantic. Although Colcord's book uses overtly offensive racist terms like "Paddy" for the Irish and "N*****" for Black people, I appreciate that Colcord transcribed her songs with a strong sense of ethnic difference, clearly identifying various ethnic groups within the maritime landscape. These types of lyrics, embedded in the songs, render cultural negotiations visible. *Roll and Go* was dedicated to the memory the author's father, Master Mariner Lincoln Alden Colcord. Its content is organized by the type of shanty—short drag, halyard, windlass, forecastle—with a foreword that begins "In the old days when American sailing ships still ploughed the seas," a clear indication that songs presented in the text are offered with a sense of nostalgia. Joanna Colcord makes sure in her book to include etchings of various vessels, including an image of the sailing ship her father commanded. Each image has a caption documenting the history of the vessel, its dimensions, construction date, and demise, as if the ships were living beings now deceased. The names are like memorabilia—*Harvard, Cambridge, Sea Witch, Young America, Andrew Jackson*—all pointing to a legacy of privileged white male conquest and masculine might. Her book is a labor of love; as the daughter of a seaman she has dedicated her text to the male singers who were able to travel. In her preface, she acknowledges shanty singers who helped her to create the text, crediting particular chanticleers with particular songs. Despite the nostalgic nature of the compilation, *Roll and Go* brings to life shanty traditions of a bygone era with all of their ethnic edginess.

It is this very edginess of the lyrics that provide an insight into the complex knowledge set of nineteenth-century seaman who worked across ethnic communities to figure out how to best survive in a rapidly changing Atlantic world. The sea shanties demonstrate that the stakes of collaboration were high as migrants worked their way to improved living circumstances. Men with limited experiences outside of their homelands felt justified in evoking the "strangeness" or "otherness" of those they encountered. Many of the songs provided verbal descriptions of places sailing men traveled to. Embedded in the song lyrics are lessons about what to expect, or whom a sailor might meet, when they land. Ports popularized through sonic storytelling were Liverpool, Cape Horn, New York, San Francisco, Greenland, and the Caribbean. Liverpool was important because its strong shipping culture offered many amenities for traveling seamen—boarding houses and pubs, tailors and cloth for garments, and a cosmopolitan environment that tolerated the ocean-bound underclass. Cape Horn off the coast of Chile was described in song because it was a dangerous crossing where many seamen lost their lives. Waters churn at Cape Horn where the Atlantic Ocean meets the Pacific Ocean. Those who successfully passed around the Horn were considered seasoned seamen. San Francisco, like Liverpool, was an active sailor-friendly port for those crossing the Pacific. Greenland was treacherous because of ice and cold weather, and the Caribbean was a unique geographic terrain where African influences were strong. In a sense, the songs provided geographic and cultural mapping of maritime landscapes for lower and underclass workers.

Sometimes in my cruise ship lectures, I sing a shanty about Paradise Street in Liverpool that tells a story about a sailor at port. It's effective on the big cruise ship stage because it is also a call-and-response song. In performance, the lead singer plays the narrator, who is the protagonist of the song. The lyrics are full of *double entendres*. Physical aspects of the woman are compared to the parts of a ship in a way that objectifies the woman but entertains those familiar with maritime jargon. She is "buff in the bow." She has a "flipper" and a "yardarm," and of course she has a "packet" that just makes it clear of the bar. The song takes a long time to sing because after each narrative line the audience responds with "Hey Ho, blow the Man Down." I robustly sing each lead phrase:

As I was a-walking down Paradise Street,
(Hey Ho, blow the Man Down . . . etc.)

Paradise Street is a street near the Liverpool docks

> A pretty young damsel I happened to meet.
> She was round in the corner and bluff in the bow,

The woman is shapely.

> So I took in all sail and cried "Way enough now"
> I hailed her in English, she answered me clear,
> I'm from the Black Arrow bound to the Shakespeare.

"Black Arrow" and "Shakespeare" would be the names of local pubs

> So I tipped her my flipper and took her in tow,
> And yardarm to yardarm away we did go.

The sailor completes the "pick up."

> But as we were going she said unto me,
> "there's spanking full rigger just ready for sea."
> That spanking full-rigger to New York was bound;
> She was very well-manned, and very well found.

Is there a ship leaving? Or is her sexuality the passage he is looking for as she offers the seaman her body as a vessel?

> But soon as that packet was clear of the bar,
> The mate knocked me down with the end of a spar,
> As soon as that packet was out on the sea.
> T'was devilish hard treatment of every degree.

This could be another man fighting for the woman, or it could be that the unnamed woman's sexual prowess was so powerful it was devilish.

> So I give you fair warning before we belay
> Don't never take heed of what pretty girls say.

As I sing the song, I discuss the meaning of the lyrics in the context of nineteenth-century seamen's lives. What's wonderful about this moment is that audience members and I are exchanging ideas about a long-lost culture across a variety of class and racial environments through the mechanism of a song that two hundred years ago may have served a similar purpose. Even as I share one interpretation of the song, I don't really know my audience or how they might view the content. There's room for negotiation. A straight, cis-gender reading of these lyrics presumes the male was girl-hunting in the bar and left with a woman who redirected him to another woman or to a ship in the harbor. But as I look at these lyrics again thinking about *double entendres* and queer perspectives, I wonder if the "spanking full rigger," which was "well manned" and knocked the protagonist down with a spar, could have been another male. There is evidence for this interpretation. Jessica Floyd has unearthed a set of homoerotic sea shanties that deal specifically with sex. While acknowledging that sex between men was one option available on long voyages, she maintains that same-sex encounters were hierarchically ordered. "Those in positions of subordination were further subordinated through their sexual domination and rape, often against their will."[59] She analyzes the lyrics of a song called "The Shaver" to illustrate her point. It is clear that the repertory of sea songs is wide and deep. I find joy in reliving and reimagining sea shanties because they conjure images of what might have occurred on the sailing ship, while leaving room for multiple interpretations as well as specific applications of meaning.

Singing sea shanties to cruise ship guests serves a purpose quite different from the way shanties were used in their original contexts. Cruise passengers are middle-class, leisure-seeking travelers and those who attend the lectures are generally elderly. In contrast, on the merchant vessels, able-bodied younger men sang to coordinate physical activity and common effort. What may be similar is that we are passing time. For cruise ship passengers, the sea shanty lecture is an interlude between meals or gambling rounds. For the merchant seamen the songs also passed time, but they simultaneously provided structure to help them endure grueling days of hard labor in the hot sun or on the cold deck. On the cruise, I am lucky if I can get the crowd to stand up or stamp their feet, to engage their bodies in even minimal physical play. Many of them are intoxicated, so activities need to be nonconfrontational and inclusive. If they have differences of opinion, they don't have time to indulge in them. Instead, they share emotions through gestures—they raise their arms while shouting "heave ho" or they clap along with song cadences. We find joy in the rhythmic play of singing together. At the same time, singing sea shanties seems nostalgic. While we travel in climate-controlled comfort with full bellies, the crowd and I can imagine ourselves as part of long-past maritime travel as the ship passes through the ocean waves and we fancy ourselves adventuring like sailors long ago.

On early sailing vessels of the eighteenth and nineteenth centuries, the forward section of the ship, located between the decks where ropes were managed, was where common sea hands gathered for song exchange. Ethnomusicologist James Revell Carr writes about an event called the "Gam," a kind of musical jam that was common on whaling and merchant ships when crews visited one another. Sailors participated in musical dialogues in the form of fiddling, challenge dancing, and sea ballad singing. This was an intimate space where bodies in proximity to one another might find a more relaxed engagement. Here, seamen, if they were not exhausted, might take a moment for performance exchange. Getting to know more about a fellow crew worker could happen during a "gam."[60]

In this cramped, tight, low-ceilinged space of the foc'sle, each man was confined to a bunk or a hanging hammock. It was a relatively unsupervised space where mariners freely told stories (yarns) or shared adventures either verbally or through their instruments. Personal memorabilia, musical instruments stored in trunks, or bags brought from home might prompt a sailor to remember and share a folk song or melody. Maritime storytelling established bonds between sailors and allowed workers from different countries to learn about customs and culture in other ports. Sailors' logs seldom describe details of foc'sle entertainments; however, they do include descriptions of conversations or exchanges between sailors. Most often the exchanges articulate frustration about the dangers of hard sea labor or express boredom with the monotony of working in a contained location, surrounded by a repeating landscape.[61] Sea songs, on the other hand, capture some of the cultural negotiations that must have preoccupied sailors as they imagined what might happen when they landed.

For instance, the song "Stormalong, Lads Stormy," somewhat of a classic within the canon, referenced the port of Liverpool. For sea workers, active ports like Liverpool, Philadelphia, or New York were markers of experiences where senses numbed by the monotony of the water could be revitalized through human interactions. Consequently, distinctive characteristics of the city of Liverpool appear in many of the songs. The all-male, hypermasculine, physical nature of sea culture, coupled with the social isolation, meant sailors often sang about women and the sexual encounters they might find in the port.

If ever you go to Liverpool,
To Liverpool the Packet School
Yankee Sailors there you'll see,

With red-topped boots an' short cut hair
There's Liverpool Pat with his tarpaulin hat,
And 'Frisco Jim the packet rat.
Wake up yer bitch 'n' let us in,
Get up yer bitch 'n' serve us gin
Oh I wisht I wuz in Liverpool Town,
Them Liverpool judies I'd dance around.
O long Stormy-stormalong,
O long Stormy-stormalong[62]

Cultural references proliferate within the song. Lyrics from "Stormalong, Lads Stormy"[63] first reference the "packet school." This alludes to shipping lines like the Black Ball that offered fast service across the Atlantic Ocean for passengers and goods. Thinking of the packet ship as a school implies that a worker would need to study the unique challenges of sailing at high speeds through the treacherous northern waters of the Atlantic Ocean in order to maintain a schedule. Adjusting to this type of hard physical labor would mint a particular type of outdoorsman used to facing challenges. "Frisco Jim" is referred to as a packet rat. The sailor, named after San Francisco, probably traveled down the Pacific coast and through the dangerous passage of Cape Horn,[64] off of Tierra del Fuego. In contrast, Liverpool Pat is probably an Irishman more familiar with the Atlantic Ocean. "Yankee soldiers" dates the song to the time of the Civil War or the mid-nineteenth century. The tarpaulin hat would have been made out of sailcloth, the most readily available fabric for a man stuck on a ship. The song references and provides guideposts for a very particular cultural community.

After the opening, the song shifts, adopting an abusive, toxic, hypermasculine tone. The location of the song changes. Apparently, we are now in a tavern where women and gin mix. "Wake up yer bitch 'n' let us in, get up yer bitch 'n' serve us gin." This is a demand made by a sailor without a thought of consent. The unnamed woman is expected to provide service and alcohol on call. Yet this may only be a fantasy dreamt up by a man who has not yet landed in the town. Expressing his misogyny binds him to the maritime culture in a manner that accentuates his masculinity, making him a part of the "in-group" while distancing himself from more subservient, feminized behavior. The final line of the song changes to a subjective tense. The protagonist wishes he were in Liverpool with the fictional women surrounding him. Most likely, he is singing the song far removed from the shore he pines for. In *Shanties from the Seven Seas*, Hugill credits his knowledge of this particular sea shanty to "a fine old coloured seaman who hailed from Barbadoes." He describes the "coloured" seaman as one who sailed on British, American, Scandinavian, and West Indian traders. "He was a master of the 'hitch'—the singing of wild yelps at certain points in a hauling song . . . he would give vent to many wild 'hitches,' absolutely impossible for a white man to copy, although white sailors did execute a poor shadow of the negro yelps."[65] Hugill's description of singing yelps underscores a core aspect of sea shanty performance—its origins in African diaspora work song practices. Yelps, chants, and cries—vocal expressions of emotion—proliferate within the work-song genre of seas shanties. In the next few sections I analyze song lyrics that evoke specific ethnic communities within the maritime world.

African Soundings

Colcord's volume contains a section dedicated to songs that she maintains originated with Negro stevedores along the Gulf Coast. During the latter half of the nineteenth century, this would have been a major port for the cotton industry as it connected all of the Caribbean with the continental United States and the tributaries of the Mississippi River. The songs were developed in response to activities of stowing cotton and ramming the bales into the ship's hold. Enslaved Africans often performed such tasks for their masters. While the chronicler writes that "their words were even more trivial and meaningless than the general run of shanties,"[66] she probably means that because they spoke African languages or a creole form of English, the sailors had trouble understanding the context and meaning of the words. I need to place her observations in the context of more contemporary scholarship in order to unearth the perspective of the subjects. Eileen Southern canonizes African American stevedore songs and Black folk music in her classic text *The Music of Black Americans*, describing a rich heritage of songs on the waterfront. Journalists and song collectors captured the supposedly lighthearted songs that served as amusement and built camaraderie among the laborers. This oft-repeated trope of Negroes singing without a care in the world validated plantation owners' beliefs about simple-minded Africans happy with their lot.

Katrina Dyonne Thompson writes extensively about how Africans were forced to sing and dance on slave ships and plantations, noting that descriptions of contented Africans fiddling and dancing were Southern propaganda. She maintains that because demonstrations of merriment were often enforced with whips, dancing was more punishment than entertainment.

"The Southern plantation became a stage, and white slaveholders, overseers, and drivers were the choreographers of the public display of enslaved blacks performing for the appeasement of white desires for dominance."[67] Even if forced to dance under contained and violent circumstances, the Africans and their descendants contributed complex vocal chants and dialogic exchanges to the canon of sea shanties. I believe the allegoric and alliterated words that Colcord found difficult to decipher were a way of creating a porous and adaptable language that could respond to various modes of forced labor.

One song, "Roll the Cotton Down," seems straightforward. Its lyric "I'm bound to Alabama, Oh Roll the cotton down" is a simple repetition of a call-and-response line. Colcord describes this as one of the most generally known shanties. She explains how a shanty could be "taken over from the colored singers, much in the same way in which they took over 'Lowlands' from the whites," becoming a shanty with "only a remote resemblance to a progenitor."[68] Katrina Thompson alludes to a cultural mixing and trading that is a by-product of the interplay between and among sailors. Undoubtedly the complex inventions devised by the workers reflected their mood and circumstances, shifting with the daily needs of the labor. Unfortunately, we cannot know today what tonality or timbre might have communicated. Emotional contexts surely added character to the shouts and cries of dockside workers. I see a textual relationship between the song "Roll the Cotton Down" and a post–Civil War shanty called "Roll Alabama Roll" about the sinking of the Confederate ship *Alabama*, but the melody is different, and from my historical distance I can't claim an evidential relationship. Nevertheless, I wonder if the sinking of the ship might have been a celebratory moment for the African American singers of the song.

Another shanty from Colcord's Negro section, "Sing Sally O,"[69] is more complex. Its lyrics include:

O I say my Mammy Dinah, What is the matter?
Sing Sally O, Fol-lol-de-day O Hurrah! Hurrah!
My Mammy Dinah, Sung Sallo O; Fol-lol-de-day.

I'm familiar with the Aunt Dinah song and its many renditions within African American folklore. Dinah, like the Anansi spider trickster character or the legendary southern animal conman Br'er Rabbit, represents sassiness and resistance even as she remains enslaved. In this iteration, she is personified as a Mammy named Dinah. The lead singer asks the Dinah character "what is the matter?" Or maybe it is a collective of singers asking the question. There could also be an inversion of character at play where the singer, in asking "what is the matter," impersonates the voice of the master, echoing an overseer's degradation of a woman named Dinah. In any event, the response is to urge Dinah to "Sing Sally O, Fol lol de day" followed by a cheer. I find several other sea shanties with songs named for Sally—Sally Brown, Sally Munro, or Shallow Brown. "Sally" seems to be the universal woman the men miss at sea. In the version above, the "negro" stevedores sing to Sally then end their call with vocables[70] —Fol-lol-de-day. The final sentence of the chant has a subtle twist. This time Mammy Dinah is referred to as <u>my</u> Mammy Dinah. In culmination, the singers communicate that they sang "Sally O Fol-lol-de- day." Could these vocables intend to communicate the phrase "for all the day," reimagined as a bastardized version of Negro speech? The song is short, and quite nonsensical without its context; the porousness of the lyrics allows African diaspora people to bend song lyrics so they reflect Black singers' perspectives. The elasticity of the lyrics and sounds within this shanty means the shanties flexibly served to communicate meaning in a variety of settings.

Black Indians

Native American seamen were an integral part of the maritime world, and many were involved in the whaling industry of the northern Atlantic. In her book *Native American Whalemen and the World: Indigenous Encounters and the Contingency of Race*, Nancy Shoemaker mines data and archives to explore the complex relationship between Native American whalers and the sea.[71] She posits that the way Native Americans strategically used their community alliances in cultural encounters around the Atlantic basin extended communication networks around whale hunting into communities already deeply invested in subsistence fishing. Because their relationship with the sea predates European colonial exploration, the whalers made use of indigenous epistemologies to collaboratively strategize whale hunting in Arctic waters. Shoemaker focuses on the New Bedford, New London, and the Mashantucket Pequot tribal communities. Her work is somewhat based upon the research of Jason Mancini, a colleague from the Mystic Seaport research center who compiled an extensive database of eighteenth- and nineteenth-century mariners who worked out of New London.[72] The Indian Mariners Project maps Native American and brown-skinned presence across international waters by documenting crew lists and ship journeys.[73] In conversations with Jason Mancini at Mystic Seaport he discussed how part of his research methodology was to note when crew lists included mariners with brown skin who were not described as "negro." Since race is a porous category, his data was based upon the perceptions of the record keeper about how race might be construed. Confusion about race and ethnicity is apparent in sea shanties, which conflate the identity of a broad cross-section of ethnic communities into generalized racial associations. Fluid categories of race, however, allowed for seamen to use shanties as flexible templates for responding to international politics through song.

There is a long history of collaboration across Black and indigenous communities in the Americas.[74] Describing these two cultural communities as discrete is slippery because of continual intermixing. Often, in popular and festival cultures, indigenous and African American communities comment upon one another's presence, articulating cultural perspectives through unique lenses. Interethnic cultural commentary captured through embodied performance appears in New Orleans carnival settings, Afro-Mexican performance, and Caribbean carnival parades, to name a few.[75] My own work on Afro-Mexico shows performers in indigenous festivals developing characters and reenactments that articulate nuanced perspectives about the making and meaning of African diaspora communities in local contexts.

A few songs in Colcord's volume capture mariners' perspectives about indigenous communities. The song "John Cherokee" in its multiple variations presents a distorted history of Black men and the Cherokee nation, but it was a perspective likely popular among working-class seamen. "John Cherokee," according to Colcord's unnamed ethnographic informant, was sung in Nassau during the Civil War by a crew loading cotton on the ship *Hilja*. The song's lyrics unfold as a storytelling narrative that is a testimony to the annihilation of a Black or Indian man. It may also have been a warning to those workers of color who might head to Alabama during the height of the Civil War. Vocables in the song, "Way-aye-yah," evoke the vocables used in many Native American communal songs. The lyrics of the sea shanty are:

John Cherokee was an Indian Man, Alabama
John Cherokee! He run away every time he can,
Alabama John Cherokee! Way-aye-yah!
Alabama John Cherokee! Way-aye-yah!
Alabama John Cherokee!
They put him aboard a Yankee ship,
Again he gave the boss the slip.
They catch him again and chain him tight
And starve him many days and nights.

He have nothing to drink and nothing to eat
So he just gone dead at the boss's feet.
So they bury him by the old gate post
And the day he died you can see his ghost.

The title of the song "John Cherokee" takes an English name and merges it with the name of a North American indigenous community, the Cherokee. Cherokee First Nations people are known for their intermingling with African Americans escaping slavery in the antebellum South. Their forced removal from the Atlantic seaboard states to Oklahoma was a bloody pilgrimage, the infamous Trail of Tears legislated by Andrew Jackson. The Indian Removal Act signed into law by Jackson in 1830 forced thousands of indigenous communities, including the Cherokee, to march along a 5,000-mile trail. In the sea shanty, John Cherokee is made into an "Everyman," representing the efforts of a Native American person to escape forced labor. He is eventually chained, starved, and forced to die at his bosses' feet. While slavery in the United States southern states is usually associated with African Americans, the song conflates the experiences of Blacks and Indians into a single narrative of slavery. Native Americans were also enslaved throughout North America and the shanty calls attention to this by connecting the title "John Cherokee" with experiences of enslavement. Two additional aspects of the song communicate indigenous epistemologies. The ghosting of John implies that his spirit still lives near the old gate post even though he is dead, and the rhythmic and melodic line of the song as recorded in Colcord's book has a beat similar to heartbeat drumming patterns heard within Native American communities when they play the communal drum.

Irish Workers

Irish workers' cultural perspectives are represented in the shanty "Paddy Works the Railroad." As the title implies, the song describes how a man named Paddy finds himself working a job laying tracks across America. Paddy is a diminutive and insulting name for people from Ireland, many of whom migrated to the Americas during the potato famine of the 1840s. Chinese and Irish workers provided the bulk of the labor on the Transcontinental Railway and other transport systems built between 1862 and 1869. The Irish were some of the first to be involved in railroad building, transferring to "iron horse" construction projects after completing canal systems in Ohio and Illinois. Railroads transported workers to the American West, creating a boom or bust economy of exhausting contracted labor. Within the masculine working-class world, the Irish formed a community that contrasted with African American and Chinese laborers.[76] The sea shanty "Paddy Works the Railroad" contributes a narrative of this experience.

> In eighteen hundred and sixty-one,
> The Yankee war had just begun,
> I put my corduroy breeches on
> To work upon the railway,
> The railway, I'm weary of the railway
> Oh poor Paddy works on the railway.
>
> In eighteen hundred and sixty-two,
> My corduroy breeches they were new.
> I took my pick with a navvy's crew
> to work upon the railway. Etc.
> In eighteen hundred and sixty-three,
> I sailed away beyond the sea
> I sailed away to Amerikee to work upon the railway. Etc.
> In eighteen hundred and sixty-four,
> I landed on the American shore
> I had a pickaxe and nothing more, to work upon the railway. Etc.

"Paddy" actually begins his work on the railway in the United Kingdom. He's got a fresh set of clothing when he decides to cross the ocean for more work. By the time he finishes working on the railroad in the United States, he has nothing more than a pickaxe for his troubles. The song speaks to migration and movement inherent in the nineteenth-century Irish experience. Leaving one's homeland and coming to a new land involves the loss of more than culture. Material goods are sacrificed along with kith and kin. Economic realities—low wages coupled with economic inequalities—result in a working man whose only possession is the tool that keeps him connected to his labor. As the Irish became "whiter" and more integrated into the American cultural imagination, communities of Irish people made economic gains. The song "Paddy Works the Railroad" moved onto the music hall stage, becoming a marker of Irish heritage.

"John Cherokee" and "Paddy Works the Railroad" are two ethnically marked sea shanties that describe historical circumstances through the lens of disenfranchised workers. The storytelling songs illustrate a particular perspective about Black, Native American, and Irish lives. John Cherokee is a victim who ends up dead, while Paddy leaves his homeland yet remains employed and productive on the railroad. If songs are understood to capture the North American imaginary, then the death of the Black Indian man, as articulated within the lyrics of these songs, seems inevitable. The song recirculates a North American myth of manifest destiny, a belief that Native American populations would eventually disappear, leaving the Americas to an empowered white population. The ideology of Manifest Destiny was used to justify the annihilation and colonization of millions of Native Americans in North America. Sea shanties circulating narratives of African and indigenous presence offer alternative perspectives about ethnic histories albeit perspectives deeply rooted in circulating narratives based upon white supremacist notions.

Mexican Histories

Sea shanties of the nineteenth century commented on Mexican presence through references to the Spanish Main and to the powerful presence of General Antonio López de Santa Ana. Santa Ana was a legendary Mexican general, an autocrat whose audacious exploits dominated the political scene for much of the first half of the nineteenth century. Multiple versions of a sea shanty titled "Santa Ana" honor his history and his exploits. The shanty, sometimes called "Santianna", was popular throughout the sailing world. Lyrics tended to idolize the general as a hero and a resister.

> Oh Santy Ana gained the day,
> Hooray Santa Ana!
> He lost it once, but gained it twice
> All on the plains of Mexico
> And General Taylor ran away,
> He ran away to Monterrey
> Oh Santy Ana fought for fame,
> And there's where Santy gained his name.
> Oh Santy fought for gold,
> And the deeds he done have oft been told.
> And Santy Ana fought for his life,
> But he gained his way in the terrible strife.
> Oh Santy Ana's day is o'er,
> And Santy Ana will fight no more.

I thought I heard the old man say,
He'd give us grog this very day.

The real Antonio López de Santa Ana, born in 1794 and dying in 1896, had a lifespan that conveniently overlapped with the height of the transatlantic merchant trade. He fought in the War of Independence from Spain and later deposed Mexico's second president, Vincente Guerrero (whose name means *warrior*). He was a self-obsessed narcissist who held a funeral for his amputated leg, a leg he lost in the battle of Veracruz while fighting the French in 1838.[77] After attaining the presidency, Santa Ana consistently granted himself outsized presidential powers, disbanding Congress when it attempted to pass a human rights bill, and insisting upon policies that gave him absolute power. He is the general who fought and won the Battle of the Alamo. When he was deposed in a revolt in 1845, "the rabid crowd went to the theater and quickly demolished the plaster statue erected to Santa Ana. They ran furiously to the pantheon of Santa Paula and with savage furiosity, exhumed Santa Ana's leg, playing games with it and making it an object of ridicule."[78]

Santa Ana, however, had a comeback. The song lyric "General Taylor ran away, he ran away to Monterrey" refers to the Battle of Buena Vista, which occurred in February 1847. Santa Ana, fighting on behalf of Mexico, surrounded a United States Army force led by Major General Zachary Taylor, which was occupying a village in the state of Coahuila. Despite the ferocity of the surprise attack, Taylor was able to keep Santa Ana from advancing through the Angostura Pass, preventing an aggressive trek northward by the Mexican forces. This, and similar incidents, made Santa Ana's colorful life fodder for sailor speculation about the grandeur of military might. The multiple variations of the song, coupled with the epic exploits of the general whose fame lasted across decades, make me wonder if the song may have been a catalyst for discussions of news or updates about international affairs. What happened before or after each encounter where workers sang the song? Could it have been used as a prelude to conversations about politics and war? If so, then shanties, like other forms of maritime embodiment, utilize the body as a megaphone for cultural literacy. Songs like "Santa Ana" demonstrate the diversity and international reach of sea shanties as a method for negotiating histories and culture in a time of rapid global institutional change. Maritime labor was part of a larger panorama of labor used for constructing new nations and industrial economies. The laboring class, often presumed to be uneducated, taught themselves about the politics and perils of various types of labor through songs. Quaint and sometimes playful lyrics that accompanied shipboard work allowed mariners to exchange ideas, contest histories, or invent new characters relevant to each sailor's experiences.

Each of the songs mentioned above is a capstan or halyard song, sung as call-and-response with little room for elaboration within the storytelling. Their purpose was to keep the workforce united around a single task. The longer songs, similar in form to Irish ballads or African griot storytelling, were sung during leisure moments when there was more time for elaboration. Longer songs provided more opportunities for improvisation and cultural exchange. Even while working, seamen would be able to listen and chime in as the storytelling developed. In Colcord's book and several others, there is a song called "The Flying Cloud" written from the perspective of an Irish seaman that describes the voyage of a slaver with fifteen stanzas of verse. The first stanza establishes the seaman's name as Edward Hollander, born in the town of Waterford. After learning the craft of a cooper (a maker of wooden casks and barrels), the protagonist shipped to Bermuda where he met the captain of the ship *Flying Cloud*, a slaver bound for Africa. There, the crew loaded 500 enslaved people onto the ship, forcing each person into a space only eighteen inches wide. Plague and fever killed half of the enslaved workers, and the narrator of the ballad helps to throw their corpses overboard. He sings "It was better for the rest of them if they had died before, than to work under the brutes of planters in Cuba forever more."[79] According to the lyrics, in Cuba the seamen sell off the Africans and then decide, with the encouragement of the captain, to become a pirate ship. Some men refuse to participate in the illegal pirate proposal and decide to disembark, but our narrator stays on board for the adventure. They sink and plunder ships in the Spanish Main, leaving women and orphans to mourn their dead family members. The last four verses describe how the pirate ship is captured by the British men of warship *Dungeness* and Captain Moore is killed. The narrator is chained and condemned to die. The song ends with the dyad: "For whiskey and bad company first made a wretch of me, Young men a warning by me take, and shun all piracy."

It's easy to see how a long narrative like this could help pass time and also teach the dangers of piracy and the ugliness and violence of slavery. Colcord dates the song between 1819 and 1825. The ships and characters of the song have not been verified,[80] but the story addresses known events around that period, and the style of the song mirrors the storytelling ballad traditions from Ireland. I'm interested in the regret the narrator expresses for participating in dangerous and morally abhorrent behavior in search of financial gain. He acknowledges the wretched state of the slaves, calls his life reckless and wild, and ultimately suffers a fate of punishment for his crimes. The song suggests a sense of morality among sailors who may never have felt that way. Singing the song meant acknowledging immoral actions might be punished, but the quest for wealth and survival is in some ways glorified in the song because the narrator/protagonist, like an ancient bard, is able to speak across time about his exploits.

Sea shanty singing is not a lost art. Its popularity at maritime festivals and maritime living history museums attest to its vitality as a living, breathing art form. Mystic Seaport hosts an annual summer event that draws hundreds of sea shanty singers to a single location. At the Sea Music Festival, enthusiasts embody sea shanties by pulling ropes or turning halyards while singing the songs. Because the museum restores whaleboats and other sailing vessels, participants young and old immerse themselves in embodied experiences of working while singing shanties. A trained troupe of performers educates those new to the genre, while more experienced chanticleers trade songs and expertise in a series of tent or outdoor performance events. There is also an academic conference, the Sea Music Symposium, where maritime scholars discuss new developments in the field and investigate singing styles of time-worn songs.[81] During active performance practice at the jam sessions, singers trade off versions of songs, improvising as they go along. When I spoke at the 2013 conference, I met poets/singers from an Alaskan fishing village as well as artists from communities in New Zealand, Australia, and other far-flung ports. In the back and forth of dialogic exchange, the festival demonstrates that storytelling still unites and excites. My sea shanty singing on a cruise ship participates in and perhaps accelerates ongoing reticulations of songs that carry meaning, messages, and politics with each refrain.

SNAPSHOT #2: Krew Kapers

Regent Seven Seas cruise line has a signature event called Krew Kapers where crew members play at sea to entertain guests. It is the best example I have seen to date of ship laborers being enlisted to perform in a theatrical setting. On the evening before guests depart the ship, the cruise director announces a special "thank you" program ostensibly organized by the crew to express their appreciation for the wonderful guests who have taken the journey with them. The fully produced event, staged in the large theatrical venue, combines a talent show with choreographed musical revue acts. Lights up on a cast selected from members of housekeeping, restaurant, bar services, and the deck department who, surprisingly, are still wearing their uniforms even though this is

Figure 23. The "YMCA" number on board the *Voyager of the Seas*, as performed by the crew.

the opening act of a staged show in a facility with the best of resources. They participate in a strange hip hop style number with lots of waving arms and "thank you" in the recorded song lyrics. The performers shift lines frequently, enabling all guests to see the array of service workers who are now stage singers and dancers.

The presentation includes several acts that feature the individual talents of crew members, performances that the cruise director refers to as the crew's "indigenous performance traditions." They don't look very indigenous to me. One woman performs a belly dance in a halter top and a skirt. Another "indigenous performance" features a singer who plays guitar in a folk music style. Perhaps the director was referring to the Tinikling bamboo stick dance performed by an all-Filipino cast from the housekeeping staff. They click their poles on the ground and hop step through the sticks in increasingly complex dance movements that eventually accelerate and broaden to include a quartet of dancers executing movements in square dance formations.

Later, a comic number features crew members wearing towels and shower caps where they pretend that they have been caught undressed. They scrub themselves with back brushes while they cavort and seem unable to find their clothing as stage-produced fog gradually envelops them. A satirical scene about the passengers comes closest to direct acknowledgment of the pretense of servitude that has been predominant throughout the journey. In a section titled "Silly Questions Guests Ask," serving staff approach the front of the proscenium two at a time. One, wearing a fashionable "smart casual" outfit, pretends to be a guest and asks with a distinctly American accent: "Do the crew live on the ship?" The second performer gives no answer, and instead responds with open palms and a quizzical look that indicates "duh!" The entire onstage performing crew laughs, and a new couple comes downstage with another question. I point to this particular charade because it gives the crew (who normally do not respond to the ignorance of the guests' onboard behaviors) an opportunity to ridicule the guests in a public forum. The short comic sketch acknowledges their expertise, their knowledge, and their understanding of both ship ways and guest behaviors.

The culmination of the Krew Kapers is a performance of the Village People's hit single "YMCA." The performers encourage the guests to sing with them and clap their hands in a great send-off, audience participation finale. I found this number to be particularly disturbing because they projected an image of the Village People upstage of the performers. The image includes a cowboy, a construction worker, and the performer Felipe Rose in his Lakota war bonnet.[82] I feel as if I am in a time warp. History folds in on itself, creating echoes of the past in these twenty-first century capricious performances. The ethnic impersonations coupled with the hyperbolic performances and the artificial fog resonate with me as a strange reiteration of the aesthetics of the Crossing the Line ceremonies with King Neptune and the native savages who are also crew workers who are also passengers. For the crew laborers who enjoy participating in this spectacle this has been an opportunity to escape from the repetitive doldrums of service and demonstrate their talents. I wonder what the rehearsals must have been like. The cruise director congratulates one of the cast members for "putting together" the spectacle. He doesn't call him the director. After the show I find an abandoned slip of paper on a bench at the side of the theater. It is titled "Krew Kapers Bow List" and it includes only the first names of each of the performers. It also states which service area they come from: John-Housekeeping-Dancer. Even as the crew members perform their expertise and their vernacular culture they are ultimately viewed as workers who have been offered a chance to escape their domestic duties for only a few hours in order to cavort for the paying guests. They will remain on board performing servitude until we reach the next port and they are, perhaps, granted shore leave.

Three

Ports

Transactions and Cultural Encounters

For cruise ship passengers and personnel, the ports they encounter distinctively bridge the maritime world with shore-based activities. Shorelines gradually descend into shallow shoals, inlets, or harbors where fishing, dredging, and docking activities continue. Cultural artifacts from human activities—anchors, dishware, and sunken ships—transverse the waterline and extend into the ocean as debris. The culture of seafaring also extends from ship to shore. Services related to maritime industry draw workers to port towns, commercial piers, or protected bays. Sea workers find respite at shoreside bars and restaurants, and land-based businesses profit from servicing oceangoing vessels and their workers. Ports, both historically and in contemporary context, are transactional zones designed to connect commercial products with consumers and terrestrial industries. Because 80 percent of the world's products travel across ocean waters to arrive in our homes and businesses, ports are an important gateway to national economies.[1] Coastlines often create spectacular landscapes, yet each port environment distinctively manages human interactions. The flurry of human activity that characterized preindustrial ports differs significantly from the sterile environment of a mechanized cargo port that unloads containers from oceanic vessels in the twenty-first century.

Before the advent of container ships, stevedores lifted cargo first into wagons, and later into motorized trucks. Since the entrepreneur Malcolm McLean adapted container shipping for commercial purposes, mechanized cranes have been used to load and unload cargo, creating commercial ports with limited active human laborers. "McLean purchased a surplus wartime oil tanker and converted it to carry the same metal containers that his semi truck hauled across the landscape."[2] On April 26, 1956, his first container was

Figure 24. A cruise ship at port in 2011.

loaded aboard the *SS Ideal X* in the Port Newark terminal headed for the port of Houston, Texas. Today, this same port in Newark, now renamed the Cape Liberty Cruise Port, is one of the most popular terminals for boarding cruises from the metropolitan New York area. However, Cape Liberty port accommodates only a fraction of the passengers who board and disembark at even larger cruise ports. The title "Cruise Capital of the World" goes to Port Miami, which accommodated more than 6.8 million passengers for the twelve-month period ending in September 2019. Port Canaveral terminal outside of Orlando and Port Everglades outside of Fort Lauderdale are in second and third place for megaship cruise passenger travel.[3] Cruise ports sit adjacent to cargo ports in most cities because the infrastructure needed to accommodate large oceangoing vessels—deep sea channels and large docking stations—are present.

Arriving for a vacation at any cruise port involves interactions with a plethora of port workers and service personnel who shuttle passengers from airline flights to ships docked at a series of piers. When one is driving or walking along the pier, ships loom high against the sky, like a series of multistory office buildings. Vessels appear monumental while the dock landing area bustles with activity. Ship workers, including entertainment staff, intermingle with onboarding passengers before guests are even aware of the multiple roles each of the service employees will play as they guide them through their immersive vacation journey. Housekeeping staff carry luggage from drop-off locations to cabins. Entertainment staff encourage onboarding passengers to take an "all aboard" photograph or welcome passengers with a champagne cocktail. While the permanent staff fulfill core tasks related to direct onboarding, local temporary employees who work only in the port—luggage porters, ushers, bus drivers, parking agents—manage the ebb and flow of passenger transfer to and from the ship.

Internationalism is inherent in port settings; port residents become accustomed to foreign goods and services moving through their shops and travelers speaking foreign tongues engaging with their establishments. I would argue that internationalism within port towns makes locals more tolerant of a spectrum of cultural behaviors. This chapter, like the previous ones, considers past and present, exploring performative spaces of shipping out where cultural communities encounter one another and negotiate ethnic identities. In this chapter, we will analyze ports and their significant contribution to this cultural exchange, focusing on four aspects: (1) the port as spectacle, (2) the port as a trading zone, (3) the port as a space for social exchange, and (4) the port as a site of tourism, particularly in the Caribbean. I am interested in both the grandiose spectacle of ports like Florida cruise ports and micro interactions in ports when ship personnel meet land-based residents, because both the grandiose and the quotidian offer opportunities for theatrical enactments. The arrivals and departures of vessels create a sensorial, visual backdrop for smaller acts of financial exchange and social fellowship. Even when there is no ship, the port encourages residents to consider cultural difference as a norm, and this aspect makes the port an evocative site for analysis of how performance mediates race and labor.

Spectacle of the Port

The spectacle of onboarding at Port Miami exemplifies how passengers experience port interactions at cargo docks where cruise ships on and offload passengers. Large ships, easily visible from airplanes, highways, and commuter trains, announce their presence through their size and branding. The waves and mouse ears of a Disney cruise ship are distinct from the rather staid blue Norwegian cruise logo, or the graphic anchor that identifies Royal Caribbean ships. Imbedded in brand marketing is an awareness that large ships will be viewed as magnificent machines coming into or exiting ports. Docking a ship places massive technological innovation on display, and the public visibility of the vessel has been used historically to reinforce military presence. An illustration of the 1859 launch of the battleship *Agamemnon*[4] demonstrates how a ship's arrival or departure centers the vessel in a performative manner.

Figure 25. The launch of the battleship *Agamemnon* from the Woolwich Dockyard in 1859. Courtesy of the Caird Collection at the Greenwich Maritime Museum.

In the image, hundreds of people stand near the docks to observe the fanfare of the ship's departure from multiple perspectives. The ship's location in the water and away from the shore gives observers an expansive perspective of the vessel.

Down left, a small steamer brings onlookers close to the ship while, on the docks, well-dressed sailors, women, and children stand attentively for the send-off. Dozens of smaller boats hold wealthier families who want to view the details of the departure. In the distance, warships and merchant sailing vessels provide background for an official launch ceremony heralded by military presence. The image, published by Rock Brothers and Payne, underscores the strength and power of the British navy. A launch event of this scale typically happened when a newly constructed ship first left port. The launch of the *Agamemnon* gains importance within the maritime archive because it marked the use of steam technology within the British navy. Later, the ship would help to lay transatlantic cable in support of a burgeoning telegraph industry.

The pomp and circumstance surrounding this steamship launch was a celebration of nineteenth-century technological innovation. The Victorian era was a time when European opera houses responded to innovations in lighting and steam technologies by introducing new systems for creating stage illusions. Richard Wagner for example, developed a vision of *Gesamtkunstwerk*, or total theater, that utilizes grand spectacle—for example, moving platforms, fog, and ghostly figures to impress audience members. Theatrical use of spectacle increased public interest in novel uses of gas and steam technologies. Just as the mechanized automation of the Wagnerian opera house publicly displayed a technological achievement,[5] so too did the launch of highly engineered ships make visible public technology that could propel larger-than-life vessels across open and dangerous sea waters. Because ship launches were freely accessible to a cross-section of the public, they dramatically excited the imagination of all types of people who, once gathered, could travel vicariously with the departing ship. The theatricality of the public ship launch was part and parcel of a broader panorama of industrial development made manifest within a rapidly expanding capitalist society. An innate by-product of any ship's landing was access to cosmopolitan goods, often long-awaited. Maritime trade brought material commodities representative of transnational culture into local living rooms.

A nineteenth-century merchant ship landing initiated a significant outpouring of labor. First, an entire crew worked to navigate the vessel into port. Seamen anchored the ship and rolled up the sails; they laid planking to create a walkway so merchandise would glide smoothly down to the stevedores. If the ship was a steamer, clouds of smoke and aural signals announced its arrival. Next, dozens of men would assist passengers as they disembarked. Other temporary laborers would offload goods, repair the ship, navigate traffic, and transport goods or people to local businesses. Eventually, the seamen would leave the vessel to enjoy shore leave in local bars or brothels. A cacophony of sounds and smells—horse-drawn carriages, vendors, rotting fish—accompanied mercantile exchange. Embodied performance interactions in the port were populist rather than erudite. The goal was to trade money quickly, and profit from financial transactions that could happen only while the ship was in port. Understanding multiple cultural codes or languages was advantageous and the most successful port workers learned foreign phrases to expedite sales. Modern street vendors in cruise ports use similar strategies, speaking English phrases to quickly attract tourists to their goods.

Cruise ship landings, particularly in Caribbean ports, replicate this spectacle. On an island, sight lines are better than what one would find in the dense port settings of Florida's departure piers. I think about an island like St Maarten where six or seven ships are easily accommodated along a long wharf visible from hillside homes. While vendors and local travel agencies become accustomed to the entry and exit of the ships, tourists staying in condos or timeshares appreciate the spectacle of ships in the harbor in much the same way that observers at the Woolwich docks must have viewed the departure of the *Agamemnon*. The spectacle, in this case, appears bucolic even though local cab drivers will bustle to pick up cruise guests while restaurants along the shoreline fire up barbecue pits in the hopes that they can lure well-fed visitors to eat if they advertise local cuisine. For vacationing passengers, the spectacle of the location draws them. Tourism feeds local economies and, as I will discuss later, islanders adjust their performance methodologies to match touristic expectations.

Trading Ports

Vacationing passengers experience ports quite differently from the way working crew members experience them. Crew members, especially those assigned to onboard service positions, have limited access to shore leave. Engineering staff use port stops for ship maintenance while staff members are frequently assigned to additional ship duties or training programs on port days. When a crew member does receive shore leave at a passenger destination port, their experience of the port depends upon the nature of the landing site. Some ports, like St. Thomas with its Kmart, have affordable box stores where staff purchase necessities like toothpaste or underwear. St. Thomas hosts a large volume of cruise ships and to support this business it has internet shops and phone services that enable workers to disembark and keep in touch with their families back home. In contrast, a crew member disembarking on an expensive island like St. Barts or a private island like Norwegian Cruise Line's Great Stirrup Cay in the Bahamas will have access to the same activities as the passengers, that is, swimming on the beach or simply experiencing the sun without having to work. When I observe crew members disembarking for leisure time at port, I reflect upon how Caribbean islands have functioned as trading ports for movements of goods and people across individual island nations. Workers arriving enslaved or conscripted encountered new cultural paradigms after crossing Atlantic waters.

For example, Christopher Columbus began his North American conquest from the island of Hispaniola (currently Haiti and the Dominican Republic). His landing on the island was the first of many transatlantic expeditions funded by the Spanish crown to extract wealth from the New World. Spanish explorers were primarily interested in finding gold circulating within indigenous empires, collecting it through military acts, and eventually sending the wealth back to Iberia to enrich King Ferdinand and Queen Isabella. Standard Spanish conquest policy was to tear down existing temples at religious sites and reuse the materials for colonial buildings in town squares. Conquistadores would force local Indigenous people to construct fortified towers, storehouses, and churches at ports to maintain Spanish dominance over shipping channels. Precious metals were stored in these buildings before they were shipped back to Europe. Collectively, Spanish ports connected to a network of interior riverways and overland highways that brought wealth from indigenous settlements in South and Central America to the coast. These early colonial settlements strategically sat where shipping routes connected to ocean routes propelled by trade winds. This strategy enabled Spanish navigators to quickly move sailing ships into direct shipping channels between the Caribbean and Iberia. The names of the ports they established—Puerto Rico (Rich Port), Santiago de Cuba, Sevilla (in Jamaica)—attest to their colonial mission of maintaining Spanish legacies through the accumulation of wealth.[6]

Colonial countries used different strategies for conquest and trade, consequently Caribbean port structures and their cultural interactions differ across islands. While the Spanish were the first to establish active trade ports in the Caribbean, other foreign nations also formed settlements. Each of these colonial powers adopted slightly different strategies for acquiring and distributing wealth. Dutch explorers used ports as trading outposts for replenishing merchant vessels with staples and for exchanging raw goods (spices, tea, or sugar) for necessities. They had limited interest in establishing permanent colonies. Portuguese entrepreneurs established mining enterprises in South America determined to send large enslaved labor forces to what is now Brazil. The French began their explorations to support fur trading in North America, moving through inland waterways into what is now the midwestern section of the United States. French Caribbean colonies—San Dominique (Haiti) and the leeward isles of Martinique and Guadeloupe—thrived from investments in sugar. These islands along with French New Orleans were part of a network of strategically important trade and military bases.

The multinational character of the Caribbean persists. Moving from island to island involves crossing multiple national boundaries. Some islands, like St. Martin/St Maarten, remain under the political tutelage of more than one colonial nation. Trade winds still define the geographic location of the islands. The Windward Islands, those a sailing ship would encounter while sailing into the wind, contrast with the Leeward Islands, those a sailing ship would encounter with the wind behind the stern. Trade winds blow from east to west; and the Windward Islands include the southern Caribbean nations of Barbados, Grenada, St. Lucia, and St. Vincent and the Grenadines, while the Leeward Islands include the more northern nations of Guadeloupe, St. Maarten, and the Virgin Islands. The Greater Antilles, the larger islands of the northern Caribbean, encompass Hispaniola, Jamaica, Puerto Rico, and Cuba.

In one of my lectures I speak about mid-Atlantic islands, land masses that were provisioning sites for vessels of all nationalities that needed a stopover before arriving in the Americas. The island of Bermuda, now a majority Black overseas territory of Britain in the middle of the Atlantic Ocean, is that kind an island. Bermuda gained notoriety when the vessel *Sea Venture*, part of a supply mission, crashed off its shores in 1609 on its way to provision the settlement of Jamestown in Virginia. One hundred and fifty people survived the wreck and stayed on the island for almost a year, raising livestock and rebuilding two new vessels from the wreckage of their previous ship. The survivors' two new ships, the *Deliverance* and the *Patience*, sailed again in 1610, eventually reaching the Virginia British settlers. The circumstances of the *Sea Venture* inspired William Shakespeare to develop *The Tempest*, about a king stranded on an unnamed island with an enslaved savage named Caliban.[7] Shakespeare's fictional account in some ways captures the feeling of isolation and abandonment that sailors felt when visiting an island deeply imbedded in oceanic waters. Often seamen would spend months in provisioning ports waiting to gather enough supplies, or in raiding passing ships for what they had on board.

St. Helena: Bridging Past and Present

The past informs the present and some spaces seem caught in a time warp. A current cruise destination on a transatlantic voyage across the southern Atlantic is the island of St. Helena, where Napoleon was banished to his final exile after his defeat at Waterloo in 1815. Established in 1659, and located off the coast of southwestern Africa, it has been primarily a provisioning island for over 360 years. Disembarking in this desolate place feels like a step back in time. Ships visit infrequently, the winds are unpredictable, and the small airport cannot easily accommodate the large planes from the African continent that would be needed to safely land in St. Helena. When I traveled there in 2023, no cruise ship had visited the island for three years and local residents had been preparing for a month for our scheduled arrival with the Regent Seven Seas *Voyager* ship. I write about the island because its location made it a stopover point for many nations—Spain, Portugal, France, Netherlands, England and others—as they traveled either around the Cape of Good Hope or across to Spanish and Portuguese colonies in South America. The ancestors of the brown-skinned islanders of Indian and African descent must have arrived as workers and then intermarried with a polyglot set of seamen or temporary settlers. When asked about their heritage, most islanders responded with a shrug. An islander in a group of EMT aids suggested: "Some people say Napoleon had a lot of children," he said. "People come from all over and stop over. We are all mixed up."

It takes a three-day journey via cruise ship from Cape Town, South Africa to arrive in St. Helena. "Saints," as the locals are known to be called, say it takes seven days for a cargo ship to make the same trip. A Portuguese sailor first identified the island in 1502, and the island continues to amalgamate rugged individuals who farm the land, work in construction, or participate in international trade with the limited set of businesses people who access the port by ship. On our cruise journey, we tendered from the ship to disembark in the harbor, a challenging exercise for the elderly passengers who had difficulty managing the active wave motion when the tenders became unstable near the rocky shore. The tenders, or small enclosed vessels used to transport passengers from ship to shore, were difficult to dock. Because of this, the ship's Filipino engineering and port staff workers spent most of their day assisting passengers through a continuous back-and-forth journey from ship to shore. I toured with the guests as an escort, visiting the grave and last residence of Napoleon.[8]

Afterwards, I took a taxi to town to learn more about the island. My taxi driver was a man in his seventies whose beat-up car had been put into service to accommodate the stream of tourists (there were about 500 guests) who would tour through the town during our six-hour stopover. Most of the taxi drivers were town residents taking advantage of a rare opportunity to earn cash with their cars and meet new people during the ship's stopover. Those who weren't driving sat on the street to get a glimpse of the foreigners who were now invading the quietude of their home island. I could see people gawking on the street, on benches, or just behind open doorways. They chatted with friends, they looked, they waved. Teenagers asked if they could take selfies with me. Many mentioned that the town had been preparing for three weeks for the arrival of this first tourist vessel in three years. It used to be—one cab driver assured me—that before the pandemic many ships passed through, the *Queen Mary*, lots of them. Now the cargo supply ship arrives only once every seven days, and the airport supports only an occasional charter flight. But what impressed me the most was the sense of overlapping time and space the islanders evoked when talking about their lifestyles. When I asked what people do for fun, the fireman who was also the tour guide who was also the security guard who looked to be in his midtwenties told me that islanders drive into town to hang out at a pub that was established in 1800. "It's where everyone meets to hang out." Or, he suggests, "You can stop in at the hotel across the street in the middle of town. You can't miss it; it's also been around for a couple of hundred years." This unique Atlantic port captures the kind of stopover mentality that is characteristic of ports where multiple nations chose not to settle, but rather to provision, raid, or copulate. While today's Caribbean ports are self-sufficient nations, they originated as distant, temporary, exotic stopovers where seamen, explorers, and settlers along with enslaved and conscripted laborers shared space and destinies.

Black Cultural Expression in the Performative Commons

Elizabeth Maddock Dillon has written provocatively about the performative commons of the Atlantic world in her book *New World Drama*, noting how late eighteenth- and early nineteenth-century performance traveled across transatlantic sites, transforming both performers and audiences engaged with aesthetics of representation. I interpret this to mean that one mode of resistance for the disenfranchised in the Caribbean was to adopt cultural forms and mannerisms of upper-class, European settlers. By adapting African and other ethnic aesthetics to reflect colonial norms, underclass and working-class individuals created a sense of belonging for themselves within the new creole cultures of the Americas. Dillon describes how Creoles, the enslaved, and an emerging planter class intermingled in London, Kingston, Charleston, and New York City to create a collective body of indigenous people, diasporic Africans, and diasporic Europeans. During the colonial and Victorian eras, each of these cities were active port towns. Playwrights of the era commented on cultural mixing within these cities, and Dillon's comprehensive study analyzes written dramatic texts performed within legitimate theaters. In particular, her chapter on "Transportation" examines how English influence, underscored by Charles II's policies (coupled with the Licensing Act of 1737), accelerated the touring of British companies to the Americas. In the process, new aesthetic cultural forms circulated around the Atlantic basin. What Dillon misses in her analysis of the performative commons of the Caribbean is the expansive archive of nonliterary vernacular performances that articulate perspectives of the underclass. Much of her study discusses how literary texts like *Oroonoko* and Shakespeare's works contributed to the formation of complex identities.[9] Yet, even though Dillon excludes the illiterate, she does reference visual aspects of workers when she describes the spectacular displays of dress that free Blacks used to upend proscribed class structures. Runaway slaves wore bright colors and fanciful outfits such as pink coats, green jackets, and Russian duck trousers. "We find in the figures of slaves who appear in pages of Jamaican newspapers a very different narrative—one which is highly material, sonic, and performative, located in display and erasure rather than in the discourse of reason and argument—located then, in the realm of the aesthetic."[10] The African sense of style and vitality, expressed through vibrant colorful palettes, persisted in the islands and contributed to a sense of self-worth in the New World. Dillon explains how the play of aesthetics unfolded in the theaters and on the streets. Dress or costuming was particularly useful in troubling assumptions about freedom and slavery, citizenship and ownership.

The docks were one setting for visual assessment of how scenes of human import and export unfolded. Africans, who once belonged to villages and clans, were recast, through the slave trade, as unpaid workers valued only for their corporeal strength. It makes sense that enslaved African communities would express cultural negotiations to affirm their humanity through physicalized and vocalized performances. Songs, dances, visual displays, and gestural storytelling were key components of the complicated maneuvers of laborers struggling for footholds within violent territories of the New World. Dress was just one component of a reimaging identity for newly arrived migrants from Europe, Africa, and Asia. Spectacles of belonging, spectacles of ownership, and spectacles of European nationalism all played out in close proximity to the docks.

Port life and town life merge in island ports because islands, smaller land masses surrounded by water, have landing docks built close to paved streets, marketplaces, customs houses, and town residences. Street and festival performances, parades, and processionals staged to process through town streets necessarily manifest geographically as an extension of the port. Carnival events, for example, could literally end with a performer's feet immersed in water. Performers, spectacularly dressed, regularly marched through the streets of Caribbean towns in festive celebrations. Because water surrounds the islands, culminating aspects of performances—libations or baptism for example—could easily acknowledge watery borders. Highbrow indoor entertainments sponsored by elites during the eighteenth and nineteenth centuries expressed Creole desires to create what Dillon refers to as a "Commons" which would reify connections to European societies. But for the working class, the streets offered opportunities for more populist cultural expressions emerging from creolization. For Blacks in particular, raucous activities in the streets were an opportunity to express humanity outside of enslavement. Folklorist Jerrilyn McGregory in *One Grand Noise* writes about how Boxing Day performances across Anglophone Caribbean nations are heterogeneous expressions of presence marked by noise. The title of her book comes from one of her informants who, when asked about the meaning of the Jamaican Jonkonnu,[11] explained that the street celebration was about making "one grand noise" to establish presence and resistance. The transgressive power of making noise at the site of forced labor constitutes working-class resistive performance within the Atlantic Commons.

Ships arriving at islands like Barbados or Jamaica might secure themselves and unload at a wharf where enslaved or free laborers could be seen moving barrels into storage areas for sale. Human cargo, offloaded and chained before going to market, would be held for individual planters. At the busy wharf, merchants claimed their goods and paid captains who were then able to distribute wages to seamen. Once paid, seamen visited nearby pubs and boarding houses or churches where they could give thanks for safe passage. There, locals exchanged Caribbean goods—sugar cane, rum, coffee, or tobacco—for cotton or weaponry from Great Britain. Notably, ports and town centers were distant from plantations, which were generally located on hills or in wooded areas away from the port. This affected the mobility of enslaved or indentured workers who would have to travel on bad roads to get to a town or port where they might interact with international travelers. In some mountainous maroon communities, escaped slaves established their own cultural codes. Consequently, insurrections tended to occur at distant locations removed from the port towns.[12]

Even though Jamaica was a key port for trade and transfer of goods to the United States, the British abolished slavery there in 1833. Previously enslaved Blacks, now legally liberated, continued to work on the same lands as indentured laborers under a system known as "apprenticeship." Some Blacks, however, attained access to freedom of movement, which allowed them to earn wages and acquire goods. On the islands, the work of moving goods to ships released laborers from the fields. The workers sang Caribbean songs and sea shanties as they moved from island to island, carrying histories and messages of liberation, spirituality, and sustenance. For those laborers relegated to plantations, Sundays and holidays were days when singing and dancing were allowed. Plantation workers united to perform Gumbey, Jonkonnu, and

Kumina dances, all drawing from African vernacular traditions. Gumbey dancers wore tall headdresses with brightly-colored fringed regalia fusing indigenous, African, and British mumming traditions[13] Jonkonnu dancers impersonated a figure named "John Canoe" as they paraded through island streets. Later, the impersonation of a single character broadened to incorporate multiple character types. Dancing Jonkonnu was a precursor for carnival traditions currently practiced throughout the British Caribbean on Boxing Day, the day after Christmas, a day when plantation owners would historically share leftover food and gifts with the enslaved.[14] More communal Kumina dances were performed in a circle and incorporated hip movements characteristic of Central Africa. Each of these dances were occasions for racial mixing and personification of European ideals through an African lens.

Narratives of Visual Display

Italian artist Isaac Mendes Belisario documents spectacular island performance displays in vibrant watercolors in his "Sketches of Character" painting series that captures the culture and artistry of Jamaican life. He illustrates habits, occupations, and costumes of the island's "negro population." Belisario was a privileged youth who wanted to celebrate Jamaica's multiracial inhabitants during a turbulent time, after the emancipation from slavery, and vernacular performance fascinated this Jewish painter and lithographer.[15] He painted stunningly intricate, detailed portraits of street musicians, actor-boys, French set girls, puppeteers, vendors, and street sweepers. Dillon reads some of Belisario's depictions as a commentary on the Black dandy, a fancified urban Black male who adopts European modes of dress. She notes politics and resistance evident in his painted, performed, parodic commentaries on British life. Assessing the impact of performance on Jamaican colonial society, she writes: "Jonkonnu, then, must be understood as a performative intellectual act: one that made the commons thinkable in both aesthetic and political terms."[16]

That nonliterary performance constitutes an intellectual act is no surprise. Complex communications embedded in embodied performance—gestural and aural exchanges—are intellectual and also contextual. Dance scholar Barbara Glass writes a more nuanced history of the "John Canoe" or Junkonnu dance where she describes its impact in North America as well as the British Caribbean. Her interpretation clarifies the festival's roots in West African traditions by highlighting the use of props and masks as storytelling. Rural manifestations of the tradition differed from urban parades. In the hills and mountains, masked performers would travel with lanterns while in Kingston in Jamaica and Nassau in the Bahamas performers dressed in variants of European attire.[17] My own experience with Jonkonnu (also known as Junkanoo) has been as witness to elaborate Boxing Day festivals in Nassau as well as rural performances in the "Out Islands."[18] In both cases, communities view the festival as an opportunity to express African cultural heritage within a British Caribbean landscape.

Belisario's art and Dillon's analysis focus on the most spectacular displays of interracial mixing, performances where two distinct racial and social classes use costuming and parades to enact difference. Not captured however are the daily interactions, many unknowable centuries later, that marked Jamaica's location along a major maritime trade route. Existing descriptions of intercultural interactions are biased, suffused with racial and social undertones. For example, the published memoir of Captain Hugh Crow, a slave trade mariner born in Liverpool who regularly transported Africans between the coast of Benin and Kingston, Jamaica implies that enslaved Africans were grateful to him for introducing them to a better life in the Americas. Describing events of 1806, he writes:

> On the first Sunday after our arrival in Kingston, a circumstance occurred on board the Mary, which was more gratifying to me as it was entirely unexpected. While I was lying in my cot, about nine o'clock in the morning, Mr. Scott, my chief mate, hurried into the cabin and said, "Sir! a great number of black men and women have come on board, all dressed in their best, and they are very anxious to see you: will you allow them to come down?"[19]

Crow links the entrance of the visitors to a mode of performance defined by dress, maintaining that the Black men and women who came on board were there to thank him for transporting them to Jamaica. He references their attire to demonstrate how their dress reflected their social improvement through assimilation.

> The women were neatly dressed in calicoes and muslins. Their hair was tastefully arranged and they wore long gold ear-rings. The men appeared in white shirts and trousers, and flashy neckcloths with their hair neatly plaited. The whole were at once clean and cheerful, and I was glad at heart to see them.

Figure 26. Socializing on the Jamaica docks at the Victoria Market. Courtesy of the National Library of Jamaica.

Crow's narrative replicates a pervasive racist belief common during the Victorian era (and beyond) that purports that subjugation and enslavement improve the character of Black men and women. Crow's description highlights what he perceives to be a newly found cleanliness in his previously enslaved cargo. They are cleaner because they are no longer in chains in the hull of the ship. Yet this sartorial display can also be considered a mode of performance, particularly in shifting cultural landscapes. Ports and islands are potential doorways to alternative lifestyles because they offer access to travelers passing through varied labor and financial scenarios. Dressing the part of an emancipated person has material outcomes if it leads to employment or liberation, and Jamaica seems to be a port where transitions were possible. Crow, Dillon, and Belisario all focus on the splendid dress of Black and Creole citizens who adorned themselves with symbols of status and inclusion. This visual performance is an important pathway for non- or semiliterate workers to negotiate themselves into enhanced work and living situations.

A 1900 photograph from the National Library of Jamaica attests to the impact of merging dress and maritime display.[20] The image documents the

Figure 27. Jamaican workers in the sugar cane fields. Source: Wikimedia Commons. https://commons.wikimedia.org/wiki/File:Sugarcane_cutters_in_Jamaica,_Caribbean_RMG_E9087.tiff

inauguration of a new statue at the Victoria Market in Kingston, Jamaica. It's a busy day. Boats are docked near the pier. The paved city streets about the wharf allow fashionable residents to stroll, watch incoming traffic, perhaps mingle and share news. Notable in the image are the Victorian summer fashions, punctuated with fancy sun hats, worn by both Black and white Jamaican citizens. Steve Buckridge, writing about the politics of dress in Jamaican society, explains that before emancipation few of the enslaved had access to European fashions. After emancipation, European dress became a passion, an outward sign of accomplishment. "For many freed persons, new raiment enabled them to participate in social activities in urban centers that required appropriate attire."[21] The inauguration of the statue illustrates how the very wharf that hosted Crow's well-dressed slaves continued to manifest as a site of social striving, revealed through the performance of dress.

In contrast, images of enslaved Africans from the mid-nineteenth century depict Blacks wearing white cotton dresses and head wraps as markers of their subservient field-laborer status. The photographer who captured this image[22] chose to display the bodies lying on the ground, close to the earth, and in need of sustenance as they gnaw on the cane. Wrapped white headcloths replicate the adornment practices of women born in Africa who wear colorful cloth wrapped around their heads when they attend public affairs. However, the same head wrap in the Americas denotes the field workers as lowly physical laborers. The plain white cotton head covering creates a uniform "work gang" look for the ensemble. The group rests in the middle of a cane field where the sharp leaves of the plant regularly cut into the limbs and hands of workers who were required to tame and harvest the cane. Sugar was the crop most cultivated in the islands; its by-products of molasses and rum sustained an emerging North American and European middle class that craved the delicacy. In the photo, the workers, seemingly caught in a moment of rest, look directly at the lens of the camera, a perspective rendering the subjects as exotic outsiders. But notice the white overseer on the right side of the frame. The photo demonstrates the man's ownership of both the people and the cultivated fields of sugar cane.

African diaspora workers were certainly not the only ethnic group exploited for their labor in the Caribbean. Irish and Indian workers derogatorily referred to as "paddies" and "coolies," respectively, also worked fields, railroads, or kitchen floors in the multinational Caribbean. Creole and racialized laborers contributed to the evolution of Caribbean ports over the course of the nineteenth century from an exchange zone for sugar and slaves to a site of international cultural capital where status and class shifted. As Belinda Edmondson has observed, "The black and brown populations of Jamaica expanded tremendously during the nineteenth century and with the expansion came rising economic and social influence."[23] The use of dress to express social affiliations was a core component of this performance of inclusion. The emergence of a Creole class of brown-skinned Jamaicans who defied identification was made possible, in part, by the geography of an island where close access to multiple transnational ports exposed residents to diverse populations.

Social Lives in Ports

How do sea workers socialize in the port? How much of ship culture transfers to the shore? The previous section described how Caribbean ports, with their easy access to downtown streets, supported public displays of ethnicity and encouraged hybridity. This section brings attention to private encounters and social interactions that transpire in port cities, past and present. Layouts of streets, demographic settlement patterns, housing options, and the locations of drinking establishments determine where crew members, historical seamen, and working-class immigrants iterate relationships. The maritime world could not accelerate social mobility without the tempestuous cacophony of the port. Black and Irish communities in particular interacted with one another through populist encounters. In this section I center my discussions around two selected nineteenth-century ports, Liverpool and New York, that supported a large sector of international trade between 1780 and 1850. There are several reasons. First, the two cities represent beginning and ending points for the voyages of the African Grove players (discussed in chapter 1) who worked on packet ships and eventually formed an early nineteenth-century theater company. This company and its performers constitute an entry point for exploring enactments of racial identities in a multicultural environment. Second, the archive is thick with descriptive writing about these two urban ports because they were primary shipping areas for trade vessels. Additionally, each of these ports benefitted financially from merchant investments in the slave trade. Black and Irish free working-class communities labored in the shadow of an industry that considered them to be subhuman manpower through which to advance industrial wealth. Third, both cities were immigrant cities where Blacks, the Irish, and others cohabited, sometimes in sensual alliances and sometimes in violent clashes over work or housing. While many ethnic workers passed through the two cities on work details, many also settled and became permanent residents of the respective countries. For example, Ira Aldridge, who first performed with the African Grove Theatre and attended the African Free School, realized that he could not effectively pursue an acting career in a nation polarized around race. Like several other mid-nineteenth-century Black artists, he became a permanent resident of the United Kingdom. Finally, both the Irish and the Africans were racially marked, making their presence visible in descriptive imagery of newspaper articles and seamen's journals pertaining to these two ports.

In any era, whether in the nineteenth century or now, ports where seamen interact with local vendors are active geographical spaces for cultural exchange. Imagine landing on a dock in a Victorian urban center. Loading docks accessed from the ship stood full of crates and barrels and burlap bags. Passengers, sailors, beggars, merchant agents, families, and shoppers looking for bargains congregated near the wharf. After the ship dropped anchor, the performance of commerce began: busking for money, package offloading, accompanied by songs, selling goods with street calls, and soliciting with gestures. Sailors on shore leave would seek out bars and boarding houses; passengers would search for relatives, food, or lodging. Beggars enticed donors by fiddling, dancing, or simply performing their poverty. Person-to-person interactions that occur in and around ports are microcosms of transactional economies, flourishing throughout port environments. Even though it was possible for sea workers to make lasting attachments onshore, in reality, it was highly unlikely. Sailors were undesirables; their bodies carried the smell of unwashed weeks at sea as well as evidence of past physical injuries. They spent their hard-earned money in brothels and bars, which were the most easily accessible points of purchase after long periods of deprivation. Unlike the popularized image of the sailor enamored of an absent lover, most sailors were romantically unattached, and likely to leave any steady employment offered to them.

Because sea workers hail from different countries, understand different customs, and speak different languages, sounds and gestures have been important communication tools in port interactions. Consequently, small acts such as asking for money with song, trading wares with gestures, and street calls are used to facilitate transactions. Those waiting for ships to arrive or depart needed temporary housing, therefore urban ports had sailor homes that provided temporary shelter. An example is the Seamen's Church Institute in Newport, Rhode Island, which continues to offer "hospitality, education, and safe haven."[24] This particular institute, like others of the late nineteenth century, had a mission of improving the moral state of seamen who, by default, were associated with a lack of Christian piety and morality. The need for economic survival and mental escape from the imposed isolation of the vessel stood in direct opposition to land-based priorities of decorous social interactions to maintain social codes. Those who survived by working on the water were caught within this dichotomy. At the site of contact between ship and land, human players negotiated moment-to-moment realities of winners and losers, outsiders and insiders.

An Incident in Cape Town

A recent cruise port incident highlights for me the precarity crew members experience when arriving and departing from a ship at a foreign port. My destination assignment for this particular transatlantic cruise required me to embark in Cape Town, South Africa and disembark in Rio de Janeiro. I flew for about twenty hours on an itinerary booked by the cruise company's travel agency—from Washington, D.C., across Nova Scotia and southward through all of Europe and the Mediterranean, then southward again, crossing the African continent. When I finally arrived in Cape Town seeking shore-to-ship transport, there was none. There was no cruise ship representative holding a sign to guide passengers to the buses; instead, a woman with a sign for "crew members only" stood looking for workers needing to connect with ships. I decided to exploit the indeterminate nature of my job title and claim to be a crew member. When I approached, the port agent looked askance because I was not dressed like a crew member. When I said I was with the Regent *Seven Seas Voyager* (a very high-end ship) she decided I was probably not a passenger either.

She checks a list, then another list. I'm not on it. "Are you with the *Nautilus*?" she asks. I assure her I am with the *Voyager*. "Oh—that one's not sailing today." "What????," I ask. "Winds are high and none of the ships can get into port," she responds. There is a long pause. "If you are a crew member then you can take the shuttle to the hotel." She checks her list, she calls someone, she agrees to add me to the crew list. It appears that crew members have assigned beds and hotels, but there is no visible infrastructure to support passengers. I decide I really want to be with the crew. Even though the specifics of my status as a destination lecturer impacted my sense of uncertainty, I am reminded that sea workers at any port before the age of the internet and cell phones would experience the need to find lodging and food after a long journey. Even in the twenty-first century it feels unstable. Knowing no one, yet waiting for a ship that is not yet in port, I seek camaraderie and, above all, information.

The port worker escorts me into a van with several Filipino port workers. We are deposited at a hotel (not the dock with the ship). I'm panicked, but the other workers are not. They seem pleased to have scored a night in a hotel before reporting to work. I ask one worker if he is headed to a ship. He says, "Yeah, but the ship isn't in port." At the hotel, he easily checks in, says good night, and goes to his room. I stand at the desk in that uncomfortable position of not knowing whether to claim status as a passenger or a crew member. And where is the ship if it's not in port? When will it arrive? The hotel clerk verifies that I belong on the ship after making a few phone calls. No one knows when the ship will port. It's currently stranded offshore with high winds. But the pick-up will be at 7:00 a.m. "Be ready," she advises.

In the morning, I come into the lobby where even more Filipino workers are gathered to have breakfast and then depart. I go to the desk and this time I explain that I am really a speaker and I won't be able to board the ship with the workers. "OK," she says. "Then don't go to the ship until after the 'boys' depart," she advises. "Get some breakfast." I say "OK" and head to the buffet. In the dining room there are now about three tables of brown-skinned crew members. Later, maybe five taller, white-skinned men come in and sit together, speaking in Norwegian. It's clear they are with the ship as well. I wonder how it is on land that nationalities separate and sit with their own, even when they will soon be sailing together. Eventually a runner from the maritime transport company calls my name.[25] "We were waiting for you in the van—come on!" I quickly gather my suitcases (there are three of them) and hurry to the van where the crew members and a couple of the passengers are heading to the ship. The maritime agent at the port (who is a Black South African) instructs us to head to Immigration, where we sit on a bench waiting to be authorized to leave South Africa. This is the most equalizing moment we will experience as passengers and crew members. Blacks, whites, Filipinos, we are travelers of varied phenotypes and class backgrounds, as we sit together on a bench in the sun and wait for Immigration to authorize us.

I have a couple of interactions with the crew members—since we are all at port together. One crew member asks me if it's OK to smoke on the bench. I say "sure." Another, taller, white-skinned woman tells me she is nervous, because this is her first time on this particular cruise line, and her first six-month contract. She looks anxious and is trying to be friendly, but the Filipino workers ignore her. They are speaking among themselves in Tagalog. I tell her it's going to be OK (as if I know) and that she'll do great. For a moment, we communicate as social equals. We acknowledge that we will be together on the ship having a collective experience, even though nationality-based groupings are already in place. We all sit together knowing that in a few hours we will all be working, although the more experienced crew members have already figured out that I will be entertainment or some kind of a privileged speaker. Our moment of worker solidarity has been brief, if it ever existed at all. This is the enigma of the port. We have to evaluate verbal, dress, and gestural clues. We have to listen to languages and inflections to ascertain where we are going and whom we should interact with.

After we finish with Immigration, we return to the cruise ship terminal where we show our passports and pass through two different doors, one labeled "Crew" and one labeled "Passengers," to enter the ship. Here any pretense of commonality ends. Holding my stamped and authorized passport, I board the ship and, in the passageway, I notice a crate with hundreds of passports stacked together. The crew members have relinquished their identity papers and secured them with the cruise company in exchange for their onboard labor opportunity. I shudder a little recognizing that management now controls each worker's ability to reintegrate into onshore citizenship.

The incident prods me to reflect on how earlier seamen must also have succumbed to shifting maritime regulations between the port and the ship. Below, I explore the precarity of "ship to shore" life through the lens of a historical seaman's journal.

William Maxon's Journey

The 1845–46 journal of William Maxon, a young Connecticut sailor, illustrates how a privileged young white seaman experienced ports and sea life during the mid-nineteenth century. The youth was a carpenter hired to work on the *Niagara*, a sailing packet traveling between New York and Liverpool. Unlike many journals that primarily recorded wind and weather data, Maxon's writings capture the perils and surprises of a journey that for more seasoned sailors may have been merely routine. Carpenter Maxon was born in 1818 in Mystic, Connecticut. The journey on the *Niagara* begins when he is twenty-seven years old. At that time, he had been a land-based ship's carpenter for about ten years. He signs onto the *Niagara*, departing from Mystic on November 18. Maxon records how they immediately hit a schooner and are forced to return for repairs. Their first stop, after relaunching and sailing through Long Island Sound, was New York City. The seaman gets his hair cut in the big city and visits his cousin John on Carmine Street. The crew spends onshore leave time celebrating Thanksgiving and attending a military parade to celebrate the anniversary of the evacuation of Yorktown. Afterward, on December 17, the ship is finally moved down to Wall Street to take on cargo. Loading and repairing the ship for departure takes another month. While they are docked, the crew continues to socialize. The captain entertains guests on board with ham, bacon, and wine on January 13. Finally, on January 20, they leave the wharf.

The following day it snows, and four feet of meltwater accumulates on the deck. After the cleanup, the ship heads south to bring on more cargo. The *Niagara* stops in Norfolk, Virginia, where Maxon notes that the weather in January feels like May in Rhode Island. Here, the carpenter documents the first performative act he sees on his journey. "The crew of negros unloading the ship go on in as fine order as I ever saw men work in my life." Maxon's observation implies that the crew of men works in unison (perhaps with a work chant) to complete their labor. In Norfolk, Maxon also sees his first slave market, where a man is on auction to be sold for $340; it disturbs him. He writes:

While passing the market saw a small collection of people at one end, called the police office. Found they had a young man up for sale. I stopped to view the scene. They were trying to raise a three-hundred-and-forty-dollar bid, could not and he was struck off, when they put up a horse for sale. This scene the first I ever saw stirred up my indignation to a high pitch I discard the country that boast of light and liberty and the[n] tolerate the system of slavery in all its worst forms it is a curse to our country.[26]

Born a Connecticut Yankee, William Maxon's firsthand experience of slavery in the near South clearly raised his consciousness about violence and racial inequality. After seeing this, Maxon establishes a relationship with the ship's cook and steward, which he documents in the log. Maxon is literate, so he uses his skills to help his fellow seamen. "Wrote a letter for the steward this evening for whom I have wrote five since in Norfolk, four for the cook, three for home, one to NY, one to Mystic." While he does not indicate the race or economic status of the two men in the domestic roles, it is clear there is a class difference that the sailor bridges in the relationship.

Finally, the *Niagara* sails across the Atlantic to Liverpool on a thirty-five-day journey. Once the ship passes through the Irish highlands and lands in Liverpool, Maxon's description makes apparent the multicultural nature of the port. He immediately goes home with an Irish tailor he describes as "poor with fine family." He buys broadcloth from the tailor for a suit and satin for a vest. Apparently, the crafty tailor picked him up at the dock where he could bring him to his residence to offer him housing and goods for sale. Four days later, the carpenter has his clothing washed by two girls who "work for the ship." Maxon finds Liverpool pleasant, but dirty: "Pleasant if were not for the smoke which is so thick that a person cannot see across the town considerable of the time." He is anxious to leave as soon as the packet ship is loaded. "Having just been 3 weeks in Liverpool a place I am not sorry to leave. I think the coal smoke has affected my stomach very much." The packet leaves Liverpool port the first weekend in May.

The brief experience Maxon has on the streets of Liverpool demonstrates the performative components of his experience in a port where his primary interaction with locals is "transactional." While at home, the traveler might self-identify as a carpenter; while at sea, he is a skilled seaman. However, on the streets of Liverpool, he is an international visitor and a potential source of cash for the local Liverpudlians. His interaction with the girls who wash his clothing and the tailor who provides cloth for his suit and vest marks him as a shopper in need of services. The simple act of stepping off the ship changes his performance parameters. At the same time, his international experience reflects a certain cultural perspective. Maxon is a member of the New England working class, a type of young, independent, and Christian worker described by Daniel Vickers in *The Young Men and the Sea: Yankee Seafarers in the Age of Sail*.[27] Maxon views England as a foreign country and compares its industrial working class with the citizens and relative tranquility of his hometown of Mystic. The Irish, in particular, represent the unfamiliar foreign. While the young sailor seems willing to trade and exchange with the Irish during his stay in Liverpool town, once his vessel goes to sea, the situation turns ugly. He begins to refer to the Irish passengers traveling in steerage as "paddy" passengers. The captain assigns Maxon the job of feeding the Irish steerage passengers, many of them escaping the potato famine. The task disgusts him, because most of them are sick from the sea travel in closed quarters. On May 12, 1846, he records: "served before 3:00 pm water for 300 persons, oatmeal and flour to 290 steerage passengers before I commenced serving water in the morning. I went fore and aft between decks several times until I got them routed out of their bearths to clean out their places before I would let them have water. It is a perplexing job to serve water and provisions to such thick heads as some of them are. The sick ones are better."

Later in the journal Maxon provides more details about the food and rations he gives to these passengers. It is bread flour accompanied by a ground corn meal similar to the dietary staple of Native Americans. Immigrant passengers were required to cook their own meals and they find the Indian meal unpalatable because when is not properly prepared with ash it expands and makes them sick.[28] Yet Maxon seems to have little sympathy for the ethnically distinct Irish.

> Served out Bread flour and Indian meal today to the passengers. 100 lb. of bread ¾ bbl.[29] flour and about 180 lb. of meal being all they would take as the Irish do not know what to do with Indian meal, quite amusing to hear their remarks about it, some thought it would take 4 hours to cook it enough, others thought it could not be eat without milk, and they could make no kind use of it, but they are great on oatmeal and potatoes. I prefer oat for pudding.

Their rations of dry goods were meant to minimally sustain them as they made their voyage. In addition to feeding the steerage passengers, Maxon has to record their names, dates, and destinations.

> I have been taking today the name, age, sex, occupation, place of nativity and where going of the steerage passengers which I found to be a tedious job taking the whole day many not knowing their age guessed at it. Some knew nothing of where they were going except to New York nor what they were going to do.

Maxon's description of the passenger inventory in steerage suggests how Irish migrants were categorized and labeled before their arrival in the United States. These immigrants, like twenty-first-century Central and South American migrants coming to North America, were hoping for hospitality and acceptance by United States government officials. In just six months, the Anglo-American artisan from Mystic, Connecticut learned a lot about transnational encounters and understandably developed a perspective about the "other" based upon his own class and social circumstances. Maxon's interactions placed him on equal footing with the Irish in Liverpool port, but once at sea, power structures shifted and the working-class Irish became subordinates. These shifting roles were realized through gestural exchanges and differential placements within the geography of the ship. Therefore, the architecture of the ship coupled with hierarchical structures on board inculcated migrating Irish travelers into new social systems that disadvantaged them. The transatlantic maritime journey affected the social status of the Irish workers from Liverpool in the same way in which free Africans might be boarded on a ship in Africa, then be redesignated as slaves once they reached American or Caribbean ports. This transformation occurs in part because of the way in which hierarchies are performed on the ship. Once the passengers land, transactions in the port may equalize status once again, depending, of course, on where the travelers disembark.

On this particular journey on the *Niagara*, the Irish eventually rebel. A fight breaks out between the passengers, and one of the mates goes into the berths with a pistol to quell the row. While the mate calms the disturbance, another man begins talk of taking over the ship in spite of the presence of passengers and crew. At this point the captain asserts his authority by bringing out more firearms. Each of the crew men loaded their pistols.

> The Capt had one of them brought aft and he put irons on him and put him in ward, they had threatened to rescue if one of their number was taken up so the Capt brought out his six-barrel pistol and loaded it in their sight examined the rest of the pistols one of the cabin passengers has a two barrel gun he brought that up and loaded it. We had

what things we could get for shelaleigh brought aft so that I should not wonder if we put a stop to fighting.[30]

The following day, the steward is placed in confinement for being insolent and stealing from the ship stores to give food to the steerage passengers. William Maxon perhaps notes this in his journal because he had merely a month earlier worked to write letters for this same steward. What is clear is that the journey at sea coupled with Maxon's experiences with the Irish migrants changed the carpenter sailor's relationship with immigrants he can now consider subordinate. However, there is one more social interaction recorded in the journal. At the end of the journal, as the ship approaches New York, Maxon writes that all aboard begin singing and talking and laughing. Once they land in the Americas, social status—alliances and relationships with other ethnic communities and class paradigms—shift once again.

Maxon's journey as recorded in his journal illustrates aspects of social interactions in port, but social life in New York port differed considerably from the staid social environment of the New England shipping community that Maxon hailed from. Mystic, Connecticut was a shipbuilding community located in the sheltered harbor of the Mystic River, where over six hundred ships were built between 1700 and the mid-1800s. It currently houses the Mystic Seaport Museum, a living history institution that reimagines and re-creates life in the 1800s. While Mystic was indeed a port, it was not an active trading port for international merchandise and enslaved laborers. Seamen could have their vessel built or repaired there, but moneymaking happened further south. A radically different, racially mixed, polyglot community populated New York during the early and mid-nineteenth century.

Landscapes and Social Lives in New York Port

Between 1830 and 1860, the port of New York was one of the most vital and vibrant places for transatlantic intercultural exchange across ethnic divisions. The neighborhood of Five Points, located on the Lower East Side just north of the main shipping docks, was legendary for grungy, working-class pastimes. An essential text for understanding the nature and function of the port of New York during the nineteenth century is Robert Greenhalgh Albion's *The Rise of New York Port*, originally published in 1939. The volume begins with a panoramic description of the port by delineating the impact maritime trade had on the developing industrial city. Images show the South Street docks packed with sailing vessels and steam-powered ships. The dock's proximity to the Hudson River on the west side of the island provided easy access to inland waterways such as the Erie Canal, which serviced Albany and Canada. The east side of the docks adjoined Long Island Sound, which connected the port to open Atlantic waters along the New England seaboard. To the south, waterways connected the port to the gardens of Staten Island and the farms of New Jersey. Geographically, the port of New York was ideally situated to reach markets throughout the northeastern and mid-Atlantic regions and to transfer raw goods from the interior to manufacturing centers in the United States and England.

New York's stock market traded personal goods and trade commodities, increasing the wealth of almost everyone interacting with the port's merchandise. Maritime historian Robert Greenhalgh Albion describes a cotton network extending into the South to bring raw goods into manufacturing districts and a coastal trade network of smaller ships that delivered transatlantic shipments to Virginia, Delaware, Boston, and the Chesapeake Bay inlets. Efficiency was important. By midcentury, steamers were more popular than other maritime vessels, overtaking paddle-wheels, sailing ships, and barges because of their speed and lack of dependency on the wind. Steamboat transport dominated maritime merchant shipping until at least World War II.[31]

A ship entering New York port would first navigate through a series of waterfront agencies and government officials. A location on the wharf was most ideal because priority was given to ships close to the markets and exchanges. Mariners paid more for the right to access these coveted spots. Cheaper slips were available at the end of the wharf where ice and traffic might damage the vessel. Lighthouses guided ships entering the area while pilot ships, required by the state, helped with navigation into the port. Traffic would bottleneck, there would be collisions, slips would be built and rebuilt. Even as ships paid for the privilege of accessing the port, agents, both foreign and local financial agencies, collected profitable fees for allowing each ship's access. New York differed from New England towns where shipping primarily brought wealth to local New Englanders because New Yorkers profited from international investments. Connective business routes between Liverpool and London meant British citizens held strong positions in shipping lines and "stock" exchanges.[32] Investors in southern and Caribbean enterprises enriched Dutch and French citizens as well as Americans.

Albion also describes the impact of the human freight of immigrants who

150 · *Shipping Out*

Figure 28. A depiction of the Port of New York from one of the "racy newspapers." Courtesy of the American Antiquarian Society.

choked New York with their ambitions and search for livelihood: "There were constant complaints, particularly from New Yorkers, that Europe was using this country as a dumping ground for its paupers, criminals and undesirables, with many a prince, parish or landlord paying the passage to be rid of a burden."[33] Similar complaints echo in this country's current anti-immigrant policies, when local governments in the southern United States ship immigrants to northern cities. Albion reports that steerage passengers arrived after being housed in the midsection of ships, where they paid $25 per person for the transport, passengers like those our young sailor Maxon fed. Once immigrants landed in New York port, they became a part of the teeming masses struggling to make do in a hardscrabble land.

Newspaper images display the social vitality of a New York port where street hawkers and vendors work the docks, support the boarding houses and slums, and distribute newspapers geared toward the underclass. Two visual archives, *The Cries of New-York* and the racy newspapers, demonstrate snippets of a street life where transnational, transactional exchanges dominated.

The newspapers and the *Cries* were popular because in a landscape of constantly shifting migrants and immigrants, receiving the latest information gave passersby an advantage on where to go, whom to see, and sometimes when to get out of town. For the illiterate, street hawkers and ballad singers were an alternative source of information. They were traveling troubadour performers who walked door to door, from street corner to street corner selling goods and offering songs or poetry for sale. Several cities published versions of the *Cries* to illustrate the sorrows of the underclass, however Frances Osgood's *Cries of New-York*, published in 1846, specifically illustrates the calls of street vendors who frequented the New York docks.

The pamphlets were originally printed to teach children about the multiethnic, impoverished people they might observe on the streets, and they promoted Christian piety by creating empathy for the poor. Each page offers an image of a character type and a description of their work activity expressed through poetical text. The introductory text proclaims: "Scorn not the rag man's poor employ! This very page, his form revealing . . ." It then explains how this character type—the rag man—goes about the city calling out "Rags! Rags! Any rags to sell!" *The Cries* places each character within a multicultural, multiracial landscape and promotes this community as an enhancement to the lifestyles of the city. Osgood explains how the rag man goes around the city with a handcart and bells purchasing rags. To underscore the cosmopolitan nature of the poor man, the author explains that many of the rags are imports from the Mediterranean, and every family should buy them. The presentation of the initial "Rag Man" character is followed by a detailed explanation of how the city of New York is located in maritime space.

> New York City, the principal city of the State of New York and, in population, wealth, and commerce, the largest city in the United States, deserves to be denominated the London of America. It is 86 miles north-east of Philadelphia, 210 miles south-west of Boston, 225 miles north-east of Washington, 670 miles north-east of Charleston, 145 miles south of Albany, 372 miles south of Montreal and 1370 miles north-east of New Orleans.

The navigational context underscores the primacy of the rag man's business within an international network, thus placing the rag man as a vital player in a network of commerce.

Osgood's text further situates New York's working-class populations geographically, naming the bridges, harbors, and inland waterways that access

Manhattan. The author notes: "There are not more than five or six cities in Europe more populous than New York."[34] This positioning of the characters within the larger world both speaks to the increasing impact of the port of New York on international and domestic shipping during the mid-1800s and normalizes the presence of the underclass within this landscape. Poverty, ethnic discord, criminality, and disease existed side by side with the growth of commerce and the accrual of middle-class wealth. Both Blacks and whites benefited as a residential and merchant class developed. Irish communities, many of them refugees from the potato famine, congregated in the dockside areas like Five Points while the suburbs north of Fourteenth Street housed free Blacks who established the African Free School and other institutions. Again, I highlight the presence of these two populations because they most visibly represent interracial and cultural mixing within an increasingly global community.

Descriptions of the auditory landscape of street cries helps us imagine some of the experience of wandering through the chaos of lower Manhattan. *The Cries*, for example, describes a Black street sweeper, humanizing the character for the children.

> Sweep! Sweep! in rags and cold,
> The poor—the lonely sweep behold!
> Yet even he—tho' dark his way—
> Tho' half his life shut out from day—
> Tho' pain and want go hand in hand,
> With him—the wanderer through the land—
> May hold some ray from Heaven, within,
> To guard his heart from grief and sin.

Here, the Christian piety behind the author's description becomes evident. Young readers are to understand that all people, even Blacks and the underclass, are children of God. Following the poem, Osgood notes that in New York, the business of sweeping chimneys is confined to colored men and boys, but in London, white men and boys perform the task. Other characters personified in *The Cries* are the Baker, the Soap Maker, the Ice Man, the Scissors Grinder, the Oyster Man, the Strawberry Girl, the Newsboy, the Radish Girl, the Milkman, the Omnibus Driver, the Match Boy, the Ice Cream Man, and the Fisherman. Interspersed between each poem with its accompanying character description are lengthy narratives about even more architectural sites in New York City—churches, parks, harbors, buildings, parks, bridges, and waterways. Each account emphasizes the dimensions and costs of the construction of these marvels of New York. *The Cries* thus captures the discrepancies between the daily lives of the poorest of the city dwellers and the magnificent infrastructure that surrounds them. The children's book offers one perspective on the types of communities prevalent in the nineteenth-century port towns.

Contrasting the sanitized portraits of *The Cries* are the "racy newspapers," a wide range of newspapers with names like *Hawk and Buzzard, Broadway Omnibus, The Pick, Evening Star,* and *Flash,* published in the mid-nineteenth century and geared toward readers in the New York underclass. A fragmentary collection of these publications housed at the American Antiquarian Society contains a variety of essays and advertisements written for immigrant readers.[35] Want ads posted by husbands beg wives to return home; bars and boarding houses advertise for customers. Printed issues include diatribes against the filth of the Bowery and impassioned pleas from women who lost their husbands to drink and wayward women. The archive is one of the few with depictions of the Black and white underclass interacting with one another, engaging in mutually beneficial enterprises to sustain themselves. Images, not always flattering, depict oyster shops and lowlife pubs. In one, a white man tries to run away when he discovers a large Black woman in his bed when he awakens. In another, titled *Debauchery in the Pub,* Black and white undesirables sit in a makeshift pub with one drunken man lying sprawled underneath a table. Other images in the collection give a sense of the seedy landscape of lower Manhattan where docks, boarding houses, and drinking establishments capitalized on the quick exchange of money by the desperate or disenfranchised.

Port Dance as Cultural Dialogue

In addition to the racy newspapers, other snippets of documentation of multiethnic working-class interactions include broadsides advertising various competitions and lowbrow theatrical events, pointing to the transactional nature of these encounters. Theater scholars will recognize the enduring legacy of dialogic performances in the development of minstrelsy, which claims its origin point in Thomas D. Rice's invention of a "Jim Crow" character, which was a crude commentary on Black presence at the docks. Rice, in one of his narratives about the origin of his "Jim Crow," says he was traveling by ship when his eye was caught by a young Black boy who was tossing coins and catching them on his tongue. The young Black beggar brought his trunk to the theater. There, Rice claims, he took the beggar's clothing to create his own version of a black "Jim Crow." Whether the specifics of the story are true or not, Rice, born in New York and immersed in its polyglot culture, saw racial difference in the Black boy and decided to capitalize on it by depicting his culture. The interplay of "I play you," and "you play me" is a basic for dialogic cultural exchange. Gestural interactions and wordplay, a sort of cultural "dozens," paved the way for offense and distancing, or at times opened common ground for further intercultural explorations.[36]

W. T. Lhamon and others have written extensively about cultural exchange implications of Black men "dancing for eels" in the Catherine Market on the Lower East Side of Manhattan. The popular mid-nineteenth-century dance displays were a marketing tool for vendors on the New York docks to draw patrons to their shops. African American men living on Long Island took the ferry to Manhattan to perform on the street for white passersby who threw coins. "Sailors and roustabouts swapped curses, verses and winks with servants and slaves," Lhamon observed. His work demonstrates how Black street gestures developed by innovative Black performers were "brought into the house and marketed"; white performers using gestural expressions they learned on the docks "shouldered their way onto established stages from The Chatham, The Bowery, and other theatres."[37]

Cultural imitations from Black performers to white appropriators were by no means a one-way exchange. Dances like the quadrille, performed by Blacks in social settings, worked the opposite way. Blacks used floor patterns drawn from French and British social dance in this vernacular dance performance style. Middle-class Blacks wove bowing patterns and steps into their own polyrhythmic social traditions. Dancers, maintaining protocols of European propriety and often clothed in high fashion, merged isolated hip rolls and complex foot patterns with upright torsos. Quadrille dance events, more common in the Caribbean islands, tended to be held on special occasions such as Christmas Day, when these activities were integrated into social balls meant to unify communities across class settings. One interpretation of the cultural impact of quadrille events was that the dances marked the assimilation of Blacks into European aesthetics, but the dances can also be interpreted as a satiric derision of these same aesthetics. As it evolved across the long nineteenth century from a social dance form for the white middle class, to a marker of assimilation for the Creole class, and finally as a national dance for Black citizens of a newly formed island society, the quadrille provides an excellent example of how a dance form can embody both migration and cultural exchange.

Yet the quadrille transcended national boundaries as well, moving around the Atlantic commons to England. In his book *Black Dance in London, 1730–1850*, Rodreguez King-Dorset writes about quadrilles as social dances originating with the French and introduced to London in 1815. Four couples arranged in a square executed floor patterns with their partners. Learning the quadrille, often a part of cotillion dance sets, was time-consuming. "The quadrille was introduced on an aristocratic level, and then spread downward. Far from refining and making the dance more complex, the quadrille was a simpler version of the cotillion, and easier to remember."[38] By the 1850s, the quadrille incorporated polkas, waltzes, and other dances adapted to a square formation for couples. The dance migrated with European settlers, appearing as a social dance for the Creole class in Antigua, Jamaica, and southern plantations in the United States. Fiddles and drums propelled dancers through floor patterns with shifting couple choreography. Black musicians and house servants watched and participated in the imported dance practice. Dance scholar Jacqui Malone chronicles the artistry of Francis Johnson, a Black musician who performed composed music for quadrilles up and down the Eastern Seaboard. The Black fiddler appears in multiple images of port and plantation performance, as if he were a mainstay of white social celebrations. The movie *12 Years a Slave*, based on the memoir by Solomon Northrup, vividly depicts a dance scene where a fiddler is forced to play for a white social dance. Even though Northrup is enslaved, his owners celebrate his musical talents as he plays for the quadrille.[39] King-Dorset describes multiple social events in Antigua where well-dressed house slaves and field slaves dance with one another on Sundays, market days, or Crop Over celebrations, marking the end of the sugar cane season. The festivities are interpreted differently by dance scholars and historians. Accounts of plantation dancers recorded by white observers describe Black performances of quadrilles as poorly executed farcical imitations of their own practices.[40] Ethnomusicologist Dan Neely, however, writing in his dissertation about Jamaica, considers the quadrille a site of evolving cultural exchange where European ballroom forms, popular on the island during the 1860s, lose favor with whites before they become a part of lower-class Black cultural expression. Eventually the dance style mixes with African folk forms to become a new kind of dance called "camp" style quadrille.[41]

The circulation of the quadrille across maritime ports shifted once again as the dance migrated to New York. In November 1858, the *Broadway Omnibus* published a short article about an occurrence at the Water Street Dance House:

On the bench nearest the bar is a fiddler and a tambourine player, each striving to out-do the other in discordant noise. The quadrille sets occupy the floor, the male partners being sailors in blue or red flannel shirts, and the "pimps" and thieves who assist in robbing the poor strangers who are unwary enough to be caught in their toils. The ladies range in age from sixteen to thirty, and they are got up in the "juvenile style" that is with short skirts reaching to the knees, pantalets and slippers with the strings crossed over the foot and tied round the ankle. The waists of their dresses are exceedingly short at the top displaying the whole of the breast and shoulders, making an exhibition disgusting in the extreme to anyone possessing the smallest particle of refinement.

The same dance that represented achievement of social status within Caribbean ports became a marker of the decadence of sailors and pimps in New York City. The voyeur who attended the Brooklyn dance characterized the spectacle as a lascivious display of absurd foolery where male sailors and pimps dance together. Women in the dance are allowed to expose their private parts in a fashion he describes as "juvenile." While the account from the *Broadway Omnibus* observer is quite derogatory, another description of a Black dance in Brooklyn is downright racist. A newspaper entry from *The Sunday Flash* (September 12, 1841) sarcastically reports on a "Grand N***** Ball."

GRAND N***** BALL IN BROOKLYN—Little did the fashionable inhabitants of the great sister city dream, while snoozing in their eider down on the night of the second instant, that an entertainment was going on in the quiet city of Brooklyn, which many would have given their great toes off of their feet to have been present at. . . . the entertainment spoken of was no more or less than a grand ball, got up by a number of the most distinguished white washers, barbers, dog-killers and street sweepers, that is to be found in the colored society of either city. The entertainment was given at Washington Hall, and at ten o'clock, there was a finer gathering of the dingy noblesse than we ever saw before. Music the most ravishing floated in the air; perfume the most *overcoming* stole through it, and such a flashing of paste pins, flirting of underclothes and shaking of black legs was never seen since the day of Jacob's roadside adventure. But the most gratifying site of all was the appearance of a number of white gentlemen who had been favored with tickets, mixing without ostentation or reserve, among the blooming, and in some cases budding damsels of Long Island.

The passage identifies the working-class occupations of the Black men in the dance hall, commenting first on the gaudy attire (perfume and paste pins), then on the presence of white men "slumming" and observing, perhaps participating, in improprieties with the Black women in the room. The style and gaudiness referred to in this description mirror how dress was used in Caribbean settings to differentiate class and status within multicultural settlement communities.

Of course, there was also a legitimate, literary theatrical scene in nineteenth-century New York. The various "racy newspapers" selectively describe some of this activity. Mr. E. Forrest appears at the Broadway Theater on February 21, 1851. Fellows' Minstrel troupe, with performers Orrister and Newcombe, present impersonations of Negro characters in their stage show. Compliments abound for their Rattlesnake Jig and Fling; Ethiopian dance events, the advertisement claims, are "alone worth the price." The Bowery Theatre presents a nautical drama titled *Yankee*. Aztec children are on display at the Society Library Room, corner of Broadway and Leonard Street. The notice suggests "Every white person in the city should visit these two interesting little strangers." And finally, the Fifth Ward Museum at the corner of Franklin Street and Broadway introduces visitors to curiosities "from every clime brought home by seafaring men, officers of the navy and travelers who have been friends to this famous private museum."

New York port thus functioned as an international center for the circum-Atlantic shipping trade—tobacco, cotton, sugar, lumber, immigrants, and the enslaved. Working-class, interethnic cultural exchange in nineteenth-century New York happened in a variety of social settings—from dance competitions to community halls, from street interactions to bar brawls. What is consistent across the settings is the way in which vernacular performance helped to articulate specific cultural frames while also supporting socioeconomic negotiations. Auditory, gestural, and even violent physicality educated the newly arrived sojourners, migrants, and immigrants about how to behave, whom to associate with, and where to find safety. If you were a seaman or an outcast in a port town, there was an easily accessible maritime highway to transport yourself to another cultural setting where your circumstance could, perhaps, improve. One popular endpoint for shipping out was the city of Liverpool in the United Kingdom, a port renowned for its role in manufacturing, financing, and insuring vessels involved in the lucrative slave trade.[42]

Black and Irish in Liverpool

Liverpool city developed rapidly. In 1664, the small village was merely a shipping stop along the rugged western coast of Great Britain. One hundred years later, as the physical infrastructure of the port improved and more sailors migrated into the area, the docks evolved into a multilingual economic hub. Overall, Liverpool ships transported half of the three million Africans carried across the Atlantic by British slavers.[43] Local merchants prospered through the exchange of human cargo for foreign goods, while working-class men excelled at building, sailing, and stocking ships for cross-Atlantic transport, activities that fueled both local and colonial economies. The vibrancy of the trade employed all types of workers—rope makers, service workers at pubs and boarding houses, carpenters, barrel makers, and so on. The result was an intercultural cauldron of peoples coming from varying economic backgrounds who vied with one another for work as laborers.

While Liverpool gained its wealth from its engagement with the slave trade, the city housed a sizable free Black community throughout the nineteenth century. The slave trade provided easy access to Africans who assisted merchants with translation and guide services as well as physical labor.[44] The city also supported isolated communities of British-born freemen in Sailortown (where Jewish, Scandinavian, Filipino, and West African communities intermingled), on Pitt and Stanhope Streets and in the Toxteth neighborhoods.[45] Because community members of varying races labored side by side, performance was used to negotiate difference.

Irish migrating eastward from across the Irish Sea due to famine or lack of opportunity joined the polyglot community as they were recruited to work in textile mills or as dockers.[46] Once settled near the Mersey, they lived side by side with enslaved and free African people. While the shipping industry ensured that Liverpool maintained an active connection with Caribbean and New York ports, workers were also needed in factories further inland where cities like Manchester processed raw cotton and sugar brought in from transatlantic ships docking in Liverpool. Clothing and goods were manufactured in Manchester, and then distributed throughout the United Kingdom. "Liverpool always was a commercial town; it left most of the dirty work of manufacturing to its neighbors."[47] If Liverpool was ocean-facing, then the sister city of Manchester was the land-bound factory town.

"Liverpool, England, where I was born and raised, is or was when I left it some fourteen years ago, the greatest seaport in the world," writes Pat O'Mara in *The Autobiography of a Liverpool Irish Slummy*. O'Mara's colorful autobiography, published in 1933, comments on life in Liverpool between 1901 and 1920. His text vividly describes an interracial and intercultural mixture of, in his words, Negroes, Chinese, Mulattos, Filipinos, and other ethnic communities in Liverpool, expanding upon observations that William Maxon had made in his 1845–46 journal.

> Over there, meandering northward from Whitechapel, just behind the Walker Art Gallery, lies that acme of all British slums, the internationally famous Scotland Road. Midway in this thoroughfare stands Paddy's Market, also internationally known where the refuse of the Empire is bought and sold. Old clothes, old boots, bits of oilcloth, turbans, frayed domestic and foreign underthings—to sell stuff brazen female hawkers seated on the flag-floor lure Coolies, Chinamen, Africa Negroes and other Empire Builders with the consumptive cackle: 'Now, John, ninepence for that coat! Come 'ere! Come 'ere!'[48]

O'Mara's recollections of Liverpool nostalgically romanticize and dramatize port life, while still capturing the sense of commerce that prevailed in the port. The New England sailor Maxon found the Irish washerwomen and the tailor exceptional enough to record in his journal because they served to further his personal cultural education. O'Mara explains that the hired women of Paddy's market specialized in waylaying foreign sailormen and leading them to particular merchants. This performance of welcome and guidance led to a lucrative transaction with an unwary foreign visitor. Similar enticements can be seen today in contemporary cruise ports, as when paid scouts bring preselected passengers to merchants for "deals" on diamonds or watches. O'Mara describes the intermingling of the Irish with other ethnic types in the ports, particularly with Blacks. Cultural groups use performative tactics in these interactions to overcome differences and successfully complete financial transactions.

Other documents in the archive document both friendly performance exchanges and violent conflict between the two ethnic groups. For example, in the New York Draft Riots of 1863 (see chapter 1) Irish longshoremen destroyed Black businesses and murdered Black laborers. Christian DuComb writes in a similar vein about the continuous taunting of Blacks by the Irish in Philadelphia in the nineteenth century during Christmas time.[49] However, violent articulations of interethnic conflict were the most extreme manifestation of tensions that were more often expressed by performances of mimicry and separation. Black and white communities, while living side by side and competing for jobs and resources, also sometimes collaborated. They also frequently imitated one another to both antagonize and learn from one another. Dance battles, wrestling contests, parades—all performance spectacles—helped to differentiate "us from them" while at the same time articulating distinctive identity categories. Difference expressed through performance also helped to negotiate new relationships within and among the communities. The popularity of blackface minstrelsy in Liverpool, primarily described by British historian John Belchem, is an excellent example of how Irish immigrants used performance to differentiate themselves from neighboring Black residents, while upholding Irish-Catholic connections to a community in flux. Blackface performance instilled a sense of whiteness in the performers at a time when the social status of the Irish was considered to be similar (and at times beneath) that of African descendants.

Whiteness studies of Irish heritage generally focus on the mid- to late nineteenth century, a historical period when Irish populations migrated en masse to mainland England and consequently to the United States. The potato famine that ravaged Ireland between 1845 and 1855 was a direct impetus for this relocation. Poor Irish migrants congregated in ghettoes and slums—the North End in Liverpool and Five Points in New York. Liverpool was often the first port-of-call in continuing immigration and emigration of Irish descendants. Even before the advent of the famines of 1846 and 1847, emigrating Irish had turned to Liverpool and the Mersey as a place for unemployed weavers to congregate. Trapped in destitute living conditions, the Irish immigrants strained the resources of Liverpool city officials. In 1834 William Henry Duncan, a physician in the north ward of the city, described the Irish as living in dirty habitations and suffering from illnesses that ran the gamut from rheumatism to lung disease.[50] Without compassion for the dire living circumstances of the Irish, the British characterized them as dirty, filthy, violent, and lacking in moral character.

Liverpool can be viewed as a pivotal social space for transforming Irish identities. From 1815 onwards, their presence was increasingly a subject of comment.[51] Belchem notes that "the Irish were labeled and stigmatized on arrival, victims of prejudice that hindered their prospects on the labor market."[52] Stereotypical representations of the Irish, while fictional, circulated and perpetuated ideas about Irish lifestyles. The Irish, like African Americans in the United States, were associated with rural practices and agricultural communities. Irish were commonly referred to as "n*****s turned inside out," while Blacks were called "smoked Irish." Noel Ignatiev, in his foundational text *How the Irish Became White*, describes how constructs of race were used by the Catholic Irish to move from their status as an oppressed "race" to an oppressing group within the Americas. Nineteenth-century racial notions fixed the Irish at the lowest rung of the Caucasian hierarchy so that "by the 1860s the 'representative Irishman' was to all appearances an anthropoid ape."[53] The real poverty of Irish living conditions was subsumed within these constructions of race. Irish presence within newly formed port communities of the nineteenth century provided a site for the alchemy of racial transformation. Trapped within unsanitary ghettos without food or running water, the two ethnicities, Irish and African, competed for jobs requiring unskilled labor. They drank and caroused together, and gave birth to mixed-race children, who further confused the racial categories designed by British and American social codes. Once again, O'Mara provides a vivid portrait of what this might have been like.

> Most of my early life was spent on Brick Street, a street of abominably overcrowded shacks nearby. Negroes, Chinese, Mulattoes, Filipinos, almost every nationality under the sun, most of them boasting white wives and large half-caste families were our neighbors, each color laying claim to a certain street.[54]

He maintains that the white women chose men of color as partners because of the men's economic status. He tells a story of a Negro man named Galley Johnson who worked as a ship's stoker and married two Irish women before retiring from the sea to run a boarding house.[55] Even if exaggerated, O'Mara's description points to continuing economic and social negotiations between Blacks and Irish as job opportunities shifted.

In both England and the United States, social codes and legal restrictions isolated Black and Irish sea workers from mainstream culture, with regulations that chose not to distinguish between the "filth" of its lowest class citizens.[56] In New York, zoning codes isolated neighborhoods like Five Points, while in Liverpool, specific sections of the city, such as Liverpool 8, became associated with distinctive ethnic communities. As poverty persisted, how were the Irish to socially advance and overcome their racial stigma? Penal codes prevented them from voting, holding public office, or living within the boundaries of incorporated towns.[57] Progressive movement toward social acceptance was a fraught path for the new settlers. Where the transplanted "white Negroes" and real Negroes rubbed shoulders and competed for resources, regulatory codes and social stigmas against both ethnic populations became nearly indistinguishable. Stigmatized but not subjugated, the

Irish, especially in Liverpool, were far from passive victims of such prejudice. Performance was a strategic, vernacular way of publicly demonstrating the differences between the two immigrant groups.

John Belcham in his book *Irish, Catholic and Scouse* describes the popularity of minstrel performance within the community halls of Liverpool.[58] Irish entertainers performed songs and dances that drew from the repertory of Black performance, yet ridiculed and inverted the forms into comedy. Father Nugent's League Hall, for example, offered cheap entertainment to Irish laborers during the 1880s. There, fishmongers, butchers, bakers, and merchants could see artists who made their fame performing with troupes like Sam Hague's minstrel show. Irish jigs and "negro absurdities," fiddlers and sketches aimed to keep Irishmen out of the pubs and better connected to their history and heritage. In an earlier essay, Belcham explains how "the minstrel format . . . provided the means to replace and render obsolete the "stage Irishman," to attract and promote reform among a population of "low Irish." He implies that Irish workers and entertainers deliberately performed African Americans as clownish buffoons in order to enhance their self-esteem, by ridiculing a class that actually resided near and often intermarried with their own.

> Blackface minstrelsy enabled the Irish to confirm their whiteness while at the same time, however, asserting their "ethnic" difference. In a bewildering process of cultural and commercial fusion and borrowing, "negro entertainment" spread beyond the professional stage to become the main attraction in the lecture halls and meeting rooms of Irish and Catholic associational culture.[59]

Black performers countered stereotypical performances with their own artistic productions staged in and around Liverpool. Two clear examples of this are challenge dances organized around William Henry Lane (also known as Master Juba), and the touring repertory of Ira Aldridge. Both of these free African American artists defected to the United Kingdom during the mid-nineteenth century—Aldridge with a repertory of Shakespeare and classical texts, and Lane with a dance competition act that featured both drag and imitative performances. I consider their performances an intervention in racist representations of Blacks as ignorant or disempowered performers. Aldridge appeared in Liverpool in 1827 and presented himself in a series of performances at the Theatre Royale. In January, he played the comic role of the slave Mungo in the play *The Padlock*. In October, he changed audience perceptions by performing the noble Othello in Shakespeare's *Othello* and Hassan, a lover, in the romance *The Castle Spectre*. Later that month, he again shifted gears, embodying Gambia in *The Slave* and the role of Zanga in the Spanish revenge play *The Revenge*. By playing multiple types of roles in the same venue, Aldridge was able to humanize both himself and his characters.[60]

William Henry Lane also played with representation. He first performed in England in 1849 when he toured London with Richard Pell's *Ethiopian Serenaders*. He was an exceptional star dancer who had gained notoriety for his challenge dances against John Diamond in New York and Boston.[61] His presence as a Black performer within a white minstrel troupe was remarkable. Lane demonstrated his versatility as a performer and an artist by performing a dance act in which he ridiculed the styles of each of his previous dance competitors in a single dance number. He was also a comic who created a female character, Miss Lucy Long, who would ridicule her fellow performers with broad humor and wit.[62] Despite Aldridge's and Lane's efforts to depict themselves as multifaceted performers, audiences and the press continued to characterize them as uniquely talented performers representing a sub-substandard race. James Cook describes how Lane decided to leave his white manager, Richard Pell, and go it alone as a self-managing Black entrepreneur. At that point, he found himself the target of racialized resentment in Manchester, and his performances began to disappear from public view.[63]

About twenty years later, in 1866, another producer attempted to tour African American performers in Liverpool. Hoping to build upon the successes of the "real negro impersonator" companies in the United States, Mr. Hague decided to bring his troupe of emancipated African Americans, Mr. Hague's Slave Troupe of Georgia Minstrels, to the city. The results were disastrous. When they traveled to Liverpool in 1866, the Black entertainers were not well received. Even though a new trend of incorporating Blacks or "real negro impersonators" had gained traction in the United States, the heavily Irish city of Liverpool preferred to see white actors ridiculing African behaviors and mannerisms. Hague eventually fired his Black actors, leaving several behind to become integrated into the Black Liverpudlian community.[64]

Nineteenth-century minstrelsy and its performance had different meanings on each side of the Atlantic Ocean. While U.S. and Cuban minstrelsy, in some ways, offered variance in its portrayal of Black culture,[65] Black minstrelsy in England reflected and commented upon a distant and exotic social "type." Entrepreneurs like Sam Hague who understood working-class aesthetics and the need for clear cultural distinctions between Blacks and the Irish were able to capitalize on their cultural literacy and accommodate to shifting social environments for their acts. Liverpool might have been a preferred ending point for African American travelers seeking to better their socioeconomic circumstance, but for Irish travelers, like those who were fed uncooked "Indian" meal by sailor William Maxon, leaving Liverpool was a better choice for social advancement. The British city, teeming with Irish farmers migrating away from the potato famine, was decidedly racist toward its Irish immigrants. For those citizens, a maritime journey away from Europe and across the waters to the Caribbean or America was an opportunistic migration. However, for African American citizens moving away from slavery, Liverpool was a fugitive refuge.

Considering how working-class men and women negotiated identities through performance during the nineteenth century provides an analytical frame for discussion of embodied performance practices in twenty-first-century ports. Ports where ships dock still function as cosmopolitan transactional zones for economic and cultural exchange. Economic and social positions still shift when travelers get off of a ship after spending time at sea. Consequently, modes of performance—busking and street trading—continue to manifest at maritime sites. Cruise ship ports today continue to function as performative settings as vibrant as Jamaica and Liverpool were during the nineteenth century. When megaships dock, releasing thousands of tourists with money, human-to-human transactional encounters are plentiful. Island locals transform from church women into lascivious Caribbean vixens, especially if it means the ship's passengers, be they midwestern construction workers or New York City brokers, will throw dollars and buy diamonds. Theatrics, formal and informal, continue to define cruise ship port transactional zones.

Tourist Ports

This section begins with ethnographic descriptions of Caribbean resident interactions with cruise ship patrons at three distinctive ports: Roatán, Honduras; Philipsburg, St Maarten: and Puerto Plata in the Dominican Republic. At each of these ports, local Caribbean residents perform scenes from local folklore to accommodate tourist imaginations about who they are. The last two discussions of the section focus on tourist sites where residents express more nuanced responses to cultural tourism. I briefly illustrate how articulations of Black identities at carnivals and museum sites demonstrate Afro-Caribbean people managing their own identity formations through strategic interactions with island visitors.

Roatán

Roatán, Honduras. The pilot boats have finished guiding the cruise ship into its slot of the extended pier at Coxen Hole. This island, once an extension of Honduras's Banana Coast, now markets scuba diving and snorkeling trips along the barrier reef. The cruise ship company Royal Caribbean owns the pier; therefore, it can control access and select appropriate activities for the guests. Today, as the passengers disembark, a collective of dancers dressed in traditional Garinagú regalia greet the guests by playing drums and dancing shuffling steps slightly reminiscent of the ceremonial *punta* dancing that characterizes Black Carib culture. Roatán once hosted British pirates who raided ships sailing out of the Spanish colonies. Later, the United Fruit Company built railroads on the nearby Mosquito Coast of Honduras and Nicaragua, displacing the Black Carib settlers. Some of the Garinagú moved north to Belize, while others settled further down the coast in less accessible villages. In the current millennium, dancing Garífuna port performers differ little from their predecessors who might have entertained early tourists. A 1927 advertisement for the Great White Fleet, a commercial ocean carrier in the region, depicts Black people carrying baskets of fruits on their heads as they welcome passengers landing in dinghies from a great white ship. Today the Garífuna dancers similarly carry baskets on their heads as they demonstrate ethnic artistry. I can easily see through the artifice of the performance. The dancers execute the more energetic dance steps between 9 and 10 a.m. as the bulk of the passengers disembark. They collect tips and other financial offerings in a painted red pail. If anyone wants to take a picture, they pay more. Later in the day, the performers will sporadically hit the drum once or twice if it looks as if a passenger might be inclined to donate.

The Afro-Caribbean ensemble includes two or three women and a couple of men so that the performers can trade off. No one wants to exert themselves too much in the midday heat. I'm not sure what the dancers do when they leave the port. This dance performance is an adaptation of their life to accommodate port trade—the busk. Tourists see them as a welcoming exotic treat to consume before they head off to snorkel the reef. The Garífuna are also transient and migratory. They stay connected to transnational communities in New York and other parts of the United States. The Bronx has the largest community of Garífuna outside of their Central American villages. The performers I see today might next week be in New York, helping an aunt or uncle manage another business. Maritime economies require managing the ebb and flow of the port performers who entertain on island shores.

The Garífuna performers are not the only ones who benefit from cruise ship traffic—they are part of a wide network of local entrepreneurs who trade with cruise clientele.

St Maarten

A port like Philipsburg in St Maarten has back-to-back shops lined with jewelry stores advertising diamonds, emeralds, gold, and Rolex watches. Individual proprietors hawk souvenirs or offer tourist services; all are involved in selling some aspect of island resources. This port trade differs little from port activities of earlier centuries. Instead of slaves and sugar, contemporary ports offer island delights and rum. The multilingual nature of the various islands offered possibilities for Creole residents, enslaved populations, and transient maritime workers to interact and develop modes of presentation incorporating multiple cultural aesthetics.

Both historically and in contemporary practice, Caribbean port entrepreneurs take advantage of tourists' stereotypical expectations of what warm waters and island "natives" can offer. In some ways, contemporary ports replicate and recirculate the same exotic tropes of earlier centuries. A 1939 poster of a Royal Mail Lines cruise displays brown bodies and placid waters as a woman carries her fruits to sell on the beach. The woman, dressed in a folkloric red headdress, blends into the landscape of sun and surf as if she were a part of West Indies commerce. In another example, vendors from the island of St Maarten sell Guavaberry liqueur, also known as Old Man Guavaberry Brand or Original Wild Island Folk Liqueur. The bottle label displays two familiar archetypes: an old grizzled Black man who looks like Uncle Remus, and a young barefoot Black woman in a colorful plaid headwrap with a matching brightly colored plaid dress. The woman smiles invitingly, visually inviting the viewer to experience both her ethnicity and the sugar-based product as tourist products. The marketing of Guavaberry liqueur demonstrates the continuing dependence on ethnic imagery to boost Caribbean sales. These representations and performances of Black, island exoticism work together to fulfill tourist expectations about the Caribbean. Consequently, island entrepreneurs, especially performers, capitulate to tourist expectations in order to bring home dollars.

If the expression of such exotic, folkloric charm is a warm enticing foreplay for a newcomer to the Caribbean, then the hard-driving act of commerce is the main event. Much as they did across the nineteenth century, proprietors invest in housing for international guests, today in the form of hotels,

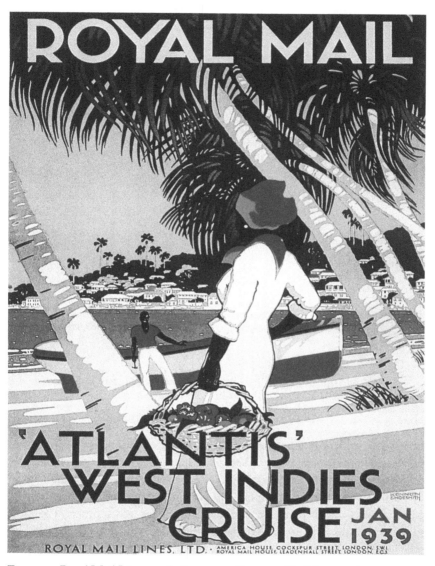

Figure 29. Royal Mail Lines marketing poster for a 1939 Caribbean cruise.

Figure 30. Marketing photo in St Maarten for Guavaberry liqueur.

timeshares, or boarding houses. They try to sell these products to cruise vacationers. Entertainment venues like bars or gambling houses (casinos) spawn sideline sex services, advertised clandestinely, which appeal to the unattached. Local tour agencies can transport and entertain large groups of cruise ship passengers as they explore local sites. Local guides add a different kind of spice to the island experience and are able to explain the nuances of history and culture. Sometimes the ship's enrichment and entertainment staff, including the destination lecturer, will accompany the guests on the excursions to ensure the continuity of the onboard experience. The most common excursions are to beaches or on sailing trips; however, bus or adventure tours are also popular.

Cruise companies are concerned about how passengers are treated once they arrive at the destinations, and some, like Royal Caribbean, build simulacra islands. Labadee, Haiti, a private cruise resort, exemplifies this setup. The

Figure 31a and 31b. Scenes at the Puerto Plata Taino Bay Cruise Terminal in the Dominican Republic, November 2022. Photo by the author.

"island" is really a peninsula located on the northern shore of Haiti where all of the amenities of the ship are available onshore. When passengers disembark in Labadee, the same cruise entertainers that performed on the boat move to the corporate-owned *palapa*[66] to play steel drums while guests water ski within the protected bay. The waiters who are working that day have an opportunity to spend time outside setting up a beach barbecue and serving drinks as the passengers collect their food from the buffet. As a gesture to the local culture, the cruise company invites a troupe of sanctioned Haitian dancers to present a fire show in the *palapa*. But the cruise companies cannot completely control the way that passengers interact with local cultures.

Puerto Plata

At some ports, local government tourist or cultural agencies stage their own performances of ethnicity to appeal to cruise industry and tourist expectations that the islands be friendly, inviting, clean, and folkloric. In 2022 I traveled to Puerto Plata in the Dominican Republic and was astonished to see how the pier and its shopping mall had been reimagined. The Taino Bay Cruise Terminal completed construction in November 2020, just before COVID-19 stalled the cruise industry for almost two years.[67] Many islands used the tourist-free time of the pandemic as an opportunity to complete infrastructure projects that would improve conditions for vacationers once the tourist trade resumed.[68]

This stunning port was adorned for the holiday season with Christmas trees and hanging baubles that looked like oversized holiday decorations. Next to the large sign identifying the destination as Taino Bay stood masked dancers wearing giant indigenous headdresses with cowry shells running the length of the dancer's leggings. I wasn't sure which cultural iconographies they were referencing, but it all looked stereotypically savage. Sounds of merengue music wafted toward me and I could soon see its source. Two conga players were drumming to a recorded version of a merengue song, and they waved at me. Next to them stood a female "greeter" with bare shoulders and a very short folkloric dress (covered with a service apron) waving at me. Next to her was Santa Claus seated in a chair with a giant nutcracker placed next to him. I wondered if I was in the North Pole, or at the Spanish Caribbean beach island I was expecting. I declined the pro-offered photo opportunity to pose with Santa and the woman and moved further into the port.

    A shopping plaza about the length of a football field and featuring Caribbean goods—rum and beach wear, Hawaiian shirts and flip flops—greeted me. My goal was to reach the taxi stands where a tour excursion of a "real-life Dominican coffee farm" awaited me. Of all of the tours offered by the cruise ship, this promised to be the most culturally enriching, as I had just lectured about coffee plantations and Taino culture. The addition of the farm tour to shore activities was likely a response to cruise passenger interest in more immersive experiences.[69] We traveled to a family home on about three acres where three generations of residents were farming cacao and coffee. Our tramp through the two-bedroom home felt invasive to me, although the residents had placed family photographs and artifacts throughout to create the feeling of rustic living. One building over, I could see that the family had gathered around a more modern concrete structure, perhaps built with funding from their new tourist engagements. I encouraged the passengers on this tour, who seemed afraid of the dark-skinned hosts, to purchase as many local items as possible since this might be a once-in-a-lifetime opportunity. Immersive port cultural experiences, while staged, give cruise vacationers an opportunity for limited experiences with local artisans, performers, and vendors. Without them the travelers on cruise circuits would be exposed to the life and lifestyles of Caribbean islanders only through my PowerPoint slides.

    Lately, I have begun to embrace my role as a destination lecturer because it helps to bridge two conflicting realities for the passengers. There is a disjunction between the land they will walk on and the histories of the people who survive and derive sustenance from the islands. Cruise passengers generally experience only beaches, jewelry shopping, or perhaps a ruin of a

Figure 32. An exhibit at the Kura Hulanda Museum in Curaçao.

plantation. The spectacle of the ship will have mesmerized them into forgetting that they were traveling to a destination. When they return home, their friends will ask—"How was your cruise?" For most, the answer will be that the food was fantastic, the service was wonderful, and the beaches had good chairs. As the cruise industry adapts to climate change and health pandemics, the entertainment bubble their passengers inhabit becomes even more restrictive, and guests are encouraged to limit their interactions to sanctioned spectacles approved by the cruise lines. These curated excursions do little to expand island economies. Within the mediated spectacle of cruise ship entertainment, I am able to educate about the histories and cultural practices of islands the passengers will never really experience. On board the ship, cruise worker interactions with passengers may provide the most intimate opportunities for cross-cultural encounters. I hope this isn't true, because the crafted nature of onboard entertainment ensures that international workers from the Global South will assume a position of deference to the wealthier, traveling middle-class passengers who purchase cruise ship excursions. This only reinforces performances of servitude that already prevail within the multicultural immersive cruise experience.

Black in Port

My experiences traveling as a Black destination lecturer are mediated by my own positionality as an African American Black woman. As I mentioned earlier, most Caribbean islands are primarily Black. When I disembark from a cruise ship to catch a tour or go shopping, port agents and vendors usually respond to our common blackness with a look, a wave—sometimes a question like "So, where are you from?" I'm clearly a tourist, but Black responses shift slightly when Black folks in port recognize and assist me. At times, narratives of local events are communicated with a little more sarcasm or salt or a knowing side-eye. Often Black tour guides and I enjoy "you know what I mean" moments, especially when visiting monuments celebrating Black histories or experiences. For example, I toured the Kura Hulanda Museum in Curaçao, a sparsely visited island history museum dedicated to African history and the African American slave trade on the island. After walking through the mostly vacant indoor and outdoor exhibits, I asked the Black museum guide why there were so many Benin headdresses and African ceremonial items on display. She responded, "The owner had them." I asked, "How did he get so many valuable items?" She responded, "They stole them." There wasn't much need for further conversation. She suggested I be sure to visit the slave trade part of the exhibition.

This part of the museum, housed in a separate building with minimal air conditioning, had rusty chains once used on enslaved Africans on display everywhere. Hundreds of chains hung against walls, casually secured with nails or wooden pegs. Next to the chains were torture devices: iron neck grips with nasty-looking spikes extending out nine inches in four different directions; mouth braces used to punish enslaved Africans who refused to eat. Anyone could touch or try out the devices by picking them up and placing them on hands or wrists or ankles. In one corner of one of the rooms, there was an entire trunk full of rusty chains, all artifacts dug up or left behind on Curaçao by the Dutch East India Tea Company's slave trade. And at the end of the building, a steep isolated ladder descended into a wooden structure, the imported hull of a wooden sailing ship which was embedded into the floor of the museum. The rounded space contained a section of two bunks removed from the inside of a vessel.

I have seen reconstructed slave ships at other museums. I experienced the Middle Passage immersive media exhibit at the Liverpool Slavery Museum, for example, where a continuous video loop flashes close-up images of a reenactment of what the enslaved would have experienced below deck. The

Liverpool exhibit, with its depictions of blood and drool, was horrific, but the Curaçao exhibit was even more impactful. The dusty hull of the ship was actual size—small—perhaps ten feet across. The bunk space was three feet high and stained with splotches. Dim lighting magnified the effect of the hot and stuffy air. Laid out across each deck of the two-tier bunk were more segments of rusty chains held in place by additional iron mounts. The exhibit appeared not to replicate a slave ship, but to be an in-situ relocation of an actual slave ship. There was no adornment in this wooden hull once used for keeping captured cargo enclosed. Visitors were able to sit in the wooden cavities and place their feet inside of chains actually used by slave traders on the island. After exiting the exhibit and entering the fresh air, I passed by the museum admissions desk on the way out. The Black woman running the desk asked how I liked the museum. I said, "There are a lot of chains." She responded, with a single word: "Yeah."

The chains of the past, the extractive nature of Caribbean histories impact both of us. I am guiding tourists who want to see beaches, not slave museums. The woman at the desk is working in a service role educating foreign visitors about subjects that are uncomfortable to them. We both hope that Black histories and Black lives will matter to our primarily white audiences who have purportedly traveled to engage with island cultures. But this is a port, and most likely our traveling publics will add this island to their checklist of visited destinations and purchase some bauble at the official cruise ship mall to remind themselves of where they have been. In this way, Caribbean cruise ports differ substantially from historical merchant trade ports of the nineteenth century. In the past, port landings and interactions were tied to personal engagements and negotiations with individual players. Today's port exchanges between cruise tourists and local residents are corporate and extractive. The largest economic profits flow to corporate entities and island governments. Even though there are opportunities for individuals and small-scale businesses to earn cash or participate in the tourist trade, economic deals are brokered in offices, not on the docks.

Carnival Practices

The Carnival—the enduring ethnic parade that brings income and recognition to Caribbean communities throughout the Americas. Many have written about the spectacle's impact in Trinidad, Barbados, Cuba, Bermuda, and other island nations.[70] Carnival originated as a Catholic colonial celebration of the beginning of Lent. Derived from the Latin phrase *carne levare*, or releasing oneself from the flesh, carnival was a chance for adherents to engage in excess before restricting bodily pleasures in preparation for the arrival of Christ. Carnival, in the Americas, allowed African descendant and indigenous people to reference vernacular spiritual practices through public masked events. By impersonating political and religious figures, and boldly wearing colorful and sometimes frightening attire, the enslaved were able to subvert social codes through public street performance. What interests me is the carnival's evolution from a march through the streets to establish African and Indian diaspora presence to a tourist attraction for foreign visitors seeking rebellious inversion of societal norms. Lyndon Gill describes the sense of exotic play engendered by the carnival, an embodied experience that in some ways parallels maritime play of the nineteenth century: "A fetish of misplaced and mistaken desires across various geographies and intimacies across, the Caribbean region itself—these affected Antilles identities—are a hundreds-of-years-old allegory for the frighteningly tangible effects of a complicated desire that both circumscribes the region and compels."[71] While carnival presents itself as representative of discrete island histories or heritages, it has always been a contested space where African and queer epistemologies brush up against religious restrictions and mannered norms of European colonial societies. Because the forms are hybrid responses invented by local communities, they resist generalized interpretation by outsiders unfamiliar with the island's community cultures. At the same time, carnival forms are a palette for outsiders to reinstate exotic imagery, find an excuse for engaging in excess, or perhaps to invest in their own expressive, embodied response to carnival song and dance.

Caribbean artists who participate in carnival reformulate performance styles and design regalia to express personal experiences. Expressive gestures—the flip of a wrist or the controlled undulation of a hip—amplify personal choices and identity associations. Dance scholar Yvonne Daniel effectively codifies and analyzes the intricacy of specific gestural acts in her book *Caribbean and Atlantic Diaspora Dance: Igniting Citizenship*.[72] Using analytical models from dance and anthropology, she details relationships between politics and performance styles in Cuba, Jamaica, and Brazil.

> You step into the anarchy of the streets; out of the crowd a ruffian appears in face paint, dreadlocks adorned with mismatched feathers and other suspicious-looking items, and a t-shirt adorned with a phrase ending in an exclamation point. The youth shouts threats in a language quite removed from your high school French or Portuguese,

or your native English or Spanish. He dances about until you hand him a five-dollar bill. If you look genuinely baffled and give him nothing, he flashes a smile and throws a handful of harmless red powder over you, and then darts away in search of another victim. . . . This is the essential Carnivalesque experience, the metaphoric challenge to quotidian rules, the mocking or satirical challenge to authority and to traditional social order.[73]

Her dance description captures the audacity of carnival performance within the cultural contexts of Caribbean islands. Each island nation's annual carnival performance discretely and distinctively promotes local communities and their politics. Dancers and community organizers deliberately honor their most talented or influential by naming them carnival kings or queens. Local practitioners and visual artists develop their craft throughout the year and vie for public recognition of their artistry during carnival season. All of these complex negotiations within local island communities are frequently interpreted as outlandish, spectacular display by tourists who have had minimal contact with island cultures. Cruise ship entertainment staff reimagine the rich cultural forms of Black-inspired carnival events and repurpose them to promote colorful exoticism throughout shipboard carnival events. Entertainment staff jump up and down to heart-racing carnival music to remind guests that the ship is traveling through the Caribbean basin. Restaurant staff develop meals with carnival themes, and the onboard store sells carnival accessories throughout the journey. For those crew members born on Caribbean islands, the funhouse mirror of cruise ship carnival perverts their traditions.

SNAPSHOT #3: Carnival Night and Alex in Port

Flashback—It's "Carnival Night" on the cruise ship and the ship is hosting an onboard rooftop party. With the COVID-19 virus ravaging the world, passengers can't interact with real islanders, so cruise staff are staging a themed extravaganza on the top deck next to the pool. Alex, who plays the steel pans as a solo act, is warming up the crowd in preparation for the entrance of the whole entertainment staff music ensemble who will join with a choreographed routine. Meanwhile, the bar staff is passing around free drinks in tall glasses to celebrate the invented special occasion. All guests were asked to wear white to better reflect the brightly colored lighting that will paint us with blue, yellow, purple, and red hues when the music gets rhythmic.

But first the cruise ship dance ensemble performs a short dance for us. It looks to me like a combination of modern dance turns and leg extensions mixed with Las Vegas formations of undulating lines and coordinated fanning of extended arms. At one point, an embodied rhythm pulses down the line of posing dancers who spread their arms wide to create a collaborative fan. When the choreographed dance ends, it's time to party.

The music accelerates and we—the guests—all wave our arms, shouting about what a great time we are having. As the live band recedes, we hear the familiar music of Bruno Mars. Activity staff member Carlos takes over and leads us in a line dance. It's the Cupid Shuffle.[74] Most of us know how to do this well. I enthusiastically perform flourishes within the phrase—extra knee wiggles and double-time foot shuffles. Alex, the steel pan player, inspired by my enthusiasm, joins in. Now the white outfits glow against the sweaty skin of the undulating crowd. We are celebrating carnival in high style. The event lasts exactly one hour, and then most people go to bed. The cruise ship has deftly captured the most spectacular elements of the Caribbean carnival without the community investment in creating a cultural event based upon history and heritage. Instead, we have danced together and sweated together without learning anything at all about island cultures. Later I have a more intimate encounter with Alex the steel pan player and he tells me how he feels about Castries, St. Lucia, the island port town that is his homeland.

The following morning I'm having breakfast in the cafeteria on the top floor of the cruise ship. We are in Castries, where the ship has just docked at a pier where the view from the upper deck overlooks the picturesque bay. The steel drum player whose rhythms have brought carnival sounds to the ship asks if he can join me. He's having poached eggs with hollandaise sauce over spinach and smoked salmon layered on top of an English muffin. A few floors below guests are dining on the same food in a much fancier dining room. Alex sits and I greet him. After a few moments, he says: "I'm back home you know." I'm confused. "St. Lucia"? He responds: "This is my home. My town is right up there on the hill." Both of us crane our heads to look out of the cafeteria windows and up the hillside. Alex tells me that he joined the ship after working as an elementary school teacher on the island. He played and studied with steel pan orchestras growing up and throughout high school and college. He went on the ship to earn money for graduate school. For a while he started teaching on the island again, but the pay was not as good as the pay on the ships and the school was not as well organized. He was accepted into graduate school at the University of the West Indies. But one day, before he filed his registration papers, he spoke with one of the graduates

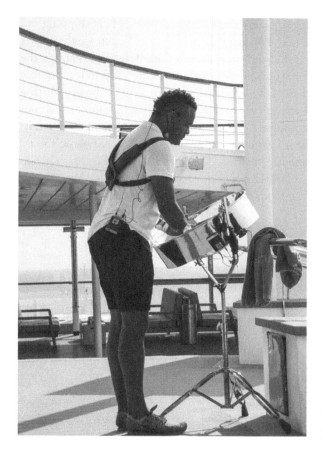

Figure 33. Steel pan player Al Alexander

from the master's program in music and asked the program alumni what he was going to do with his degree. The graduate asked Alex if he could help him play on cruise ships. Discouraged, Alex decided not to pursue professional arts training in music.

Now Alex has a new dream. He wants to open a tourist attraction on the island in his village: a botanical garden where visitors can learn about island culture and see the beauty of the vegetation. Maybe spend some time learning about the rich history of St. Lucia. I suggest that business school might be the best way forward. He agrees. With management training, owning a business and learning to profit from tourist dollars might be productive and emotionally fulfilling. He says maybe then he could train other musicians to work as ensembles on cruise ships. I encourage Alex to follow the advice of Karl Marx and own the means of production. Alex has been cruising and playing the steel drum on ships for about a decade now. He is shipping out hoping to make it back home. We are at his home now. We can see the streets he used to walk and play on. From our seats in the cafeteria we can see the school where he used to teach. But Alex can't get off the ship today. Because of the COVID-19 pandemic, all ship workers must stay on board. With a heavy heart, I tell Alex I am getting off the ship today and taking a bus tour of the island (managed completely by the cruise ship). "OK," he says. "Mention my name and maybe someone will remember me." "What name should I use?," I ask him. He responds: "Just say Alex the steel pan player says hello." We finish the eggs. I get off the ship. No one has time to discuss Alex and his instrument because they are working too hard to make tips before the ship leaves port.

Coda

Improvisations and Cultural Reflections

My coda describes a series of encounters on cruise ships that evolved into moments of improvisation at sea. I have written extensively about the ship as a space where culture and meaning shift for those on board. But as in all venues of performance, there are times when one must improvise. When things go wrong on a ship, the superficial façades of social structures are upended. Mechanisms behind the coordinated entertainment spectacle of the cruise become visible. In particular, the crew responds differently. For passengers, being at sea can be a fantasy and many engage in living out previously unattainable dreams, even if only in their imaginations. The cruise enables both passengers and crew members to enact moments of nostalgia with delight. I sometimes wonder why people choose to stay at sea, but when I see the joyful way in which people live in the alternative universe of the ship, I understand. These brief vignettes illustrate some of the improvisational moments I have observed or participated in on the ship, highlighting the fantasies and the reflections they evoke. The improvisational moments reveal the true liminality of the seascape and highlight the significance of social exchange and the performance of self. Improvisation exposes the performative nature of the ship at sea.

When Things Go Wrong

Time

When you cruise on a ship, time becomes decoupled from customary schedules or routines. Staff alter time to match upcoming destinations and to smoothly guide passengers from ship activity time frames to shore activity time frames. This becomes somewhat complex when Caribbean cruises transition across geographic time zones or when various nations observe different conventions of when to change from daylight savings time to standard time. In a similar manner, travelers taking transatlantic cruises shift their clocks across five or six hours of time. In either case, it is important for passengers to know when to change the clocks, because this will affect when they attend programmed activities on board. Housekeeping crew members and engineering staff facilitate this by changing public clocks and sometimes resetting bedside clocks in cabins to match the correct ship time. On a recent cruise, the system failed. The housekeeping staff, the engineering staff, and the entertainment staff did not coordinate with one another regarding which days to shift the clocks. Passengers, responding to the daily planner (a printed schedule published by the entertainment staff), awakened an hour early and arrived to the destination lecture, only to sit in an empty theater wondering what went wrong. The hall clocks broadcast a time that did not match the cabin clocks. Meanwhile, the restaurants refused to serve breakfast to the wakeful passengers, because the kitchen staff were adhering to a later time schedule. A disruption of time also disrupts passenger abilities to settle and plan, distancing then from land-based structures and encouraging them to improvise new ways of responding to slippery time frames. Their experience differs from the crew members who become accustomed to the fluidity of time and space. Such incidents of temporal dislocation are uncomfortable for passengers who travel on the ship for only a limited time, yet they help the guests to adjust to the spontaneity of ship life and inculcate them into the necessary improvisations of sea activities. A fluidity of time in some way creates a fluidity of thought where new ideas percolate, ready to be explored.

No Port

Cruise ships change itineraries more than you expect. Even though destinations are announced and passengers pay to travel to specific locales, it doesn't always work out. Sometimes the weather whips up the waves and prevents tender boats or port piers from functioning. Sometimes there are immigration or medical restrictions (this happened frequently during the COVID-19 pandemic) that won't allow passengers to disembark. When this occurs, the captain will simply add another sea day or occasionally shift to another port, a process that disrupts timing and planning for all cruise ship guests. Those who complain are asked to accept the new itinerary or book another cruise in order to access the missed port. These instances of missed ports underscore the fragility of the ship at sea and the limited controls cruise operators have over nature's impacts. Under these circumstances, it is even more important to acknowledge that the vacation is more about the ship than the destination.

Slow Food

Chapter 2 discussed how the dining room with its sympotic space becomes one of the primary locations where passengers spend their time. When it rains, or when limits are placed on ship activities because of weather, guests tend to head for food venues. Most ships no longer have assigned dinner times for guests, and, consequently, an open seating arrangement means diners can choose to eat dinner any time between 6:00 p.m. and 9:00 p.m. Even so, this is a limited time frame for dining room staff to accommodate 2,000 or more guests. As a result, food service sometimes backs up. Under those circumstances, the serving staff must move into overdrive. The orderly division of hostesses, headwaiters, sommeliers, and associate waiters breaks down and everyone does whatever is necessary to quickly bring the food out to the clientele. Surprisingly, I have seen uniformed first mates and engineering staff who were dining with guests jump up and serve platters to ensure that the façade of excellent food service was maintained. Like good team players on a theatrical production, everyone chips in to deliver the promised dining entertainment.

Finding Your Fantasy

On the Dance Floor

Elderly couples sometimes dance in the central rotunda where the staircase meets the main corridor floor, waltzing and turning in sequined dresses with sturdy heels. When I see them, I recognize how easily the cruise creates an improvisational performative space for clients to immerse themselves in activities difficult to do on shore. It's a safe and convenient walk from the cabin to the cruise atrium, one that can be managed with aching legs and unsure steps. When senior guests join a cruise, they are easily able to participate in physical activities like partner dancing. The romance of dancing to a Frank Sinatra song accompanied by a string quartet might continue into the tea room, where the couple will be able to sit and sip from a fancy ceramic cup. For some, this might be the realization of a lifelong or adolescent dream come true, a dream that can easily manifest in the immersive seascape of the cruise.

Bossa Nova

I traveled on a long cruise with another destination lecturer who in his youth played the guitar. He was a regular lecturer, meaning that he spent more than half of his year lecturing on back-to-back cruises. On this particular voyage, he decided to live out his fantasy of playing bossa nova with a backup band, so he convinced musicians from the entertainment team to join him in an educational musical set where he lectured about the bossa nova while the staff singers and the cruise ship band demonstrated riffs from bossa nova songs. My co-lecturer could barely play the guitar, but he left the event beaming. Through his cruise ship event, he was able to improvise within the structures of the destination lecturer role and revisit his youthful experience of performing, only this time he played before a full-house audience in the fantasy world of the ship. I think that many performers on cruises also experience this joy. The cruise ship provides seemingly endless opportunities for both guests and passengers to improvise with different identities and skill sets. Comedians, and even cruise directors, have guaranteed audiences when they perform on ships. If they are regulars, they can experiment with new routines or new character types.

Connections

On my most recent journey, I reported for work only to learn that the associate cruise director, who was my direct supervisor, went to the same high school in Flemington, New Jersey, that I attended. This was an odd moment. We were both theater students (albeit during different years) and we had studied under the same drama teacher. He had moved into comedy and television, perfecting a character similar to Groucho Marx that he used as his cruise performance persona. Under this guise, he had developed a hornpipe dance where he impersonated a sailor. While I had become Dr. Anita, the cruise ship lecturer, he had become the awkward physical comedian who dances the hornpipe. Responding to this unusual circumstance, we together agreed to play in hyperbole by creating a special event in our unique environment. We would have a sea shanty sing-in with the passengers, and he would show me his infamous hornpipe. My schoolmate reserved the top-floor lounge for our special midday event, and ship guests attended. We sang and danced and shared a moment of collective fantasy about who-we-could-have-been-if-we-were-sailors. It was magical. Exploring this imaginative world was uniquely possible because we were at sea and away from traditional theater structures of tickets and audiences, venues and auditions. Both of us understood the ship as a play space for experimentation where we could "try out" theatrical innovations without censure. Of course, the experience ended when we arrived at the last port. We waved (hugs would have broken the maritime codes) knowing we will probably never meet again.

Death and Dying

Cruising appeals to senior citizens who sometimes have limited mobility. Once you get onto a ship, there is no need to unpack bags or take public transportation in order to see miraculous sites around the globe. Some elderly guests choose to cruise until they die, and why not? Food and libraries and serving personnel are readily available. There are medics on board and a housekeeping staff member is always available to clean up. I have met guests who have taken over two hundred cruises, or who cruise regularly for four to six months each year. Widows and widowers cruise when they have lost their partners. They sometimes seek companionship in the game rooms or libraries on board. I have met elderly gay couples who support one another by cruising together even when only one person can actually get off to see the port. This is a fantasy of living life to its conclusion in a space of luxury and privilege where the world passes by, just beyond the balcony. Contemplating death while staring at the endless ocean is surely something most who have spent days on the open water have experienced. Encountering the power of the water with its vast expanse brings human beings face to face with their mortality. And in these moments of consciousness many passengers reevaluate the meaning and purpose of their lives. Seamen of the past who worked on treacherous waters undoubtedly felt the power of nature as a life-and-death circumstance. Improvisation would have been essential for survival. Even though elderly cruise passengers travel within a luxury environment, the ever-present ocean facilitates contemplative reflection about who they are.

Self Reflection

On my most recent cruise, I presented a lecture about African heritage roots, where I discussed indigenous epistemologies and cultural recuperation efforts in South Africa. I showed a video about a contemporary South African artist named Zana Masombuka who has developed artwork around the concept of the Ndebele Superhero. Masombuka believes African people will set trends for the next waves of artistic innovation and her warrior is a Black woman who is empowered to unite her cultural history with her contemporary presence in a rapidly changing Africa.[1] I presented the artist's work hoping in a nonanthropological way to educate my audience members about the humanity of African people. After the presentation, an elderly white Danish man approached me with tears in his eyes. He explained how he was now living in Canada with an American woman and had unwittingly purchased land in the middle of territory once held by an indigenous community. My talk was triggering for him because he was regularly paying thousands of dollars in fines for the right to remain seated on property that was once ceremonial land for the original peoples. The Danish man was unable to resolve for himself the complicated conundrum of his colonial presence on indigenous land when he felt that he, as a foreign immigrant, deserved ownership because he had spent his hard-earned fortune to acquire land in his own name. My talk had emphasized the humanity of native people, the importance of territorial rights, and the injustice of colonial occupation. He opened by saying he liked my presentation, but he was disturbed because he felt he was on the wrong side of the political issue. This was complicated. Cruise ships mandate a lack of controversy in presentations and I wanted my talks to be informative and not disturbing, yet merely acknowledging the presence of an empowered global majority shifted the self-perception of this traveler who had never really reflected on his role in the transnational puzzle of cultural mixing.

I felt empathy, because he was troubled. Both of us agreed that there was no immediate solution to this uncomfortable moment of vacation travel turned into guilt-ridden recognition of the impacts of global inequity. What could he as an eighty-one-year-old traveler and I as a destination lecturer do to resolve this? In the moment, nothing, but each of us left the encounter transformed in our consciousness. He reflected. I reflected. I realized how impactful it can be to reach new audiences, audiences who, if I were not on the cruise ship, would never attend a formal performance centering on global majority artistry. There is a power in using theater to educate, when it foregrounds the humanity of the disempowered and brings new stories to individuals who have never heard them. This kind of reflection was facilitated by the unstructured time we had, traveling through the liminal space of an unmoored vacation ship, to sit with self and experience something new. Of course, not everyone experiences this. Many people cruise to drink and laugh, dance and party, and forget about thoughtful reflection. Still, there is something about this geography of the ocean, where we are neither here nor there, that opens a portal for cultural encounter and transformation that has nothing to do with the destination.

Disembarking

Eventually the time comes when I have to get off of the ship. The final day before a ship arrives at a disembarkation port is usually a difficult day. The passengers are sad, and they take it out on the crew. The crew is stressed because they know that disembarkation days are also embarkation days, and they will not get much sleep. On my last day of my most recent journey, I see the white woman crew member with whom I had such a fruitful conversation back at the Cape Town port. Then, she was nervous about starting her first cruise contract, and excited about our pending transatlantic voyage together. I spotted her in the dining room where she was off in the distance wiping tables and attentively serving coffee. I asked her crew chief, a Filipino gentleman, about greeting her. Acknowledging my interest, he first pointed me toward her serving area and then alerted her, with a nod, that I wanted to have a conversation with her. It was then that I realized that the amicable friendship we felt in the bright Cape Town sun sitting on the concrete barrier at port could not be replicated within the hierarchical space of the cruise ship. I said, "Hi, I just wanted to see how you were doing," and she said, "Oh, I'm doing OK, I'm fine." After she spoke, she glanced around furtively, looking to see if anyone watched our interaction. I asked if she was getting off the ship and a shadow passed over her eyes. "No," she said . . . "no." I leave her, knowing she cannot get off the ship and I hope that the other crew workers will bring her into their community. I can see that her performance of servitude has been well instated. She had stepped into the repeating pattern of sea workers from the past who understand their prescribed subservient space within the hierarchies of the ship. This woman has more mobility than they did. Still, she does not lift her eyes, or express her emotions in a public place. It feels a little odd to see this performance imprinted on a white body, but she has chosen to be at sea. I wonder how long she will stay in this position, or if she will sign another six-month contract.

I am about to disembark. The housekeeper has removed my bags from the room. I sit in the theater waiting with other guests for the cruise director to announce that our group has been called to exit. I think about my next cruise. There is something about this entertainment space. It aims for utopia despite the history of servitude and containment inherent in the long history of ocean ships and shipping out. Only in these moments of improvisation do the cracks begin to show and the dystopian cultures of containment and servitude reveal themselves. It's easy to be cynical about the use of labor at sea, to question the politics of "shipping out"; the prescriptive roles of the service industry within this environment seem insurmountable. But as I exit, I see retail staff and waiters talking to one another and exchanging ideas. I remember how, on this maritime circuit, I had a great conversation with the Surinamese sommelier in a quiet corner of the dining room where she talked about Dutch slavery in the ABC (Aruba, Bonaire, and Curaçao) islands. Then I recall how I discussed community activism among elders in Jamaica with the gentleman who was wiping the tables in the cafeteria. I am getting off, but the service workers will continue the circuit. Home, wherever home might be, is merely a referent for a place where we will all return some day.

Appendix

Gonzalez Lecture Circuits

Ship	Date	Line	Destination
Century	September 27, 2003	Celebrity	Cozumel, western Caribbean
Summit	December 22, 2003	Celebrity	Cozumel, Panama Canal, Pt. Limon, Aruba
Century	June 2004	Celebrity	Cozumel, western Caribbean
Mariner of the Seas	October 2–9, 2005	Royal Caribbean	Nassau, St. Thomas, St Maarten
Rhapsody of the Seas	March 19–26, 2006	Royal Caribbean	Western Caribbean
Explorer of the Seas	May 11–20, 2007	Royal Caribbean	Bermuda, St Maarten, St. Thomas, San Juan
Explorer of the Seas	May 22–31, 2008	Royal Caribbean	Labadee, Casa del Campo, St. Thomas, San Juan
Equinox	January 4–15, 2010	Celebrity	Southern Caribbean
Solstice	July 18–25, 2010	Celebrity	Western Caribbean
Explorer of the Seas	February 18–27, 2011	Royal Caribbean	San Juan, St. Thomas, Samana, Labadee
Eclipse	November 19–26, 2011	Celebrity	San Juan, St Maarten, St. Kitts
Explorer of the Seas	May 19–24, 2012	Royal Caribbean	Bermuda
Oasis of the Seas	January 7–11, 2013	Royal Caribbean	
Equinox	February 22–March 4 2016	Celebrity	Cozumel, Puerto Limon, Colon, Cartagena, Grand Cayman
Equinox	May 15–26, 2017	Celebrity	St. Thomas, Tortola, Antigua, Barbados, St. Lucia
Paradise	September 7–11, 2017	Carnival	Cuba (Cozumel)
Victory I	October 13–22, 2017	Victory Cruises	Great Lakes
Summit	July 31–August 14, 2021	Celebrity	St Maarten, Curacao, Barbados, St. Lucia, Aruba
Riviera	December 3 to 13, 2022	Oceania	Antigua, Bahamas, St Maarten, St. Lucia, Puerto Rico
Sirena	November 18–28, 2022	Oceania	St. Barts, St. Vincent, Dominica, St. Lucia, Puerto Rico
Voyager	January 6–18, 2023	Regent Seven Seas	Namibia, St. Helena, Rio de Janeiro

Notes

Introduction

1. David Krasner and Harry J. Elam Jr., *African-American Performance and Theater History: A Critical Reader* (New York: Oxford University Press, 2001), 4.
2. The speaker, Antonio Disla, made this commentary when he was a student in an African American Theater class at Florida State University. He is currently an assistant professor at the University of Michigan in Ann Arbor.
3. David Foster Wallace, "Shipping Out: On the (Nearly Lethal) Comforts of a Luxury Cruise," *Harper's Magazine*, January 1, 1996.
4. See the appendix for a list of cruises on which Gonzalez lectured.
5. Christina Sharpe, *In the Wake: On Blackness and Being* (Durham, N.C.: Duke University Press, 2016).
6. Jasmine Nichole Cobb, *Picture Freedom: Remaking Black Visuality in the Early Nineteenth Century* (New York: New York University Press, 2015).
7. Marcus Wood, *The Horrible Gift of Freedom: Atlantic Slavery and the Representation of Emancipation* (Athens: University of Georgia Press, 2010).
8. Douglas A. Jones Jr., *The Captive Stage: Performance and the Proslavery Imagination of the Antebellum North* (Ann Arbor: University of Michigan Press, 2014).
9. The Mende are an ethnic group from what is now Sierra Leone in Africa.
10. Others have written extensively about the *Amistad*, most notably maritime scholar Marcus Rediker in *The Amistad Rebellion: An Atlantic Odyssey of Slavery and Freedom* (New York: Penguin Books, 2013). The rebellion and trial are also the subject of the film *Amistad* directed by Steven Spielberg in 1997.
11. Jasmine Nichole Cobb, *Picture Freedom: Remaking Black Visuality in the Early Nineteenth Century* (New York: New York University Press, 2015), 29–65. Cobb describes the conundrum of the Amistad travelers in chapter 1 of her book where she writes about fugitive freedom in the Atlantic.
12. Hester Blum, *The View from the Masthead: Maritime Imagination and Antebellum American Sea Narratives* (Chapel Hill: University of North Carolina Press, 2008).

13. Maritime studies is a broad interdisciplinary field of study encompassing scientific analysis of the oceanic environments, naval histories, chronicles of working seamen, and analysis of maritime artifacts.

14. Alex Roland, W. Jeffrey Bolster, and Alexander Keyssar, *The Way of the Ship: America's Maritime History Reenvisioned, 1600–2000* (Hoboken, N.J.: John Wiley and Sons, 2008); Benjamin Woods Labaree et al., *America and the Sea: A Maritime History* (Mystic, Conn.: Mystic Seaport Museum, 1998); Donald S. Johnson and Juha Nurminen, *The History of Seafaring: Navigating the World's Oceans* (London: Conway Maritime, 2007).

15. W. Jeffrey Bolster, *Black Jacks: African American Seamen in the Age of Sail* (Cambridge, Mass.: Harvard University Press, 1997).

16. Ray Costello, *Black Salt: Seafarers of African Descent on British Ships* (Liverpool: Liverpool University Press, 2012).

17. Marcus Rediker, *The Slave Ship: A Human History* (New York: Penguin Books, 2008). Sowande' M. Mustakeem, *Slavery at Sea: Terror, Sex, and Sickness in the Middle Passage* (Champaign: University of Illinois Press, 2016).

18. J. Welles Henderson and Rodney P. Carlisle, *Marine Art & Antiques: Jack Tar; a Sailor's Life 1750–1910* (Woodbridge, England: Antique Collectors' Club, 1999).

19. Kimberley A. Peters, Jon Anderson, Andrew Davies, and Philip Steinberg, eds., *The Routledge Handbook of Ocean Space* (London: Routledge, 2022); Eric Paul Roorda, *The Ocean Reader: History, Culture, Politics* (Durham, N.C.: Duke University Press, 2020).

20. Peters et al., *Routledge Handbook of Ocean Space*, xxii.

21. Christina Sharpe, *In the Wake: On Blackness and Being* (Durham, N.C: Duke University Press, 2016).

22. Diana Looser, *Moving Islands: Contemporary Performance and the Global Pacific* (Ann Arbor: University of Michigan Press, 2021).

23. Jordan Waiti and Belinda Wheaton, "Indigenous Maori Knowledges of the Ocean and Leisure Practices," in *The Routledge Handbook of Ocean Space*, ed. Kimberley A. Peters, Jon Anderson, Andrew Davies, and Philip Steinberg (London: Routledge, 2022), 85–100.

24. Alexander G. Weheliye, *Phonographies: Grooves in Sonic Afro-Modernity* (Durham, N.C.: Duke University Press, 2005).

25. Performance studies scholars have for decades investigated how meaning resides in embodied practices of dance and theater. For example, in the 1990s Jane Desmond asked: "How does dance signal, enact, or rework social categories of identity?" Jane C. Desmond, *Meaning in Motion* (Durham, N.C.: Duke University Press, 1997), 2. Scholars interested in cross-cultural embodiment, especially those relating to diaspora performance, greatly expanded the field. *Everynight Life: Culture and Dance in Latin/o America*, written in the same year as the Desmond anthology, provided an insider, Latinx perspective on the popular dance implications of "politics in motion." Celeste Fraser Delgado and Muñoz José Esteban, *Everynight Life: Culture and Dance in Latin/o America* (Durham, N.C.: Duke University Press, 1997), 4. Other performance studies scholars built upon early explorations

of embodiment to include personal ethnography as a way of expressing interactions within diverse cultural communities: Melissa Blanco Borelli, *She Is Cuba: A Genealogy of the Mulata Body* (New York: Oxford University Press, 2016); A'Keitha Carey, "Visualizing Caribbean Performance (Jamaican Dancehall and Trinidadian Carnival) as Praxis: An Autohistoria of Kiki's Journey," *Journal of Dance Education* 16, no. 4 (2016): 129–38, https://doi.org/10.1080/15290824.2016.1124436; N. Fadeke Castor, *Spiritual Citizenship: Transnational Pathways from Black Power to Ifá in Trinidad* (Durham, N.C.: Duke University Press, 2017); Thomas F. DeFrantz and Anita Gonzalez, *Black Performance Theory* (Durham, N.C.: Duke University Press, 2014). These earlier writings privileged embodiment as a way of knowing even as they provided theoretical context for understanding how bodies shift cultural understandings across time.

26. I refer to the work of Katherine Profeta, *Dramaturgy in Motion: At Work on Dance and Movement Performance* (Madison: University of Wisconsin Press, 2015).

27. These texts deeply analyze how gesture communicates meaning. Eugenio Barba and Nicola Savarese, *The Secret Art of the Performer: A Dictionary of Theatre Anthropology* (New York: Routledge, 2005); Jan N. Bremmer and Herman Roodenburg, *A Cultural History of Gesture* (Ithaca, N.Y.: Cornell University Press, 1991).

28. Even nineteenth-century performers such as Henry Siddons (b.1807) catalogued physical stances of emotions in his *Practical Illustrations of Rhetorical Gestures in Action*. Henry Siddons, *Practical Illustrations of Rhetorical Gesture and Action, Adapted to the English Drama* (London: Richard Phillips, 1807). These gestural studies of linkages between emotion and movement circulated widely during the nineteenth century and beyond.

29. Antony S. Manstead, "The Psychology of Social Class: How Socioeconomic Status Impacts Thought, Feelings, and Behaviour," *British Journal of Social Psychology* 57, no. 2 (2018): 267–91, https://doi.org/10.1111/bjso.12251; Michael W. Kraus, Jun Won Park, and Jacinth J. Tan, "Signs of Social Class: The Experience of Economic Inequality in Everyday Life," *Perspectives on Psychological Science* 12, no. 3 (2017): 422–35, https://doi.org/10.1177/1745691616673192

30. Gillian M. Rodger, *Champagne Charlie and Pretty Jemima: Variety Theater in the Nineteenth Century* (Urbana: University of Illinois Press, 2010), 5.

31. Other cultural studies books—Carla L. Peterson, *Black Gotham: A Family History of African Americans in Nineteenth-Century New York City* (New Haven, Conn.: Yale University Press, 2011); Christian DuComb, *Haunted City: Three Centuries of Racial Impersonation in Philadelphia* (Ann Arbor: University of Michigan Press, 2017); Joanna Bourke, *Working-Class Cultures in Britain, 1890–1960: Gender, Class and Ethnicity* (New York: Routledge, 1994)—focus on sociocultural lives of ethnic communities in coastal cities and tangentially reference performance practices and describe how social life in port cities impacted the polyglot mariners who traveled through them.

32. "Employees of Cruise Industry U.S. 2019," Statista (Statista Research Department, November 11, 2022), https://www.statista.com/statistics/201342/employment-in-the-cruise-line-industry-since-2007/

33. Dorinne K. Kondo, *Crafting Selves: Power, Gender, and Discourses of Identity in a Japanese Workplace* (Chicago: University of Chicago Press, 1990), 24.

Chapter 1

1. Sea days are times when the ship is not at port. Because all passengers are on board with nothing to do but explore the ship, the majority of entertainment activities are scheduled during sea days.

2. John P. Pittman, "Double Consciousness," Stanford Encyclopedia of Philosophy (Stanford University), March 21, 2016, https://plato.stanford.edu/archives/sum2016/entries/double-consciousness/

3. Dan Benedict, "So You Want to Be a Cruise Ship Lecturer?" Cruise Critic, January 8, 2020, https://www.cruisecritic.com/articles.cfm?ID=1176

4. James Frieze, *Reframing Immersive Theatre: The Politics and Pragmatics of Participatory Performance* (London: Palgrave Macmillan, 2016), 5.

5. Frieze, *Reframing Immersive Theatre*, 23.

6. "Welcome to Virgin Voyages," Virgin Voyages (Virgin Cruises Intermediate), accessed January 12, 2023, https://www.virginvoyages.com/

7. Jennifer A. Kokai and Tom Robson, *Performance and the Disney Theme Park Experience: The Tourist as Actor* (London: Palgrave Macmillan, 2019), 14.

8. "Cruise Lines," Cruise Line Industry Association, 2023, https://cruising.org/en/cruise-lines

9. Dorinne K. Kondo, *Crafting Selves: Power, Gender, and Discourses of Identity in a Japanese Workplace* (Chicago: University of Chicago Press, 1990), 24.

10. Denys Bulikhov, May 2009.

11. Christine B. Chin, "Labour Flexibilization at Sea," *International Feminist Journal of Politics* 10, no. 1 (2008): 1–18, https://doi.org/10.1080/14616740701747584

12. Jess Peterson, "Medium," *Medium* (blog), July 29, 2016, https://medium.com/@jesspeterson/the-10-kinds-of-nationality-in-the-cruise-industry-450ebfdac165

13. Ester Ellen Bolt and Conrad Lashley, "All at Sea: Insights into Crew Work Experiences on a Cruise Liner," *Research in Hospitality Management* 5, no. 2 (2015): 199–206, https://doi.org/10.1080/22243534.2015.11828345

14. Maria Borovnic, "Seafarers: The Force That Moves the Global Economy," in *The Routledge Handbook of Ocean Space*, ed. Kimberley A. Peters, Jon Anderson, Andrew Davies, and Philip Steinberg (Oxfordshire: Routledge, 2022), 149.

15. Ester Ellen Bolt and Conrad Lashley, "All at Sea: Insights into Crew Work Experiences on a Cruise Liner," *Research in Hospitality Management* 5, no. 2 (2015): 204, https://doi.org/10.1080/22243534.2015.11828345

16. Bolt and Lashley, "All at Sea," 205.

17. James Revell Carr, *Hawaiian Music in Motion: Mariners, Missionaries, and Minstrels* (Champaign: University of Illinois Press, 2014).

18. Thomas Hamilton, "Ira Aldridge," *Anglo-African* magazine, 1860.

19. Tomas Alberto Avila, *Black Caribs—Garifuna: Saint Vincent's Exiled People and the Roots of Garifuna: A Historical Compilation* (Providence, R. I.: Milenio Publishing, 2008).

20. Marvin McAllister, *White People Do Not Know How to Behave at Entertainments Designed for Ladies and Gentlemen of Colour* (Chapel Hill: University of North Carolina Press, 2003), 177.

21. Shane White, *Stories of Freedom in Black New York* (Cambridge, Mass.: Harvard University Press, 2002). White writes extensively about James Hewlett, the African Grove Theatre, and the quest for freedom within the free Black New York City community. His book uniquely uses storytelling as a methodology for unpacking how individuals mobilized their freedom to ensure their success in a society where slavery was present, but freedom and agency were achievable.

22. Anna Mae Duane and Thomas Thurston. "The History of the School," n.d., https://www.nyhistory.org/web/africanfreeschool/history/curriculum.html

23. Larry Tye, *Rising from the Rails: Pullman Porters and the Making of the Black Middle Class* (New York: Macmillan, 2004). Tye writes about how southern Black porters working on luxurious sleeping cars were able to move from bondage to secure positions in the Black middle class where they created an intellectual culture of activists and political leaders.

24. Michael Sokolow, *Charles Benson, Mariner of Color in the Age of Sail* (Amherst: University of Massachusetts Press, 2003).

25. "New York Daily Advertiser," *New York Daily Advertiser*, 1820.

26. W. Jeffrey Bolster, "Every Inch a Man," in *Iron Men, Wooden Women: Gender and Seafaring in the Atlantic World, 1700–1920*, ed. Margaret S. Creighton and Lisa Norling (Baltimore: Johns Hopkins University Press, 1996), 152.

27. Alex Roland, W. Jeffrey Bolster, and Alexander Keysaar, *The Way of the Ship: America's Maritime History Reenvisioned, 1600–2000* (New York: Wiley, 2007), 69–81. These three maritime historians write extensively about the importance of coastal shipping in the formation of American identity because it led to the development of small businesses that helped to establish the United States as an independent trading entity.

28. John Bull, "Letterbook Of Capt. John Bull, Falmouth Packet Service," *Letterbook Of Capt. John Bull, Falmouth Packet Service* (1800).

29. J. Welles Henderson and Rodney P. Carlisle, in *Marine Art & Antiques: Jack Tar; a Sailor's Life 1750–1910* (Woodbridge, England: Antique Collectors' Club, 1999), 65.

30. Kelly K. Chaves, "Before the First Whalemen: The Emergence and Loss of Indigenous Maritime Autonomy in New England, 1672–1740," *New England Quarterly* 87, no. 1 (2014): 46–71, https://doi.org/10.1162/tneq_a_00344

31. William Page, J. Hill, and C. B. Hulsart (Boston, Mass., n.d.).

32. Herman Melville, *Moby Dick* (New York: Harper & Brothers, 1851). The novel *Moby Dick or The Whale* by Herman Melville is available in multiple formats and is a staple of English literary studies. Its contents describe a fictional journey on a whaling ship the details of which form a romanticized, yet historically accurate,

portrait of whaling. Melville's other two maritime novels, *Redburn* and *White Jacket*, also recount maritime exploits.

33. Marvin McAllister, *White People Do Not Know How to Behave at Entertainments Designed for Ladies and Gentlemen of Colour* (Chapel Hill: University of North Carolina Press, 2003). The Grove was the first name for the African Grove. It was first an entertainment garden, then later adapted into a theater.

34. A caulker is a worker who inserts oakum into the seams of a ship to make it airtight and waterproof. Oakum is a tarred fiber, usually made of jute, pine tar, and linseed oil.

35. Frederick Douglass, in *The Life and Times of Frederick Douglass* (Hartford, Conn.: Park Publishing Co., 1881), 246.

36. W. Jeffrey Bolster, "Every Inch a Man," in *Iron Men, Wooden Women: Gender and Seafaring in the Atlantic World, 1700–1920*, edited by Margaret S. Creighton and Lisa Norling (Baltimore: Johns Hopkins University Press, 1996), 139.

37. "Jack Tar" is the generic name used to describe the common sailor. It refers to the tar used by sailors to seal the seams in wooden boats. The term is derogatory because it alludes to the dirtiness of both the job and the person.

38. John C. Williams, *New York Spectator*, 1827, 2.

39. *Evening Post*, 1824, 3.

40. Charles Foy, "Seamen Love Their Bellies: How Blacks Became Ship Cooks," *Uncovering Hidden Lives: 18th Century Black Mariners* (blog), August 10, 2014.

41. Charles Foy, "Uncovering Hidden Lives: 18th Century Black Mariners," *Uncovering Hidden Lives: 18th Century Black Mariners* (blog), August 10, 2014, https://uncoveringhiddenlives.com/tag/old-seamen/

42. Thomas Francis Adkins, *The Nautical Cookery Book* (London: Wilson and Whitworth Limited, Steam Printers, 1899). The inside first page reads "Silver Medalist, Universal Food and Cooking Exhibition, 1896. Instructor of Nautical Cookery under the Technical Education Board L.C.C. at The Sailors Home, Well Street and Dock Street, London E." Accessed at Greenwich Maritime Archives, August 2017.

43. Rufus Fairchild Zogbaum (1849–1925) was known for his naturalistic drawings of scenes from the U.S. Navy.

44. Douglas A. Jones Jr., "'The Black Below': Minstrelsy, Satire, and the Threat of Vernacularity," *Theatre Journal* 73, no. 2 (June 2021): 129–46, https://doi.org/10.1353/tj.2021.0038

45. Jones, "'The Black Below'," 117.

46. Iver Bernstein, *The New York City Draft Riots: Their Significance for American Society and Politics in the Age of Civil War* (Oxford: Oxford University Press, 1990), 27.

47. Bernstein, *New York City Draft Riots*, 28.

48. Carla L. Peterson, *Black Gotham: A Family History of African Americans in Nineteenth-Century New York City* (repr., New Haven: Yale University Press, 2011), 182.

49. William Powell (Mystic, Conn., n.d.).

50. Carla L. Peterson, *Black Gotham: A Family History of African Americans in Nineteenth-Century New York City* (repr., New Haven: Yale University Press, 2011), 239.

51. "Alaska Cruise Association," CLIA Alaska Cruise visitor profile comments, accessed July 13, 2021, https://akcruise.org/cruising-in-alaska/cruise-visitor-profile/

52. I have not yet met a female cruise ship captain although I have seen women in the bridge. I hope there are some.

53. Elizabeth Doyle, *Banana Boats: A Missing Link in the Rise of the Cruise Vacationing 1881 to 1958*, an unpublished manuscript shared at the 2012 Mystic Seaport, Munson Institute, National Endowment for the Humanities America, and the Sea symposium, 2012.

54. Helen M. Rozwadowski and Sylvia A. Earle, *Fathoming the Ocean: The Discovery and Exploration of the Deep Sea* (Cambridge, Mass.: Harvard University Press, 2005), 62.

55. William H. Miller, *First Class Cargo: A History of Combination Passenger-Cargo Ships* (repr., Cheltenham, Gloucestershire: History Press, 2016).

56. Kristoffer A. Garin, *Devils on the Deep Blue Sea: The Dreams, Schemes, and Showdowns That Built America's Cruise Ship Empires* (New York: Viking, 2005); Alex Roland, W. Jeffrey Bolster, and Alexander Keyssar, *The Way of The Ship: America's Maritime History Reenvisioned, 1600–2000* (repr., New York: Wiley, 2007).

57. "Cruise Industry: Revenue Worldwide 2007–2027," Statista, accessed February 4, 2021, https://www.statista.com/statistics/204572/revenue-of-the-cruise-line-industry-worldwide-since-2008/#:~:text=In%202016%2C%20the%20global%20cruise,approximately%2035.5%20billion%20U.S.%20dollars

58. "About CLIA—Cruise Lines International Association," Cruise Line Industry Association, accessed February 4, 2021, https://cruising.org/en/about-the-industry/about-clia. Partner members are suppliers, port agents, ship building companies, and so forth.

59. Helen M. Rozwadowski and Sylvia A. Earle, *Fathoming the Ocean: The Discovery and Exploration of the Deep Sea* (Cambridge, Mass.: Harvard University Press, 2005), 62.

60. "Hotel History in Mackinac Island, Michigan—Grand Hotel," Historic Hotels Worldwide, accessed October 5, 2022, https://www.historichotels.org/us/hotels-resorts/grand-hotel/history.php

61. "Mackinac Island," Lakeshore Excursions, accessed January 17, 2023, https://lakeshoreexcursions.com/mackinac-island/. I traveled with Bob in July 2019 when I cruised from Chicago to Toronto on a Great Lakes tour. He boarded the ship just before we arrived at Makinac Island. He was both an onboard speaker and an island tour guide. The booking agent sponsoring lecturers for these Great Lakes destination immersions is Lakeshore Excursions.

62. Steve Maxwell, "More Than Money: How an Old-Time Builder Created a Hotel Icon," Baileylineroad, July 5, 2021, https://baileylineroad.com/more-th

an-money-heroic-contractor-shows-what-it-means-to-ride-risk-manage-people-and-make-good-things-happen/. The same article appears in the *Ottawa Citizen*. https://ottawacitizen.com/life/homes/house-works-contractor-shines-in-challenge-of-building-1880s-great-lakes-grand-hotel

63. William H. Miller, *First Class Cargo: A History of Combination Passenger-Cargo Ships* (repr., Cheltenham, Gloucestershire: History Press, 2016).

64. Kristoffer A. Garin, *Devils on the Deep Blue Sea: The Dreams, Schemes, and Showdowns That Built America's Cruise Ship Empires* (New York: Viking, 2005), 14–19.

65. Peter Quartermain and Bruce Peter, *Cruise: Identity, Design, and Culture* (New York: Rizzoli, 2006), 39–40.

66. Sue Denning works on Celebrity cruise ships and she has been interviewed extensively about her work. She states that the Celebrity entertainment director organizes all of the guest entertainers, but she has a significant say in who is selected. Denning also performs sections of her own cabaret act on the ship. Like many of the cruise directors, she has an entertainment specialty.

67. Audrey Williams June and Brian O'Leary, "How Many Black Women Have Tenure on Your Campus? Search Here," *Chronicle of Higher Education*, May 27, 2021, https://www.chronicle.com/article/how-many-black-women-have-tenure-on-your-campus-search-here. Only 2.1 percent of tenured professors are Black females.

68. Gabriella Gutiérrez y Muhs, Yolanda Flores Niemann, Carmen G. Gonzalez, and Angela P. Harris, *Presumed Incompetent: The Intersections of Race and Class for Women in Academia* (Logan: Utah State University Press, 2012).

69. Madelyn Mette, "Map of North Atlantic and Gulf Stream | U.S. Geological Survey," USGS Science for a Changing World, 2021, https://www.usgs.gov/media/images/map-north-atlantic-and-gulf-stream

70. Bruno Tavernier, "The Spanish Routes—Gold and Silver," in *Great Maritime Routes: An Illustrated History*, trans. Nicholas Fry (New York: Viking, 1970), 101–18.

Chapter 2

1. "The Firm," Gem, February 17, 2022, https://gemsrl.com/thefirm

2. "Celebrity Solstice Cruise Design," Wilson Butler Architects, January 3, 2018, https://www.wilsonbutler.com/project/celebrity-solstice-cruise-design/

3. Ballast during the nineteenth-century was usually rock or iron. In modern-day shipping water loaded on and off of the ship is used as ballast. The intake and offloading of ballast whether it is water or geological matter can be an environmental hazard as organisms or invasive species are moved from one geological environment to another.

4. "Ballast Water Management," Bawat, accessed February 1, 2023, https://www.bawat.com/. This is an example of a cruise ship ballast water management system.

5. David Wiles, *A Short History of Western Performance Space* (Cambridge: Cambridge University Press, 2009), 19.

6. Wiles, *A Short History of Western Performance Space*, 4.

7. Wiles also discusses the Empty Space as a space of the imagination where theatrical visioning can take place. I have two thoughts about this. On the one hand, the empty space does not exist on the cruise ship because it cannot be monetized. On the other hand, passengers may choose to take the long slow voyages of the cruise ship precisely because they want to access the imaginative potential of the empty space as they break away from their land-based associations and connections.

8. This excerpt is from the November 4, 2022 onboarding letter for the *Sirena*, Oceania cruises. Others are similar although perhaps less prescriptive.

9. Shipboard entertainment for upper-class patrons, those paying more than $5,000 for a midrange cabin, is usually quieter. Those guests are usually older and prefer to read and sun when they are on the pool deck.

10. David Wiles, *A Short History of Western Performance Space* (Cambridge: Cambridge University Press, 2009), 64.

11. Both the musicals *42nd Street* and *Gold Diggers of Broadway* feature grand staircases where women in glitzy costumes parade and dance during musical numbers. *The Story Behind the 42nd Street "Stair Dance"* YouTube, 2019, https://www.youtube.com/watch?v=fEMHUyY2DVs; *Lullaby of Broadway* YouTube, 2016, https://www.youtube.com/watch?v=Yx6s-YReOJY

12. Different cruise lines name this event differently, but the essentials of the game are the same.

13. David Wiles, *A Short History of Western Performance Space* (Cambridge: Cambridge University Press, 2009), 131.

14. Wiles, *A Short History of Western Performance Space*, 137.

15. Wiles, *A Short History of Western Performance Space*, 161.

16. "Le Petit Chef: A One-of-a-Kind Dining Concept," Celebrity Cruises, 2023, https://www.celebritycruises.com/things-to-do-onboard/eat-and-drink/restaurants-and-cafes/le-petit-chef-at-qsine

17. Cruise directors plan event sequences within each sailing voyage to correspond with rising and falling guest moods. At the beginning of a journey there is excitement about simply being on the ship and enjoying its amenities. Toward the end of the journey activities like cooking shows and participatory programming keep guests involved in ship play culture.

18. Wiles, *A Short History of Western Performance Space*, 209.

19. Harold M. Otness, "Passenger Ship Libraries," *Journal of Library History* 14, no. 4 (1979): 486–95.

20. J. Welles Henderson and Rodney P. Carlisle, *Marine Art & Antiques: Jack Tar: A Sailor's Life, 1750–1910* (Woodbridge, England: Antique Collectors' Club, 1999), 183–85.

21. Simon J. Bronner, *Crossing the Line: Violence, Play, and Drama in Naval Equator Traditions* (Amsterdam: Amsterdam University Press, 2006), 8–26, 46.

22. José Esteban Muñoz, *Cruising Utopia: The Then and There of Queer Futurity* (New York: New York University Press, 2009), 1–3.

23. Steven Zeeland, *The Masculine Marine: Homoeroticism in the U.S. Marine Corps* (Abingdon, England: Routledge, 2013); Judith Butler, *Gender Trouble: Feminism and the Subversion of Identity* (New York: Routledge, 2006).

24. "Crossing the Line," Naval History and Heritage Command, July 9, 2019, https://www.history.navy.mil/browse-by-topic/heritage/customs-and-traditions0/crossing-line.html

25. "NHHC," Naval History and Heritage Command, accessed May 24, 2014, https://www.history.navy.mil/

26. Graham Seal, "Burying the Dead Horse," *Gristly History* (blog), June 24, 2018, https://gristlyhistory.blog/2018/06/24/burying-the-dead-horse/; Richard King, "Poor Old Horse," National Maritime Historical Society, accessed February 1, 2023, https://seahistory.org/sea-history-for-kids/horse/; Rachel Conley, "The Dead Horse Festival," Mariners' Museum and Park, October 22, 2014, https://www.marinersmuseum.org/2014/10/the-dead-horse-festival/

27. Brian David Bruns, *Cruise Confidential: A Hit below the Waterline: Where the Crew Lives, Eats, Wars, and Parties—One Crazy Year Working On* (Palo Alto, Calif.: Travelers' Tales Guides, 2008).

28. Bruns, *Cruise Confidential*, 327–28.

29. Ester Ellen Bolt and Conrad Lashley, "All at Sea: Insights into Crew Work Experiences on a Cruise Liner," *Research in Hospitality Management* 5, no. 2 (2015): 199–206, https://doi.org/10.1080/22243534.2015.11828345

30. Christine B. Chin, "Labour Flexibilization at Sea," *International Feminist Journal of Politics* 10, no. 1 (2008): 9, https://doi.org/10.1080/14616740701747584

31. Minghua Zhao, "Emotional Laborer in a Globalised Laborer Market: Seafarers on Cruise Ships." Working Paper Series No. 27. Wales: Seafarers International Research Centre, Cardiff University.

32. This event was a special event on Celebrity cruise lines between 2004 and 2010. Events and activities change regularly and differ across cruise line companies.

33. Interestingly, Thomas Tegg, who published the print, came from a rather troubled childhood. Even though he attended boarding schools as a child, I would not characterize his life as upper class. He did, however, understand how to appeal to upper-class sensibilities.

34. José Esteban Muñoz, *Disidentifications: Queers of Color and the Performance of Politics* (Minneapolis: University of Minnesota Press, 1999), argues that queer disidentifications remake worlds through a politics of performance. By this he means that nonnormative performance is a political act of foregrounding and reinterpreting the world from queer perspectives. Later, in *Cruising Utopia: The Then and There of Queer Futurity* (New York: New York University Press, 2009), Muñoz posits that this type of resistant performance is a gesture toward queer futurities that may not be realized in the present.

35. Angelique V. Nixon, *Resisting Paradise—Tourism, Diaspora, and Sexuality in Caribbean Culture* (Jackson: University Press of Mississippi, 2015); Melissa

Blanco-Borelli, *She Is Cuba: A Genealogy of the Mulatta Body* (New York: Oxford, 2016); Elizabeth S. Manley, "Imagining the Tropics: Women and Tourism in the Caribbean," National Humanities Center, October 12, 2022, https://nationalhumanitiescenter.org/elizabeth-manley-imagining-tropics-women-tourism-caribbean/; Kamala Kempadoo, "Gender, Race and Sex: Exoticism in the Caribbean," *Revista/Review Interamericana* 22, no. 1–1 (Summer 1992): 208–25; Nickesia S. Gordon, Jonathan Schroeder, and Janet Borgerson, "Folk and Fantasy: Colonial Imaginations of Caribbean Culture in Mid-Century Calypso Album Cover Art," *Howard Journal of Communications* (2022): 1–21, https://doi.org/10.1080/10646175.2022.2148226

36. Dorinne K. Kondo, *Crafting Selves: Power, Gender, and Discourses of Identity in a Japanese Workplace* (Chicago: University of Chicago Press, 2009), 300–304.

37. Mid F. Bland, "Log" (London, n.d.).

38. Esther Newton, *Cherry Grove, Fire Island: Sixty Years in America's First Gay and Lesbian Town* (Durham, N.C.: Duke University Press, 2014).

39. George S. Emmerson, "The Hornpipe," *Folk Music Journal: The English Folk and Dance Society* 2, no. 1 (1970): 12–33.

40. Brenda Dixon Gottschild, *Waltzing in the Dark: African American Vaudeville and Race Politics in the Swing Era* (New York: Palgrave Macmillan, 2000), 15.

41. James W. Cook, "Master Juba, the King of All Dancers! A Story of Stardom and Struggle from the Dawn of the Transatlantic Culture and Industry," *Discourses in Dance* 3, no. 2 (2006).

42. Barbara Glass, *African American Dance: An Illustrated History* (Jefferson, NC.: McFarland & Company, 2007).

43. Jerrilyn McGregory writes about Black communities in the Caribbean and in southern communities of the United States that come together on Boxing Day (December 26) to deliberately participate in parties that make a grand noise and announce their presence; Jerrilyn McGregory, *One Grand Noise: Boxing Day in the Anglicized Caribbean World* (Jackson: University Press of Mississippi, 2021). Anita González writes about how sounding the deck in Jarocho dance unites communities around an imagined Afro-Mexican cultural heritage; Anita González, *Jarocho's Soul: Cultural Identity and Afro-Mexican Dance* (Lanham, Md.: University Press of America, 2004).

44. Anita González, George O. Jackson, and Pellicer José Manuel, *Afro-Mexico: Dancing between Myth and Reality* (Austin: University of Texas Press, 2010).

45. Julius Sherrard Scott, *The Common Wind: Afro-American Currents in the Age of the Haitian Revolution* (New York: Verso, 2018).

46. Alexander G. Weheliye, *Phonographies: Grooves in Sonic Afro-Modernity* (Durham, N.C.: Duke University Press, 2005), 3, 19.

47. Danielle Fosler-Lussier, *Music on the Move* (Ann Arbor: University of Michigan Press, 2020).

48. The area of West Africa near Ghana was known for the gold and minerals that were transferred from the interior and sold to sailing vessels along the coast.

49. Horatio Bridge and Nathaniel Hawthorne, "CHAPTER III," in *Journal*

of an African Cruiser: Comprising Sketches of the Canaries, the Cape De Verds . . . and Other Places . . . on the West Coast of Africa (London: Wiley and Putnam, 1845), 13.

50. Diane Frost, "Diasporan West African Communities: The Kru in Freetown & Liverpool," *Review of African Political Economy* 29, no. 92 (2002): 285–300.

51. Stan Hugill, *Shanties from the Seven Seas: Shipboard Work-Songs and Songs Used as Work-Songs from the Great Days of Sail* (repr., New London: Mystic Seaport Museum, 1994), 361.

52. Horace Beck, *Folklore and the Sea* (Mystic, Conn.: Mystic Seaport Museum, 1970); Hugill, *Shanties from the Seven Seas*; Craig Edwards, interview by Anita Gonzalez, in person (repr., Mystic Seaport, 2015); John Holstead Mead, *Sea Shanties and Fo'c'sle Songs, 1768–1906*, in the G.W. Blunt White Library, Mystic Seaport, Mystic, Connecticut (Lexington: University Press of Kentucky, 1973); Robert Young Walser, *The Shantyman's Canon* (Madison: University of Wisconsin Press, 1995).

53. Roy Palmer, "Shanty," *Grove Dictionary of Music and Musicians* 29, no. 23 (2001): 205.

54. Nina Sun Eidsheim, *The Race of Sound: Listening, Timbre, and Vocality in African American Music* (Durham, N.C.: Duke University Press, 2019), 3, 7.

55. "What Is a Sea Shanty?," Sea Shanty Facts, History and Meanings (Royal Museums Greenwich), accessed July 10, 2021, https://www.rmg.co.uk/stories/topics/sea-shanty-facts-history-meaning

56. Roy Palmer, *The Oxford Book of Sea Songs* (Oxford: Oxford University Press, 1986). Palmer collected and compiled songs sung by sailors into a handbook, *The Oxford Book of Sea Songs*, which pairs melodies with lyrics to capture the experiences of English-speaking seamen through their sung stories. In *Shanties from the Seven Seas* (repr., New London: Mystic Seaport Museum, 1994), Stan Hugill focuses on work songs, compositions that differ from sea ballads because their cadence and structure match the rhythmic patterns of shipboard tasks—pulling in ropes or turning the capstan, for example. While Palmer takes a more expansive and academic approach to the literature, including ballads and port songs in his anthology, Hugill writes in a folksy style as if trying to capture the imagined, romanticized rowdy camaraderie of the jolly sea worker. Even though this approach fails to engage with the hard labor and unpleasant circumstances of men stranded at sea, he offers a glimpse into the complex messages communicated within the songs. His collection includes lyrics, scores, and analyses of over four hundred shanties. If you consider the global reach of sea songs, Hugill's lens is limited. His historiography of sea shanties is based upon archives of sailing men from New England and mid-Atlantic villages in the United States. These sailors were some of the more privileged of those who worked transatlantic vessels because they were connected to ship-building communities where families owned or managed workshops. Those who went to sea were often skilled craftsmen, able to secure higher status employment within the trade.

57. W. B. Whall, *Ships, Sea Songs and Shanties* (Glasgow: James Brown & Son, 1913; repr., Forgotten Books, 2018, with a new introduction on folk music), is a vintage collection of traditional sailing songs. Originally appearing in the *Nautical*

Magazine and Yachting Monthly, the songs come complete with lyrics and sheet music, as well as pictures of celebrated sailing ships of the time. William Boultbee Whall (1847–1917) was a master mariner famous for writing this book. He became a member of the merchant navy when he was fourteen and became acquainted with the songs during his eleven years aboard ships of the East India Companies. In addition to this volume, Whall also wrote a number of books related to practical seamanship and navigation.

58. Joanna C. Colcord and Lincoln Colcord, *Roll and Go: Songs of American Sailormen* (Indianapolis: Bobs Merrill Company, 1924).

59. Jessica Floyd, "Jib-booms, Barrels, and Dead Eyes: Singing Sex in Sea Chanteys," PhD diss., University of Maryland, Baltimore County, 2017, 142–43.

60. James Revell Carr, *Hawaiian Music in Motion: Mariners, Missionaries, and Minstrels* (Champaign: University of Illinois Press, 2014), 91.

61. Frederick Pease Harlow, *The Making of a Sailor; or, Sea Life Aboard a Yankee Square-Rigger* (Salem, Mass.: Marine Research Society, 1928); John Holstead Mead, *Sea Shanties and Fo'c'sle Songs, 1768–1906, in the G.W. Blunt White Library, Mystic Seaport, Mystic, Connecticut* (Lexington: University Press of Kentucky, 1973); Clement Cleveland Satwell, *Captain Nash DeCost and the Liverpool Packets*, 1st ed. (Mystic, Conn.: Marine Historical Association, 1955); Michael Sokolow, *Charles Benson, Mariner of Color in the Age of Sail* (Amherst: University of Massachusetts Press, 2003).

62. Shanty singers sing the chorus "O Long Stormy Storm-along" between each line of verse recorded here.

63. Stan Hugill, *Shanties from the Seven Seas* (repr., New London: Mystic Seaport Museum, 1994), 70.

64. E. I. (Ezekiel I.) Barra, *A Tale of Two Oceans: A New Story by an Old Californian: An Account of a Voyage from Philadelphia to San Francisco around Cape Horn, Years 1849–50, Calling at Rio De Janeiro, Brazil, and at Juan Fernandez, in the South Pacific* (San Francisco: Press of Eastman Co., 1893).

65. Stan Hugill, *Shanties from The Seven Seas* (repr., New London: Mystic Seaport Museum, 1994), 71.

66. Joanna C. Colcord and Lincoln Colcord, *Roll and Go: Songs of American Sailormen* (Indianapolis: Bobs Merrill Company, 1924), 15.

67. Katrina Dyonne Thompson, *Ring Shout, Wheel About: The Racial Politics of Music and Dance in North American Slavery* (Champaign: University of Illinois Press, 2014), 70.

68. Thompson, *Ring Shout, Wheel About*, 18.

69. Thompson, *Ring Shout, Wheel About*, 16.

70. Vocables are utterances in indigenous and popular song that refer to form rather than meaning. Pitch and tone enhance vocables, so they are able to communicate without language, stirring emotions in both the singer and the listener.

71. Nancy Shoemaker, *Native American Whalemen and the World: Indigenous Encounters and the Contingency of Race* (Chapel Hill: University of North Carolina Press, 2017).

72. Jason R. Mancini, "Beyond Reservation: Indians, Maritime Labor, and Communities of Color from Eastern Long Island Sound, 1713–1861," in *Gender, Race, Ethnicity, and Power in Maritime America: Papers from the Conference Held at Mystic Seaport, September 2006*, ed. Glenn S. Gordinier (Mystic, Conn.: Mystic Seaport, 2008). Also, Jason R. Mancini, "New London's Indian Mariners," Connecticut History, a CTHumanities Project—Stories about the people, traditions, innovations, and events that make up Connecticut's rich history, November 18, 2021, https://connecticuthistory.org/new-londons-indian-mariners/.

73. "Maps," Indian Mariners Project, January 22, 2014, https://indianmarinersproject.com/maps/

74. William Loren Katz, *Black Indians: A Hidden Heritage* (New York: Atheneum Books for Young Readers, 2012); Jack D. Forbes, *Africans and Native Americans: The Languages of Race and the Evolution of Red-Black Peoples*, 2nd ed. (Champaign: University of Illinois Press, 1993).

75. Michael Smith, *Mardi Gras Indians* (New York: Pelican Press, 1994); Anita González, *Afro-Mexico: Dancing between Myth and Reality* (Austin: University of Texas Press, 2010); Milla Cozart Riggio, *Carinal: Culture in Action—The Trinidad Experience—World of Performance* (New York: Routledge, 2004).

76. Ryan Dearinger, *The Filth of Progress: Immigrants, Americans, and the Building of Canals and Railroads in the West*, 1st ed. (Oakland: University of California Press, 2015).

77. G. M. Joseph and Timothy J. Henderson, "Décimas Dedicated to Santa Anna's Leg," in *The Mexico Reader: History, Culture, Politics* (Durham, N.C.: Duke University Press, 2003), 213–16.

78. G. M. Joseph, Timothy J. Henderson, and Prieto Guillermo, "The Glorious Revolution of 1844," in *The Mexico Reader: History, Culture, Politics*, ed. Gilbert M. Joseph and Timothy J. Henderson (Durham, N.C.: Duke University Press, 2003), 211.

79. Joanna C. Colcord and Lincoln Colcord, *Roll and Go: Songs of American Sailormen* (Indianapolis: Bobs Merrill Company, 1924), 74.

80. Roy Palmer, "Shanty," *Grove Dictionary of Music and Musicians* 29, no. 23 (2001): 185.

81. https://www.mysticseaport.org/press-release/mystic-seaport-to-host-34th-annual-sea-music-festival-june-6-9/

82. Felipe Rose is a gay performer who claims Puerto Rican and Lakota descent and is known to controversially wear a war bonnet and other indigenous regalia in his public performances. His activist approach to gender and ethnicity includes recognition of his two-spirit identity in his musical performances. Andrew Fenton, "The Village People's Alex Briley Says Any Indian Headdress Ban Won't Apply to the Group at the Golden Plains Festival," News Corp Australia Network, 2015, https://www.news.com.au/entertainment/music/tours/the-village-peoples-alex-briley-says-any-indian-headdress-ban-wont-apply-to-the-group-at-the-golden-plains-festival/news-story/aaff8e46a20efa418f80fa3cf432a6cf; K. A. Dilday, "The Village People's 'Indian' Remembers Stonewall," Bloomberg.com, June 26, 2019,

https://www.bloomberg.com/news/articles/2019-06-26/the-village-people-s-indian-remembers-stonewall

Chapter 3

1. Charmaine Chua, "Docking: Maritime Ports in the Making of the Global Economy," in *The Routledge Handbook of Ocean Space*, ed. Kimberley Peters, Jon Anderson, Andrew Davies, and Philip Steinberg (New York: Routledge, 2022), 126

2. Eric Roorda and Hamlett Roz, "The Container Ship," in *The Ocean Reader: History, Culture, Politics* (Durham, N.C.: Duke University Press, 2020), 199–202. For dimensions of containers and a more detailed description of the container's interaction with the railroad and trucking industries, see Matthew Heins, "Containers: The Shipping Container as Spatial Standard," in *The Routledge Handbook of Ocean Space*, ed. Kimberley Peters, Jon Anderson, Andrew Davies, and Philip Steinberg (New York: Routledge, 2022), 138–47.

3. Susan B. Barnes, "Big and Busy," *Global Traveler* 2023, 36–37.

4. Greenwich Maritime Archives, Launch of the H.M.S. Agamemnon 90 Guns at Woolwich Dock, May 22, 1852. The ship-rigged steam battleship *Agamemnon* was the first warship to be built with screw propulsion, though other sailing vessels had been fitted with engines after commissioning. *Agamemnon*'s success was such that she remained the basic model for the first decade of Britain's steam battle fleet.

5. Oscar G. Brockett and Margaret Mitchell, *Making the Scene: A History of Stage Design and Technology in Europe and the United States*, ed. Linda Hardberger (San Antonio: University of Texas Press, 2010), 196–97.

6. Ida Altman, "Key to the Indies: Port Towns in the Spanish Caribbean: 1493–1550," *The Americas* 74, no. 1 (2016): 5–26, https://doi.org/10.1017/tam.2016.79

7. Joseph Kelly, *Marooned: Jamestown, Shipwreck, and a New History of America's Origin* (New York: Bloomsbury, 2018).

8. On this particular cruise line, destination lecturers were only allowed to disembark on shore excursions by offering to lead groups as an escort. This involves counting passengers, making sure they are safe, and vouching for the accuracy and appropriateness of the tour.

9. Elisabeth Maddock Dillon, *New World Drama: The Performative Commons in the Atlantic World, 1649–1849* (Durham, N.C.: Duke University Press, 2014).

10. Dillon, *New World Drama*, 169.

11. Jerrilyn McGregory, *One Grand Noise: Boxing Day in the Anglicized Caribbean World* (Jackson: University Press of Mississippi, 2021), 16. Jamaica's Jonkonnu tradition was the site of the earliest recorded Jonkonnu galas in the nineteenth century.

12. Rhiney and Cruse, eds., "Maroons in the Caribbean," Caribbean Atlas, 2013, http://www.caribbean-atlas.com/en/themes/waves-of-colonization-and-control-in-the-caribbean/waves-of-colonization/maroons-in-the-caribbean.html;

Lynn Brown, "The Obscured History of Jamaica's Maroon Societies: Maroon Societies in Jamaica and the Rest of the Americas Have Survived for Hundreds of Years," *JSTOR Daily* (blog), August 31, 2016, https://daily.jstor.org/maroon-societies-in-jamaica/

13. Jerrilyn McGregory, *One Grand Noise: Boxing Day in the Anglicized Caribbean World* (Jackson: University Press of Mississippi, 2021), 33–40.

14. McGregory, *One Grand Noise*, 55–78.

15. Jackie Ranston, *Belisario: Sketches of Character; A Historical Biography of a Jamaican Artist* (Kingston, Jamaica: Mill Press, 2008).

16. Elizabeth Maddock Dillon, *New World Drama: The Performative Commons in the Atlantic World, 1649–1849* (Durham, N.C.: Duke University Press, 2014), 214.

17. Barbara S. Glass, *African American Dance: An Illustrated History* (Jefferson, N.C.: McFarland and Company, 2009), 67–77.

18. The "Out Islands" are the smaller islands of the Bahamas where residents live rural lifestyles away from the urban centers of Nassau and Freeport. Most of the author's experiences have been on Cat Island where her grandmother was born.

19. Hugh Crow and John R. Pinfold, *The Memoirs of Captain Hugh Crow: The Life and Times of a Slave Trade Captain* (Oxford: Bodleian Library, Oxford University, 2007).

20. Charles Rodman Pancoast, *National Library of Jamaica Digital Collection* (NLJ Glass Slide Collection), accessed February 15, 2023, https://nljdigital.nlj.gov.jm/items/show/4921

21. Steve Buckridge, "Black Skin, White Mask: Race, Class and the Politics of Dress in Victorian Jamaican Society, 1837–1901," in *Victorian Jamaica*, ed. Tim Barringer and Wayne Modest (Durham, N.C.: Duke University Press, 2018), 583.

22. Unknown, *Sugar-Cane Cutters in Jamaica, Caribbean*, photograph (Greenwich, London, n.d.), National Maritime Museum. This photograph shows life in Jamaica in the latter part of the nineteenth century. The sugar industry, although in decline in this period, did not end with the emancipation of slaves in 1838. Instead, it continued, with Black people becoming employees rather than slaves.

23. Belinda Edmondson, "Most Intensely Jamaican: The Rise of Brown Identity in Jamaica," in *Victorian Jamaica*, ed. Tim Barringer and Wayne Modest (Durham, N.C.: Duke University Press, 2018), 555.

24. "Serving Our Maritime Community," Seamen's Church Institute, Newport, accessed January 27, 2021, https://seamensnewport.org/

25. The transport company in South Africa was Albatross, https://albatrossms.co.za/

26. "Log of the Ship Niagara, Mystic CT," n.d., Collection at Mystic Seaport, Mystic Seaport Museum.

27. Daniel Vickers, *Young Men and The Sea: Yankee Seafarers in the Age of Sail* (New Haven, Conn.: Yale University Press, 2007).

28. "Shipboard: The 19th Century Emigrant Experience > Emigrating > Life on Board," State Library New South Wales, https://www.sl.nsw.gov.au/stories/shipboard-19th-century-emigrant-experience/life-board. Accessed February 11, 2024.

29. "bbl" references barrels of flour.

30. Shelaleigh (or shillelagh) is an Irish walking stick or weapon. Here, the author refers to gathering weapons to use for a fight.

31. "New York Stock Exchange," in *Encyclopedia Britannica* (New York: Encyclopædia Britannica, 2021).

32. "New York Stock Exchange," in *Encyclopedia Britannica*.

33. Robert Greenhalgh Albion, *The Rise of New York Port, 1815–1860* (New York: Scribner, 1939), 337.

34. Frances Sargent Osgood, *The Cries of New-York: With Fifteen Illustrations* (New York: J. Doggett, Jr., 1846).

35. "American Antiquarian Society," American Antiquarian Society, accessed February 15, 2021, https://www.americanantiquarian.org/

36. The "dozens" is a verbal game where participants exchange insults in rapid verbal dialogue. The goal is to use insulting street language more effectively than your challenger. Think of it as a fast rap challenge full of insults.

37. W. T. Lhamon, *Raising Cain: Blackface Performance from Jim Crow to Hip Hop* (Cambridge, Mass.: Harvard University Press, 2000), 34.

38. Rodreguez King-Dorset, *Black Dance in London, 1730–1850: Innovation, Tradition, and Resistance* (Jefferson, N.C.: McFarland & Company, 2008), 68.

39. Solomon Northrup, *Twelve Years a Slave* (1853 manuscript; repr., independently published, 2022).

40. Rodreguez King-Dorset, *Black Dance in London, 1730–1850: Innovation, Tradition and Resistance* (Jefferson, N.C.: McFarland & Company, 2008), 97–99.

41. King-Dorset, *Black Dance in London, 1730–1850*, 651.

42. The city of Liverpool houses the Slavery Museum, one of the few museums dedicated to the history of the transatlantic slave trade.

43. "Europe," National Museums Liverpool, accessed May 25, 2019, http://www.liverpoolmuseums.org.uk/ism/slavery/europe/liverpool.aspx.

44. James Walvin, *England, Slaves and Freedom, 1776–1838* (Jackson: University of Mississippi Press, 1986), 2.

45. Ray Costello, *Black Salt: Seafarers of African Descent on British Ships* (Liverpool: Liverpool University Press, 2012), 90–93, 101–3.

46. Frank Neal, *Black '47: Britain and the Famine Irish* (London: Macmillan, 1998); John Belchem, *Irish, Catholic and Scouse: The History of the Liverpool-Irish, 1800–1939* (Liverpool: Liverpool University Press, 2007).

47. Colin Wilkinson, *A Cruise along the Manchester Ship Canal* (Liverpool: Bluecoat Press, 2010), 6.

48. Wilkinson, *A Cruise along the Manchester Ship Canal*, 4–5.

49. Christian DuComb, *Haunted City: Three Centuries of Racial Impersonation in Philadelphia* (Ann Arbor: University of Michigan Press, 2017), 6.

50. Frank Neal, *Black '47 : Britain and the Famine Irish* (London: Macmillan, 1998); John Belchem, *Irish, Catholic and Scouse: The History of the Liverpool-Irish, 1800–1939* (Liverpool: Liverpool University Press, 2007), 20.

51. Neal, *Black '47*, 13.

52. John Belchem, *Irish, Catholic and Scouse: The History of the Liverpool-Irish, 1800–1939* (Liverpool: Liverpool University Press, 2007), 27.
53. Noel Ignatiev, *How the Irish Became White* (London: Routledge, 2009), 2.
54. Pat O'Mara, *The Autobiography of a Liverpool Irish Slummy* (Liverpool: Bluecoat, 2007), 11.
55. O'Mara, *Autobiography of a Liverpool Irish Slummy*, 12.
56. Tyler Anbinder writes extensively about the living conditions of the Irish in New York's Five Points district, in chapter 3, "How They Lived," of his book *Five Points: The 19th-Century New York City Neighborhood That Invented Tap Dance, Stole Elections, and Became the World's Most Notorious Slum* (New York: Penguin, 2002), 72–106. In a similar way, John Belchem writes about the decadence and poverty of the Irish slums in his chapter "The Lowest Depth: The Spatial Dimension of Irish Liverpool" of the book *Irish, Catholic and Scouse: The History of the Liverpool-Irish, 1800–1939* (Liverpool: Liverpool University Press, 2007), 56–69.
57. Noel Ignatiev, *How the Irish Became White* (London: Routledge, 2009), 34.
58. John Belchem, *Irish, Catholic, and Scouse: The History of the Liverpool-Irish, 1800–1939* (Liverpool: Liverpool University Press, 2007), 216–45.
59. John Belchem, "The Whiteness of Ireland under and after the Union. Comment: Whiteness and the Liverpool-Irish," *Journal of British Studies* 44, no. 1 (2005): 146–52, https://doi.org/10.1086/424984
60. Anita Gonzalez, "19th Century Acts," 19th Century Acts, 2016, http://19thcenturyacts.com/
61. Eileen Southern, *The Music of Black Americans: A History, 3rd Edition* (New York: W.W. Norton, 1997), 95.
62. "Local and Provincial (1828–1900)," *Manchester Guardian*, 1848, https://www.proquest.com/docview/473675124/7222E1DEFC304457PQ/1
63. James W. Cook, "Master Juba, the King of All Dancers! A Story of Stardom and Struggle from the Dawn of the Transatlantic Culture and Industry," *Discourses in Dance* 3, no. 2 (2006).
64. Eileen Southern, "The Origin and Development of the Black Musical Theater: A Preliminary Report," *Black Music Research Journal* 2 (1981): 10, https://doi.org/10.2307/779408
65. Jill Lane, *Blackface Cuba, 1840–1895* (Philadelphia: University of Pennsylvania Press, 2005).
66. A *palapa* is an open-sided palm-covered hut.
67. "New Cruise Terminal in Puerto Plata Will Be Operational in 2020," *Dominican Today*, December 14, 2019, https://dominicantoday.com/dr/tourism/2019/12/14/new-cruise-terminal-in-puerto-plata-will-be-operational-in-2020/
68. Robert McGillivray, "Construction Underway on Two New Caribbean Cruise Ports," Cruise Hive, August 1, 2022, https://www.cruisehive.com/construction-underway-on-two-new-caribbean-cruise-ports/77863
69. Shivani Vora, "Five Ways to Get Some Culture on Your Next Cruise," *New York Times*, April 13, 2018, https://www.nytimes.com/2018/04/13/travel/culture-cruise-tips.html; Donna Tunney, "Cultural Exchange Programs Grow on Shore and

Onboard," *Travel Weekly*, December 20, 2011, https://www.travelweekly.com/Cruise-Travel/Insights/Cultural-exchange-programs-grow-on-shore-and-onboard; Erica Silverstein, "4 Luxury Cruise Lines That Are Rocking Destination Immersion," Cruise Reviews, Cruise Deals and Cruises—Cruise Critic, October 10, 2019, https://www.cruisecritic.com/articles.cfm?ID=3056. This voyage was an Oceania cruise, one of the lines specializing in more immersive experiences.

70. Garth L Green and Philip W Scher, *Trinidad Carnival* (Bloomington: Indiana University Press, 2007); Kevin Adonis Browne, *High Mas: Carnival and the Poetics of Caribbean Culture* (Jackson: University Press of Mississippi, 2018); Jerrilyn McGregory, *One Grand Noise: Boxing Day in the Anglicized Caribbean World* (Jackson: University Press of Mississippi, 2021); Lia T. Bascomb, *In Plenty and in Time of Need: Popular Culture and the Remapping of Barbadian Identity* (New Brunswick, N.J.: Rutgers University Press, 2019); Lyndon K. Gill, *Erotic Islands: Art and Activism in the Queer Caribbean* (Durham, N.C.: Duke University Press, 2018).

71. Gill, *Erotic Islands*, xxii.

72. Yvonne Daniel, *Caribbean and Atlantic Diaspora Dance: Igniting Citizenship* (Champaign: University of Illinois Press, 2011).

73. Daniel, *Caribbean and Atlantic Diaspora Dance*, 108.

74. *Cupid—Cupid Shuffle (Music Video)*, AsylumRecordsTV, YouTube, 2007), https://www.youtube.com/watch?v=h24_zoqu4_Q

Coda

1. Lamide Akintobi, "Proudly Ndebele: South Africa's Zana Masombuka Showcases Her Heritage through Modern Expressions of Art," CNN (Cable News Network), February 8, 2022, https://www.cnn.com/style/article/zana-masombuka-ndebele-superhero-south-africa-spc/index.html

Index

Page numbers in *italics* refer to illustrations.

Adkins, Thomas Francis, 36
African Americans: folk songs, 102, 111–13; Native Americans and, 114–15; racial prejudice against, 38–39, 159–64; railway porters, 27, 193n23
African American studies, 1
African Free School, 27, 140, 152
African Grove Theatre, 25–27, 29, 31–32, 140, 193n21, 194n33
Afro-Mexican performance, 114
Agamemnon (battleship), 125–27, *126*, 128, 203n4
Alabama (Confederate ship), 112
Albion, Robert Greenhalgh, 148–50
Aldridge, Ira, 140, 162–63
"America and the Seas" seminar, 5
Amistad (slave ship), 4
Andersen, Jon, 6
Antigua, 155
Arawak indigenous people, 53
Arison, Ted, 43
Aristophanes, 94
Aristotle, 94
Aruba, 186
Asian seamen, 33
Australia, 19

Bahamas, 128, 136, 204n18
Baker, Dow, 43

Bakhtin, Mikhail, 83
ballads, 97, 101–3, 109, 119–20, 151, 200n56
ballast, 58, 196nn3–4
banana industry, 43. *See also* United Fruit Company
Barbados, 130, 134, 173
Belchem, John, 160, 162
Belisario, Isaac Mendes, 135–37
Belize, 26
Benedict, Dan, 15
Benson, Charles, 27–28
Bermuda, 130, 173
Bernstein, Iver, 39
Black actors, 25–32, 162–63. *See also* African Grove Theatre
Black Ball line, 29, 110
blackface minstrelsy, 38, 153–54, 160, 162–63
Black seamen, historical, 5–7, *24, 28;* cooks, 33–41, *34–35, 37;* dancing and, 99–101; longshoremen, 39; stewards, 25–32, 40–41
Blum, Hester, 4
Bolster, W. Jeffrey, 5, 29, 31, 193n27
Bolt, Ester Ellen, 21, 90
Bonaire, 186
Boston Banana Company, 43
Bowery Theatre, 157

Boxing Day, 134–36
Brazil, 174
British colonialism, 53, 131. *See also* colonialism
British navy, 126
British West Indies, 103
Bronner, Simon, 87
Brown, William Alexander, 25, 31
Bruns, David, 88–89
Buckley, Burnett, 40
Buckridge, Steve, 138
busking, 140, 164–65
Butler, Judith, 87
Butler, Wilson, 55

call-and-response songs, 101, 103, 106, 112, 119
Cape Horn, 106
Cape Liberty Cruise Port, 124
Cape of Good Hope, 18, 131
Cape Town, South Africa, 141–44, 185
capstan songs, 104, 119, 200n56
captains, 42, 44–45, 56, 195n52
cargo ports, 123–24
cargo ships, 18, 58; cargo-passenger ships, 43–44
Caribbean islands: Black populations, 54; history, 19, 52–54. *See also* ports; *specific islands*
Caribbean tourism, 1–3; Black travelers and, 172–73; destinations, 16–18; folkloric exhibitions, 26, 164–71; local economies and, 128, 164–73; origins of cruises, 43; sexualized exoticism and, 94, 166–68, *167, 168,* 174
Caribe indigenous people, 26, 53, 165–66. *See also* indigenous people
Carnival Cruise Line, 15, 17, 42, 44, 66, 71, *71,* 83–84, 89
carnival practices, 164; on Caribbean islands, 114, 173–75; on cruise ships, 175–78
Carr, James Revell, 22, 109
Caskey, Charles, 46

Castries, St. Lucia, 176–78
Celebrity cruise line, 44, *65, 68,* 70, 73, 80, 83, 91, 94, 95, 196n66, 198n32
celebrity culture, 66, 72, 91
Chappelle, David, 94
Charles II, 132
Chatoyer, Joseph, 26, 32
Cherokee nation, 114–15
Church, Andrew B., 88
class hierarchies, 22, 42, 56, 90, 94
class status, 6, 42, 47–48, 67, 191n31. *See also* steerage passengers; upper-class passengers
Cobb, Jasmine, 4
coffee plantations, 170–71
Colcord, Joanna and Richard, 105, 111–12, 114, 115, 119
colonialism, 52–54, 128–32, 172, 184
Colored Sailor's Home, 39–40
Columbus, Christopher, 128
commerce, 125, 127, 151; busking, 140, 164–65; in cruise ship ports, 128, 164–73; in historic port cities, 127–28, 134, 140–41, 159; performance and, 159; shopping areas on cruise ships, 62; street hawkers, 151, 164, 166
competitions: on cruise ships, 71–72, 82–84, 91–92, 94; on nineteenth-century ships, 92–96, *93,* 98–101. *See also* dance competitions; games
container shipping, 123–24
Cook, James, 100, 163
cooks: on cruise ships, 33, *34* (*see also* dining spaces on cruise ships); on merchant ships, 33–41, *35, 37*
Costa Cruises, 44
Costello, Ray, 5
COVID-19 pandemic, 78, 131, 169, 175, 178, 180
Creole cultures, 132–34, 139, 154–55, 166
crew members: diverse international identities, 8, 19–25, 30, 34 (*see also* cultural exchange); front-facing staff, 21; immersive performance by,

1–2, 49, 91; maritime labor hierarchy, 12, 42–44, 51, 69, 77; participation in passenger/crew games, 73–75, 95; performance ratings, 14; "play at sea," 88–92, 95–96; sea culture and, 6–7; shore leave, 128, 203n8; theatrical performances events by, 120–22, *121*; wages, 90. *See also* captains; cruise directors; dining spaces; engineering staff; entertainment staff; housekeeping staff; stewards; waiters

The Cries of New-York (Osgood), 150–53

Crop Over celebrations, 155

Crossing the Line ceremonies, 122; on cruise ships, 89; historical, 84–88, *85, 86*

Crow, Hugh, 136–38

cruise directors, 15, 19, 21, 48–49, 52, 62, 69, 197n17

Cruise Lines International Association, 44

cruise ship passengers, 1–2; demographics, 14; elderly, 181–83; onboard activities, 16–18; onboarding, 10–54, 124–28. *See also* dining spaces on cruise ships; entertainment activities on cruises

cruise ships: history of, 42–45; moments of improvisation at sea, 179–86; numbers of employees, 7; spectacle of landings, 127–28; theatricality of, 1–2, 5; workers (*see* crew members). See also *specific cruise lines*

cruise ship space: architectural design, 45, 47–48, 55–61, 81; cave spaces, 61, 79–82, *80*; cosmic circles, 61, 71–75; deck plans, *50* (*see also* lower decks; upper decks); empty space, 61, 197n7; entertainment venues, 49; as performance space, 55–56; processional, 60–68, *64, 65*; public plazas, 61, 68–71; sympotic spaces, 61, 75–79

Cuba, 119, 130, 173, 174

cultural exchange, 1–2, 5, 9, 15–16; crew members and, 20, 25–33, 90–91; liminality and, 184–85; in ports, 125, 140–41, 153–57; sea shanties and, 96–97, 101–11; in tourist shore excursions, 26, 164–73, 178. *See also* dialogic performances and exchanges; gestural exchanges; interracial and cultural mixing

Cunard Line, 48

Curaçao, 186

currents and trade winds, 26, 53, 58, 129–30

dance competitions: on cruise ships, 71–72, 82–83, 91–92; on historical sailing ships, 98–101; in Liverpool, 160, 162–63

dances: African traditions, 83, 134–35; carnival practices and, 174–76; cruise ship parties, 74; European, 154–55; performers at tourist ports, 165–66; quadrille events, 154–57

Daniel, Yvonne, 174

Davies, Andrew, 6

Dead Horse Ceremony, 84, 88

Deliverance (sailing ship), 130

Denning, Sue, 49, 196n66

destination lecturers, 2–3, 10–12, *11*, 11–12, 18–19, 46, 51–54, 63, 76, 90, 96, 141–43, 170–71, 195n61, 203n8

dialogic performances and exchanges, 84, 101–3, 112, 120, 153–54

Diamond, John, 100, 163

Dickens, Charles, 100

Dillon, Elizabeth Maddock, 132–33, 135–37

dining spaces on cruise ships, 33, *34*, 61–63, 66–67, 75–80, 181. *See also* waiters

disembarking, 185–86

Disney cruise line, 17, 125

Disneyland, 17

Dixon-Gottschild, Brenda, 99

Dominican Republic, 128, 164, *169*, 169–71

double consciousness, 13, 38
Douglass, Frederick, 31
The Drama of King Shotaway (play), 26, 32
dress: formal, 70; identities and, 133, 136–39; symbolic cues and, 70–71
"Drunken Sailor," 96, 102
Du Bois, W.E.B., 13
DuComb, Christian, 159
Duncan, William Henry, 160
Dutch colonialism, 53, 129, 131, 172. *See also* colonialism
Dutch East India Tea Company, 172

Eclipse (cruise ship), 80
Edmondson, Belinda, 139
Eidsheim, Nina Sun, 104
Elam, Harry J., Jr., 1
embodied performances, 7, 23, 86, 96–105, 114–20, 127, 135, 154, 164, 174–76, 190n25
engineering staff, 18, 21, 69, 73, 91–92, 128, 131, 180, 181
enrichment offerings, 15
enslaved Africans, 3–4, 10, 22–23; cultural expression and resistance, 133–34, 136–37; maritime escapes, 4, 30–31; singing and dancing, 111–13, 155. *See also* slavery
entertainment activities on cruises, 11, 13, 15–16, 192n1; in cave spaces, 79–82; cooking shows, 79; in cosmic circles, 71–75; "edutainment" lectures, 3, 11; fantasy and, 181–83; passenger-crew interactions in, 91; "play at sea," 82–84, 95–96; in processional corridors, 61–68; in public plazas, 68–71; on sea days, 11, 52, 192n1; sequences of, 197n17; sexualized, 94–95; shore excursions, 26, 164–73, 178; special interest lecturers, 15; in sympotic spaces, 75–79; theatrical performances by crew members, 120–22,

121; time zones and, 179–80. *See also* competitions; games; partying
entertainment staff, 19, 48–52; Black performers, 52; onboarding, 124–25. *See also* destination lecturers
Equinox (cruise ship), 65
Erie Canal, 149
European aesthetics, 154
exoticism, 94, 166–68, *167, 168*, 174
Explorer of the Seas (cruise ship), 70, 73

Father Nugent's League Hall, 162
Ferdinand and Isabella, King and Queen of Spain, 129
field labor, *138*, 138–39
Filipinos: in Liverpool, 158–59, 161; workers on cruise ships, 20, 41, 89, 121, 131, 142–43, 185
Florida cruise ports, 124–25
Floyd, Jessica, 108
"The Flying Cloud," 119–20
folkloric exhibitions, 26, 164–71
folk songs, 100, 102, 103, 109, 111–13. *See also* sea shanties
food service staff. *See* dining spaces
42nd Street (musical), 197n11
Fosler-Lussier, Danielle, 103
Foucault, Michel, 60
Foy, Charles, 34
free Black people, 3, 30–31, 193n21, 193n23
French colonialism, 53, 129, 131. *See also* colonialism
Frieze, James, 16
fugitivity, 4, 39, 41, 164, 189n11

"gam" (musical jam), 109
games: on cruise ships, 73–76, 95; game rooms, 61; historical maritime rituals, 84–88
Garífuna (Black Caribe) cultures, 26, 165–66
Garinagú, 165
Gem (cruise line architect), 55

Index · 213

gender: crew members and, 21; gender play, 87; maritime work and, 12, 195n52. *See also* masculinity; racialized and gendered stereotypes
Gesamtkunstwerk (total theater), 127
gestural exchanges, 22–23, 141, 147, 154
Gill, Lyndon, 174
Girard, Stephen, 56
Glass, Barbara, 135
Global North, 21
Global South, 1–2, 20–21, 171
Gold Diggers of Broadway (musical), 197n11
Goombay (music form), 101
Gordinier, Glenn, 5
Grand Hotel, Mackinac Island, 45–46
Grand Staircase, 69–70, *70*, 197n11
Greater Antilles, 130
Great Lakes: cargo shipping, 18; cruises, 46, 195n61
Great Stirrup Cay, 128
Great White Fleet, 43, 165
Greek workers, 19, 21
Greenland, 106
Grenada, 130
Guadeloupe, 129, 130
Guavaberry liqueur, 166, *168*
Guerrero, Vincente, 118
Gumbey dances, 134–35

Hague, Sam, 162, *163*
Haiti, 128–29, 168–69
Haitian Revolution, 102
halyard songs, 105, 119–20
Hamilton, Thomas, 25, 27
hazing, 85–87
Hewlett, James, 25, 26, 193n21
"Hey Ho, blow the Man Down," 106–8
hierarchies: gendered, 34–37; maritime, 12, 42–44, 51, 69, 77; racial, 12, 21–22, 34–37; social, 22, 42, 56, 90, 94; transformation of social status and, 147

Hilja (ship), 114
Hispaniola, 128, 130
homoeroticism, 87, 108
Honduras, 26, 164–66
hornpipe dance, 36, 98–99, 182
hotel industry, 45–47
housekeeping staff, 12, 19, 32–33, 67, 124, 185
Howe, Alphonse, 46
Hugill, Stan, 104, 105, 110–11, 200n56

identity, 4–5; in Caribbean tourist ports, 164–73; crafting of, 97; of cruise ship crew members, 20, 41–42; of destination lecturers, 3, 12, 42; of displaced laborers, 8; dress and, 133, 136–39; experimental, 84–96, 181–86; liminal spaces and, 4, 6, 9, 11, 16, 31, 36, 61, 94, 179–86; in nineteenth-century ports, 144–64; in port settings, 125; racial and ethnic boundaries, 41–42, 114; social status and, 160–61
Ignatiev, Noel, 160
immersive cruise experience: entertainment activities, 8, 16–18, 181–83; port excursions, 170–71; spatial design and, 56, 81; worker performance and, 1–2, 49, 91
immersive theater, 16–17
immigrants. *See* migration
improvisation, 179–86
India, workers from, 19, 33, 104, 139
Indian Removal Act, 115. *See also* indigenous people
indigenous people, 26, 53, 146, *169*, 170; carnival practices, 174; colonialism and, 117, 129, 184 (*see also* colonialism); Native American seamen, 113–15
International Labor Organization, 21
interracial and cultural mixing, 19, 103–4, 112–14, 131–39, 152, 204n18

Irish communities: folk songs, 103; in Liverpool, 140, 145–47, 158–64; in New York, 39, 140, 152; social status and whiteness, 160–64; workers and sailors, 39, 41, 100, 115–17, 139
Irish Longshoremen's Benevolent Society, 39

Jackson, Andrew, 115
Jack Tar, 31, 194n37
Jack Tar: a Sailor's Life, 5
Jamaica, 129–30, 133–38, *137*, 155, 164, 174, 186, 203n11
Jarocho dance, 101, 199n43
jig dancing, 98–100, 162
"Jim Crow" character, 153–54
"John Cherokee," 114–17
Johnson, Francis, 155
Johnson, Galley, 161
Jones, Douglas A., Jr., 38
Jonkonnu dance, 134–36, 203n11

Keysaar, Alexander, 193n27
King-Dorset, Rodreguez, 155
kitchen tours, 78–79
Kondo, Dorinne, 8, 20, 97
Krew Kapers, 120–22, *121*
Kru people, 103
Kumina dance, 135
Kura Hulanda Museum, Curaçao, *171*, *172–73*

Labadee, Haiti, 168–69
labor, 7–8; national development and, 118. See also crew members; seamen, historical
Lane, William Henry (Master Juba), 100, 162–63
Lashley, Conrad, 21, 90
Leeward Islands, 129–30
leisure travel, 14; upper-class nineteenth-century, 22, 42, 45–47. See also cruise ship passengers
Lhamon, W. T., 154

Liar's Club (event), 84, 95
libraries, 61, 79–82, *80*
liminality, 3–4, 6, 9, 11–12, 14, 16, 31, 36, 52, 61, 94, 179–86
Liverpool, 103; Black and Irish communities, 140, 145–47, 158–64; dance competitions, 160, 162–63; packet ships to New York, 25, 29, 144–48; sea shanties about, 106, 109–10; slave trade, 158, 205n42
Long Island Sound, 149
Looser, Diana, 6
The Love Boat (television show), 17, 94
lower decks, 2, 44, 56–58; kitchen tours, 78–79
luxury travel. See upper-class passengers
Lyons, Albro, 39–40

Mackinac Island, 45–46
Main Street passageway, 61–66
Malone, Jacqui, 155
Mancini, Jason, 113
Manifest Destiny, 117
Mariner of the Seas (cruise ship), *64*, *82*
maritime studies, 5–6, 190n13
Marley, Bob, 102
maroon communities, 134
Martinique, 129
Marx, Karl, 177
masculinity, 14, 34–36, 87, 105, 109–10, 116
Mashantucket Pequot community, 113
Masombuka, Zana, 184
Maxton, William, 144–48, 150, 159, 164
McAllister, Marvin, 26
McGregory, Jerrilyn, 134
McLean, Malcolm, 123
McLean, Thomas, *35*, 35–36
Melville, Herman, *Moby Dick*, 30, 193n32
Mende people, 4, 189n9
merchant ships: cooks on, 33–41, *35*, *37*; photographs of, *24*, *28*; port activities,

127; servitude on, 34; steamships and, 149; stewards on, 25–32; workers, 2, 5–7, 18, 22–24
Mexicans, 114, 117–18
mid-Atlantic islands, 130
middle-class passengers, 67, 171
Middle Passage, 3, 172–73. *See also* enslaved Africans; slavery
migration, 4, 22, 25–33, 39, 47, 140, 146–53
Miller, William, 43, 47
minstrelsy, 38, 153–54, 160, 162–63
misogyny, 87, 110
Moby Dick (Melville), 30, 193n32
Moel Ellian (merchant ship), 23–24, *24*
Monarch of Bermuda (passenger ship), 48
mortality, 183
Mr. Hague's Slave Troupe of Georgia Minstrels, 163
Muñoz, José Esteban, 87, 94, 198n34
music, 67, 70–72, 82–84, 170, 175–78, *177*. *See also* ballads; dance competitions; dances; sea shanties
Muskateem, Sowande, 5
Mystic, Connecticut, 144, 146–48
Mystic Seaport Museum, 113, 120, 148

Napoleon, 130, 131
Native Americans, 146; seamen, 113–15, 117. *See also* indigenous people
Nautical Cookery Book (1896), 36
naval seamen, 18, 36, *86*, 87–88, 126
Ndebele Superhero, 184
Neely, Dan, 155
Newark, 124
New Bedford, 113
New England, 149. *See also* Mystic, Connecticut
New London, 113
New Orleans, 30, 103, 114, 129; Congo Square, 101
New York City, 7; Black communities, 25, 29, 39–40, 100, 140, 152–57, 165, 193n21; cruise terminals, 124; draft riots (1863), 39, 41, 159; Five Points neighborhood, 100, 148, 152, 160–61; Irish communities, 39, 140, 152; packet ships to Liverpool, 25, 29, 144–48; port of, 109, 148–53, *150*; sea shanties about, 106; shipping industry, 149, 152, 157; social life in nineteenth century, 144, 148–57; theater scene, 157
Niagara (packet ship), 144–48
Nicaragua, 26, 165
Norfolk, Virginia, 144–45
Northrup, Solomon, 155
Norwegian Cruise Line, 17, 44, 125, 128

Oasis of the Seas (cruise ship), 62
Oceana cruise line, 62, *75*, 80, 207n69
oceanic studies, 5–6
O'Mara, Pat, 158–59, 161
onboarding, 10–54, 124–25; spectacle of, 125–28
Orion (passenger ship), 48
O'Rorke, Brian, 48
Osgood, Frances, *The Cries of New-York*, 150–53

packet ships, 25, 29, 110, 144–48; architecture of, 56–58, *57*, *59*
"Paddy Works the Railroad," 115–17
Palmer, Roy, 105, 200n56
Paradise (cruise ship), *71*
partying, 15, 66, 72, 74, 82–83
passenger ships: nineteenth-century, 43–45, 47–48, 81. *See also* cruise ships
Patience (sailing ship), 130
Pell, Richard, 163
performance, 5–7; cruise ship space and, 55–84; of leisure, 14; in long nineteenth century, 7; paradigms, 12–19; social negotiations and, 4–5. *See also* embodied performances

performances of servitude, 1–8, 11, 13–14, 18–19; by Black and brown cruise ship workers, 2–4, 11, 32–33, 63, 76–79, 89–90, 120–22, 185–86; by Black seamen in nineteenth century, 35–38; cross-cultural encounters and, 171 (*see also* cultural exchange); excellent behavior, 14
performance studies, 1, 5–7, 190n25
Peters, Kimberley, 6
Philadelphia, 7, 109, 159
Philippines, 19. *See also* Filipinos
Philipsburg, St Maarten, 164, 166–69
photographers on cruise ships, *64*, 65–66, 84, 170
pirates, 13, 51, 53, 119, 165
pool decks, 66–68
Port Canaveral, 124
Port Everglades, 124
Port Miami, 124–25
ports, 18, 123–78; Black cultural expression in, 132–35; cargo ports, 123–24; Caribbean cruise ports, *124*, 124–25, 164–73; changes in cruise ship itineraries, 180–81; crew members and, 141–44; cruise ship tourists and, 164–73; dance forms and, 99; economic aspects, 123 (*see also* commerce); internationalism in, 125; in nineteenth century, 127, 137, 144–48, 173; port dance as cultural exchange, 153–57; social lives in, 4–5, 139–41, 191n31; social mobility and, 140; as spectacle, 125–28; as stopovers, 131–32. *See also* Liverpool; New York City
Portuguese colonialism, 129, 131. *See also* colonialism
Powell, William, 39–41
private cruise resorts, 168–69
privateers, 53
processional space, 60–68, *64, 65*
proscenium spaces, 56, 68
Puerto Plata, Dominican Republic, 164, *169*, 169–71
Puerto Rico, 129, 130

quadrille dance events, 154–57
Queen Mary (passenger ship), 48, 81, 131
Queen of Bermuda (passenger ship), 48
queer epistemologies, 174
queer performance, 94, 198n34

race, 3–5; definitions of, 31; intersections with performance and labor, 1–2, 14–16; as porous category, 114; voice and, 104. *See also* interracial and cultural mixing
racial hierarchies, 12, 21–22, 34–37
racialized and gendered stereotypes, 35–38, 86–87, 92–94, *93*, 122, 166, *167*, *168*. *See also* blackface minstrelsy
racial prejudice, 38–39, 159–64
"racy newspapers," 150, *150*, 153, 157
rag man, 151
railroads, 46; African American porters, 27, 193n23; Irish workers on, 115–17
Rediker, Marcus, 5
Regent Seven Seas cruise line, 120, 130, 142
Rice, Thomas D., 153–54
Riley, William, 40
Roatán, Honduras, 26, 164–66
Rodger, Gillian M., 7
Roland, Alex, 193n27
"Roll the Cotton Down," 112
Roorda, Eric Paul, 5
Rose, Felipe, 122, 202n82
Rosseau (packet ship), 56, *57*
Royal Australian Navy, 86
Royal Caribbean cruise line, 17, 44, 62, *64*, 70, 73, 82, 95, 125, 165, 168–69
Royal Mail Lines, 166, *167*

sailing ships, 2, 5, 22–23, 58. *See also* merchant ships
sailor homes, 39–40, 141
San Francisco, 106, 110
Santa Ana, Antonio López de, 117–18
"Santa Ana," 117–18
Santiago de Cuba, 129

Scott, Julius, 102
seamen, historical: competitions and, 92–96, *93*; cultural exchange through music and dance, 96–101, *98*, 199n43; hazards faced by, 45; maritime rituals and, 84–88; mortality, 183. *See also* Black seamen, historical; merchant ships; naval seamen; sailing ships
Seamen's Church Institute, 141
Sea Music Festival, 120
Sea Music Symposium, 120
sea shanties, 6, 182–83; African songs and, 111–13; contemporary performances of, 120; cultural exchange and, 96–97, 101–11; Irish workers and, 115–17; labor and global institutional change, 118–20; Mexicans and, 117–18; Native Americans and, 113–15; storytelling lyrics, 97, 105–11, 200n56, 201n62
Sea Venture (sailing ship), 130
self-reflection, 75, 183–85
Seven Seas Voyager (cruise ship), 142
Sevilla, Jamaica, 129
sexuality, 83, 94–96, 107–9
Shakespeare, William, 26, 130, 133, 162–63
Sharpe, Christina, 3, 6
Sheridan, Richard Brinsley, 26
shipping industry, 21, 29–30; New York port and, 149, 152, 157; nineteenth century routes, 24, 149. *See also* merchant ships
Shoemaker, Nancy, 113
shore excursions, 164–73, 178
shore leave, 128, 203n8
Siddons, Henry, 191n28
Sierra Leone, 103
singing and songs, 87; ballads, 97, 101–3, 109, 119–20, 151, 200n56; call-and-response songs, 101, 103, 106, 112, 119; capstan, 104, 119, 200n56; folk, 100, 102, 103, 109, 111–13; halyard, 105, 119–20. *See also* sea shanties
"Sing Sally O," 112

Sirena (cruise ship), *75*, 80
slavery, 3–4; Black sailors and, 30–31, 38, 41; museums on, 172–73, 205n42; Native Americans and, 115; slave ships, 4–5, 58, 119, 172–73; slave trade, 5, 38, 41, 53, 134, 136, 140, 144–45, 157–58, 205n42. *See also* enslaved Africans
social fellowship, 29, 91, 125, 182–83
social norms, 36, 83–84, 132; alternative, 94–96, 174; group identity and, 92
Sokolow, Michael, 27
songs. *See* singing and songs
South Africa, 183–84
South Carolina, 103
Southern, Eileen, 111
space, 4; types of, 60–61. *See also* cruise ship space
Spanish colonialism, 53, 128–29, 131. *See also* colonialism
SS Ideal X (container ship), 124
St. Barts, 128
steamships, 22–23, 45, 47, 126, 203n4; merchant shipping and, 149. *See also* passenger ships
steel pan music, 175–78, *177*
steerage passengers, 29, 47, 146–48, 150
Steinberg, Philip, 6
stevedores, 103, 111, 113, 123, 127
stewards: on cruise ships, 32–33 (*see also* housekeeping staff); on merchant ships, 25–32, 40–41
St. Helena, 130–32
St. Lucia, 130, 176–78
St Maarten, 54, 127, 129, 130, 164, 166–69
"Stormalong, Lads Stormy," 109–10
street hawkers, 151, 164, 166
St. Thomas, 128
St. Vincent, 26, 32–33, 130
sugar trade, 52–54; sugar cane plantations, 53–54, *138*, 138–39, 155, 204n22
Summit (cruise ship), *68*, 70

Tagatz, Bob, 46, 195n61
Taino Bay Cruise Terminal, 169–70

Taino indigenous people, 53
Taylor, John, II, 31
Taylor, Zachary, 118
Tegg, Thomas, *93, 198n33*
The Tempest (Shakespeare), 130
theaters: main-stage, *68,* 68–71; spectacle and, 127
Theatre Royale (Liverpool), 162
Thompson, Katrina Dyonne, 111–12
Titanic (film), 17, 42
Titanic (ship), 45
tourism. *See* Caribbean tourism
trade winds. *See* currents and trade winds
transactional economies, 141, 145–46, 153; in cruise ship ports, 164–73. *See also* commerce
Trinidad, 173
troubadour performers, 151
12 Years a Slave (film), 155
Tye, Larry, 193n23

United Fruit Company, 43, 165
United States: coastal shipping, 29, 193n27; free Black communities, 30–31. *See also* African Americans; New York City
United States Navy, 87–88
Universal Studios, 17
upper-class passengers, 22, 42–43, 45–48, 77, 197n9
upper decks, 17, 18, 27, 33, 35–36, 44, 56, 58, 66–67, 72, 91, 103, 176
utopia, 67, 87, 92, 185

Vickers, Daniel, 146
Victory I (Great Lakes ship), *75*

Village People (band), 122, 202n82
Virgin Islands, 130
Virgin Voyages, 17
Voyager of the Seas (cruise ship), *121*

Wagner, Richard, 127
waiters, 12, 13, 28, 33, 41–42, 63, 76–78, 169, 181. *See also* dining spaces on cruise ships
Waiti, Jordan, 6
Wallace, David Foster, 2
Washington, Frances, 40
Weheyliye, Alexander G., 102
West Africa, 103, 135, 158, 199n48
whaling ships, 29–30, 40, 56, 97, 109, 113, 193n32
Whall, W. B., 105, 200n57
Wheaton, Belinda, 6
White, Shane, 193n21
Wiles, David, 8, 60–61, 67, 76–77, 79, 197n7
Williams, John C., 31
Windward Islands, 129–30
women: Black academics, 51–52, 196n67; maritime work and, 12, 195n52. *See also* exoticism; racialized and gendered stereotypes; sexuality
working-class entertainment, 7. *See also* dances; singing and songs
working-class passengers, 47–48. *See also* steerage passengers

Xenophon (merchant ship), 31

Zeeland, Steven, 87
Zogbaum, R. F., 36–37, *37,* 194n43